Remains: Non-Viewable

John Sacret Young

FARRAR, STRAUS AND GIROUX · NEW YORK

Farrar, Straus and Giroux
19 Union Square West, New York 10003

Copyright © 2005 by Sacret, Inc.
All rights reserved
Distributed in Canada by Douglas & McIntyre Ltd.
Printed in the United States of America
First edition, 2005

Grateful acknowledgment is made to the following for permission to reproduce
excerpts: to A. P. Watt Ltd. on behalf of Michael B. Yeats for *The Circus Animals'
Desertion* by W. B. Yeats; to Ned Broderick for his poem "Each face will . . ."; and
to Warner Bros. Television for the opening scene of the script from the pilot episode
of the television series entitled *China Beach*.

Library of Congress Cataloging-in-Publication Data
Young, John Sacret, 1947–
    [Weather tomorrow]
    Remains : non-viewable / John Sacret Young.— 1st ed.
      p. cm.
    ISBN-13: 978-0-374-24903-8
    ISBN-10: 0-374-24903-2 (alk. paper)
    1. Young, John Sacret, 1947– —Family. 2. Young, John Sacret, 1947– —
Childhood and Youth. 3. Screenwriters—United States—Family relationships.
4. Screenwriters—United States—Biography. 5. Vietnamese Conflict, 1961–1975—
United States. I. Title.

PS3575.O795Z477 2004
813'.54—dc22

                                                                    2003017794

www.fsgbooks.com

10 9 8 7 6 5 4 3 2 1

To Jeanette MacPhere Young
John Van Wic Young
Julia Ruth Sacret Young
Riley McCormick Young

I sought a theme and sought for it in vain . . .
Out of what began?
A mound of refuse or the sweepings of a street,
Old kettles, old bottles, and a broken cane
Old iron, old bones, old rags . . .
Now that my ladder's gone,
I must lie down while all the ladders start,
In the foul rag-and-bone shop of the heart.

—WILLIAM BUTLER YEATS

Each face will lose its name
And time will not defer
But there will always be the bond
Between what we are
And where we were.

—NED BRODERICK, VIETNAM VETERAN

One

walking from Plymouth to North Plymouth through the raw air of Massachusetts Bay at each step a small cold squudge through the sole of one shoe

looking out past the grey framehouses under the robinsegg April sky across the white dories anchored in the bottleclear shallows across the yellow sandbars and the slaty bay ruffling to blue to the eastward

this is where the immigrants landed the roundheads the sackers of castles the kingkillers haters of oppression this is where they stood in a cluster after landing from the crowded ship that stank of bilge   on the beach that belonged to no one   between the ocean that belonged to no one and the enormous forest that belonged to no one that stretched over the hills where the deertracks were up the green rivervalleys where the redskins grew their tall corn in patches forever into the incredible west

for threehundred years the immigrants toiled into the west

and now today

—JOHN DOS PASSOS, THE BIG MONEY

1

CALL UP A STORY: a writer makes them up and sets them down but it is what we all do to make shape of our days.

Some years ago I fell in love with Hawaii. I'd rent little houses on the beach on one of the islands, nothing fancy, a kitchen, a bed, an outdoor shower, and some ceiling fans. The water was warm and salutary. I would read and write, or try to write, and to think and decompress. It was funny to come six thousand miles to one ocean when I'd grown up on the edge of another, along Cape Cod Bay south of Duxbury but north of the two bridges, the Bourne and the Sagamore, in a part of Plymouth, Massachusetts, where my family still lived, at least some of them, some of the time.

In 1999 in Wailea Bay on the Big Island, a tiny, largely unpopulated and unknown beach tucked between two famous resorts, I found I hadn't brought any writing with me. For close to thirty years it is what I have done, write screenplays and books, and I had no idea what it meant or that in fact it wasn't an ending but a beginning, one that had been waiting for me—the pipe well laid—for decades.

While I was there a message passed from my mother through my wife, Jenny, whom I was separated from then, and through my office to me: my uncle George was ill. My uncle—Big

George, we often called him—was a tall, bald, smiling man, long and lanky, six foot six, and the head of the family, as much as there can be one in a big and sprawling family. A tremendously competitive athlete under the guise of his great grin, even if age had slowed him—he had had both his hips replaced—he still was up before seven every day as a matter of pride and New England principle. He was an Old Yankee.

The message was puzzling, for I knew he was sick. Six weeks before doctors had unearthed a stomach tumor, but it hadn't seemed a life-threatening emergency. He wasn't rushed into surgery; in fact the operation was postponed while the recommended doctor, an acquaintance, scooted away for a vacation. That was early May. Now, mid-June, the operation had been performed and declared a success. Recovery, naturally at George's age, eighty-nine, would be slow and arduous. Now this message.

Communication within a large family can often become comedy, waylaid by malfunction or misinformation, ending up feeding on itself erroneously. I got on the phone to sort out what it meant. It was too late to reach my mother on the East Coast, so I called Jenny, and to my surprise she answered.

"Oh, it's you," she said.

"I got this message—"

"Well, it's true."

"Wait a minute. I haven't even said—what's true?"

"Your mother called me."

"Nice of her to call *me*."

"Why would she?"

"Oh, stop."

"She knew she could reach me."

"Jen."

"Don't call me that."

"Time out. Please."

I could hear her take a deep breath, and she did what she could do, wend inside herself through our torturous history, much of it my fault, and find her ample generosity. She told me then what she had heard was simple and declarative. George wasn't sick; rather, he'd been taken off life support and wasn't expected to live through the night.

Sunset was soon to be. I walked down to the beach as the sun broke free of the clouds in its slide into the sea. Maui etched itself into sight in the distance and the epic shape of Haleakala sat along a section of the horizon like a splayed pyramid. The water ran through deepening shades and ceased to roil. The sun bloated and flattened into the shape of a mushroom cloud as it lanced the Pacific. In less than three minutes it was gone. The water lost any burnish and was calm. A parade of clouds remained, long and low and loosely in the gray shapes of battleships. They offered up a reminder that Pearl Harbor was not so far away.

Suddenly the last upslants of light pulled bright handkerchiefs out of a hat. They turned upside down the color spectrum. In afterglow the clouds gathered up a fever of hues—pink, watermelon, blood orange, and carnelian. The migrant shades held an aching, transient beauty. Thousands of miles away where my uncle lay it was six hours later, well into the night he wasn't supposed to live through.

THIRTY YEARS BEFORE, the week before Christmas in 1969, I had answered another phone call. I had returned home for the holidays after moving to California. It was Big George on the other end of the line.

"George," I said. "Is that you?" In my family we had long since dropped the use of "uncle" or "aunt."

"John?" he asked. "What are you doing home?"

"Snuck in for Christmas."

"Well, is your dad around?"

"No, both Dad and Mom are at some party or other."

"Oh."

"Maybe I can help. You want me to give them a message?"

He didn't respond and I thought that perhaps I'd lost the connection. I said his name and when he made a sound I lifted my voice and my attitude to meet the man where I was so used to experiencing him: always positive, up, even if falsely so, powerfully so. I chimed into the phone: *"George, how are you?"*

"Not so good."

"What is it?"

He started to speak, broke off, an unsteadiness to his tone. "What?"

"It's Doug," my uncle said. "He's been killed in Vietnam."

After I got off the phone I looked up the number where my parents were and called them. I could hear the murmurs and laughter that surround cocktails and sound not unlike the sea as I waited for my mother or father to come to the phone.

Christmas was a time of such get-togethers in our town and maybe every town. This particular one had a special flavor, the first party hosted by a family that was recovering from a tragedy of their own. Somewhere over a year before one of their two sons left a note to a girl he barely knew. He had fixated on her, pursued her futilely, and somehow felt spurned by her when her family sequestered her and shipped her out of town. He locked himself in the garage and turned on the motor of the family's Buick Riviera. The parents were away in Florida on a boat they had just bought, and Stevie wasn't discovered for three days. His brother, checking the house, came upon him.

By 1969 the casualty list in many families wasn't small. The decade that had started with such promise and new frontiers had been hijacked by assassinations and an undeclared war and a loss of center that split generations and suddenly, wrenchingly, was pushing its way into radical behavior, avowedly political, that would often collapse upon itself in subsequent years.

It was my mother who came to the phone. My parents left the party immediately, and as soon as they arrived home they set to helping call other members of the family. My father and

George, two brothers born only fifteen months apart, were two of ten, and Doug, just over fifteen months younger than I am, was one of twenty-two first cousins we had on that side of the family.

George and Betty lived in West Hartford, Connecticut, then, and before the day was done my brother, Mason, and I flew down to be with them. Their oldest son, George Jr., had already arrived and their one daughter, Samantha, was living at home while her new husband, serving in Korea, waited to see whether he would go to Vietnam.

It was cold and getting colder by the time we reached the house. The forecast had changed from rain to snow, but the temperature was dropping faster than that. It was in the teens, and single digits were expected by morning; zero after that. We were there to wait. Doug was being shipped home. Da Nang to Dover, Delaware to West Hartford. The timetable of his arrival was not yet clear.

It had been a little after eleven o'clock that Sunday morning when the government sedan had pulled up in front of the house. George had already played a round of golf, knowing with the weather report it could be the last for the winter. He had shot a 77. For years he had been a scratch golfer and a local champion. His handicap had begun to rise, sneaking up to a six and now an eight, but it seemed to have found a solid resting place. After all, he was almost sixty.

Betty was talking on the new yellow wall phone in the kitchen that would still be there thirty years later. She was the one who answered the door. The officer asked for George and the three men went into the study and closed the door. Betty was left outside to wait. They didn't tell her. She didn't know what to do or where to go. She knew and yet had to wait to know. She sat in a straight-back chair in the hall and waited. The wait was terrible.

The two men had brought with them and left behind a telegram:

I MOST DEEPLY REGRET TO INFORM YOU ON BEHALF OF THE
UNITED STATES MARINE CORPS THAT YOUR SON LANCE COR-
PORAL DOUGLAS W. YOUNG USMC WAS KILLED IN ACTION
20 DECEMBER. HE SUSTAINED A FATAL INJURY TO THE HEAD
WHILE ON PATROL IN THE VICINITY OF DANANG REPUBLIC
OF VIETNAM. I WISH TO ASSURE YOU OF MY HEARTFELT SYM-
PATHY AND THAT OF YOUR SON'S FELLOW MARINES AT THIS
TIME OF HEARTACHE AND LOSS.

> LEONARD F. CHAPMAN, JR.
> GENERAL USMC COMMANDANT
> OF THE MARINE CORPS

Quite quickly a follow-up one was delivered. It told no
more of how Doug had died. I found it sitting on the desk in
the small study that sat opposite to the living room. A yellow
Western Union envelope opened, read, refolded, and placed
back. I took it out and this is what it said:

THIS CONCERNS YOUR SON LANCE CORPORAL DOUGLAS W.
YOUNG.

THE MARINE CORPS WILL RETURN YOUR LOVED ONE TO A
PORT IN THE UNITED STATES BY FIRST AVAILABLE AIRLIFT. AT
THE PORT REMAINS WILL BE PLACED IN A METAL CASKET
AND DELIVERED BY MOST EXPEDITIOUS MEANS TO ANY FU-
NERAL DIRECTOR DESIGNATED BY THE NEXT OF KIN OR TO
ANY NATIONAL CEMETERY IN WHICH THERE IS AVAILABLE
GRAVE SPACE. YOU WILL BE ADVISED BY THE UNITED STATES
PORT CONCERNING THE MOVEMENT AND ARRIVAL TIME.
AT DESTINATION, FORMS ON WHICH TO CLAIM AUTHORIZED
INTERMENT ALLOWANCE WILL ACCOMPANY REMAINS.

THIS ALLOWANCE MAY NOT EXCEED $75 IF CONSIGN-
MENT IS MADE DIRECTLY TO THE SUPERINTENDENT OF A
NATIONAL CEMETERY. WHEN CONSIGNMENT IS MADE TO A
FUNERAL DIRECTOR PRIOR TO INTERMENT IN A NATIONAL
CEMETERY, THE MAXIMUM ALLOWANCE IS $250. IF BURIAL

TAKES PLACE IN A CIVILIAN CEMETERY, THE MAXIMUM AL-
LOWANCE IS $500.

IT IS ALSO INCUMBENT UPON THE UNITED STATES MA-
RINE CORPS TO MAKE CLEAR THAT ANY AND ALL EXPENSES
IN EXCESS OF THESE AMOUNTS CANNOT AND WILL NOT BE
COVERED.

DO NOT SET DATE OF FUNERAL UNTIL PORT AUTHORITIES
NOTIFY YOU DATE AND SCHEDULED TIME OF ARRIVAL DES-
TINATION.

This telegram was not signed.

WHEN WE WERE YOUNG Doug and I were thrown together by several kinds of proximity.

Among so many cousins we were the closest in age, two boys barely a year apart. My brother, Mason, was the next older by almost two years, and that seemed a lot, and only more as we got older. Suddenly he and Doug's brother, George, a year and a half older still, sprouted in height ("a bunch" was the family expression) and dwarfed us. Suddenly they turned into teenagers. Suddenly they were driving and dating girls. Doug and I were left inches and licenses and tons of testosterone behind.

This was Plymouth, Massachusetts, hailed as "America's Home Town" since the *Mayflower* may or may not have landed on a jokingly small rock there that had cracked open like an egg at some point and been slapped back together. It took the town three hundred years to scrabble together twenty thousand people, but in the millennium now it was struggling with a population explosion.

A generation ago, when we were growing up, there had been another landing: Pilgrim Station, a nuclear power plant. The town had bought into its promise of prosperity, cheap energy, and a giant jack to the tax base. It didn't pan out, and the boondoggle it became stretched for decades. It was off-line more than on-, cropped up with lousy safety ratings, didn't hold back hikes in taxes until, finally, it was sold and at last shut down. But there it sat, a hazardous albatross. Plymouth's latest lightbulb was building golf courses. A sudden epidemic of them was eating up the low-lying landscape, eradicating cranberry bogs and wrapping around the ponds that spackled the county, the largest in square miles in Massachusetts. The tally of ponds in Plymouth was startling. There were three hundred and sixty-five of them, as many as the days in the year. From the air it could have been bayou country.

We lived south of the center of the town and within sight at the lowest of solstice and equinox tides of the several out-croppings of rock that stretched out from Manomet point called the Mary Anns. We used them as markers when fishing and their beautiful brute shapes were sharp with warning and augur. In a winter storm in 1928 we had often heard about and a plaque memorialized, a steamship, the *Robert E. Lee*, foundered on them and a boatswain and two surfmen from the Coast Guard station lost their lives.

While we were all in Plymouth, between Memorial Day and Labor Day, we seldom bathed, and went barefoot, except to play tennis or go to Fenway Park. The bottoms of our feet callused. Doug and I tested them on the narrow road that ran between the houses our parents at first rented and later owned. Noon on the hottest days put them to the fire. The road could have been a kiln. The blacktop made us dance. We did a cha-cha up the road then, trying not to let our feet touch down and vowing not to abandon the scorching surface. That would be to admit defeat. It was one more of our many con-tests, a youthful variation of Chicken. Once in a while the tar would melt and bubble like molten lava and carry a sweet heavy scent and stick to our feet. Licorice patches on the toughened soles. Still we didn't bathe; showers were for sissies. For us the only place to wash was in the ocean.

That was where we went every sunny afternoon. Soft sand ruled the beach above the high-tide line and before we were ten we played with boats there. Our toy ones left wakes in the soft sand that didn't last. At full or new moon the tide rolled up several extra feet and then pulled way out. The beach became immense for an hour or two. Those were game days on the sand flats—stickball, Fox and Geese, and Capture the Flag. There seemed little or nothing we couldn't turn into games.

Or we would build dams. Pools formed and the toy boats found safe harbor until the tide swept our handiwork away. Once or twice a summer we'd attempt a Hoover Dam to hold the incoming sea back, digging out wet sand and reinforcing the walls and making them higher still. Sometimes while on vacation my uncle George or my dad pitched in. With his huge hands, George scooped out great hunks and, if only for a while, would help stem the tide.

After age ten we sailed. We crewed on one Thistle or Puffin or mutt of a boat, fun grunt work, eager to hold the tiller and steer until my uncle bought one of the first Sailfish. For a few years they were everywhere, the hot ticket, their sails jiggering across the bay. They're no longer made now, though the next generation of innovation, the Sunfish, still exists. The Sailfish was little more than a flat plank wrapped in fiberglass, but it seemed revolutionary. We had taken a ride up to a Marblehead factory and watched this magical stuff, fiberglass, being manufactured and molded into Boston Whalers, the other rage of the day. Along the tour there were piles of samples the thickness of coins and the size of cupcakes. We snuck some under our shirts thinking we were very smart, and got payback when their unfinished underbellies rubbed our own bellies raw. The nylon-like fibers set right into the skin and fired up a nasty, itchy, ugly rash.

Along Cape Cod Bay a southwest wind comes up almost every afternoon. An easterly or northeasterly breeze tends to stitch the mornings with patterns of corduroy and lend the water a sapphirelike cast. By three o'clock the wind swings around. The water, never warm, takes on additional chill and changes color, altering to a rough roiled green that has no luster and little beauty and is often chopped by whitecaps. The wind can keep picking up until there are small craft warnings. It takes dusk to quiet it down again.

This was the time we set out each day. Quickly, we'd shake the rioting outboards loose. We'd tack the Sailfish out beyond the points of land that extended toward Provincetown, where the wind was stinging and the water was rougher still. We'd be soaked with spray, hiking out, laughing, and hanging on to the tiller and the sheet for our lives, waiting for and wanting the next gust.

We loved to gamble with capsizing. Sometimes we'd do it to each other; sometimes we'd do it together: let the simple plank of a boat heel higher and higher, holding too hard a close haul until we were sliding despite ourselves—or, even better, tossed despite ourselves, laughing and cursing into the drink.

The water sobered us up. It was freezing and, shivering, one of us would haul up onto the dagger board while the second hung on to what would have been the gunwale on a real boat and kicked. Together, using weight as leverage, using the water for traction and thrust, we'd draw the Sailfish upright again. The sail loosed itself from the bay, like an animal shaking itself off, flapping and showering water on us, rising and readying to catch the wind again.

For an instant we'd be at a standstill. A last luffing into the wind. With a jolt, a kick—a *swock*—the boom would swing then and the sail would take on the stiff snap of the southwest wind and be full again. And laughing again and still shivering, we'd be off.

Before August every year Doug's hair paled from red through tawny to towhead. Our tans were deep and burned in, shoe-polish brown that darkened to umber at the base of our backs in the inch above our bathing suits. When we came in from sailing, the shadows from the high bluff lengthening across the beach, our bodies were spattered with salt. We were as dark and salted as roasted almonds.

We didn't talk much while we sailed. The Red Sox might merit mention. Certainly the summer of Ted Williams's final season, when the *Boston Herald* charted his climbing home run total, the headlines increasing in size until they were huge, 32-point, when he hit his 521st in his final at bat. There was the Democratic Convention in Los Angeles in 1960. We were aware of it. We were in southern Massachusetts and Hyannis Port wasn't far away. In other places and other families there may have been deep discussions, arguments loud and long across the dinner table, but not for us, not on the water or anywhere else.

Our conversations had a functional and sweet simplicity: "Tighten the sheet." "Yank the dagger board." "We're planing!" "Look at that rooster tail!" "Ready about, hard alee." "Jibe ho!" "Here we go!" "Man overboard!" and "HOLY SSSHHHHIIIIIIIITTTTTTTTTTTT!" For the rest the water and the wind did the talking.

I can only remember a single instance when we did. Sort of did. There were two-mile and three-mile buoys then and we sailed out to the first, a bell buoy. It was a fire-engine red that had dulled from wind and salt and wet. It rocked with the waves, but was broad enough at its base to stand on—or so we thought, and so I had to try. We tacked close by and I dropped off the Sailfish and swam to it. The water was very cold. It lacerated the skin and then began to work its way in. The climb onto the buoy looked easy until I attempted it. The buoy was bigger than I had realized and there was nothing to get ahold of. The metal was slick and the discoloration along the water line was deep with sea grunge. It was no longer even red there—a greasy bottle-green that was racing toward black. I had the greatest trouble getting up and the victory of success was tempered by exhaustion.

Standing was easier. The casing around the bell wasn't solid and there were places for my hands to grip. Using my body, I rocked the buoy until the bell sounded. It was dull and deep. It had never seemed loud but now, so close, it shut my ears down. It jolted me and made me let go and blew away the image I had imagined of riding the buoy like a bronco, one arm aloft in triumph.

I was in the cold drink again and, jibing to pick me up, Doug went over. In a few strokes I reached the Sailfish and the two of us clambered up onto the narrow edge. We were side by side shivering and the buoy was still tolling and we could see back to land—the dazzle of the westerly sun and the bluffs and the Pine Hills that lay beyond—and all of it looked very small.

"Maybe we should just stay out here," Doug said.

"It's certainly warm enough," I said, my teeth clacking away.

"Not so back in."

"I forgot my sleeping bag."

"I'm serious."

"I was afraid of this."

"It's beautiful."

"It's freezing."

"But take a look," he said. "Take a look around. It's beautiful. Well, not beautiful, but it's something."

"It's something freezing," I said.

"It's something—peaceful," he said, but the word broke up in stuttering syllables, his own teeth chattering, and I laughed.

"I mean it," he said. "I'll remember this."

"Oh, great."

"And so will you."

"Fine," I said, "but now can we get out of here?"

We did, and of course he was right, I do, and in my memory the way the cold screwed down and ran through my limbs and the muscle soreness and deep fatigue like a bone bruise all over that came from that day are still there, but what he said and the quality he described—the peacefulness—is what I most recall.

THE OTHER TIMES we talked were the rainy days. In sou'westers, still barefoot, we'd tromp from one home to the other, hide out in our rooms, or best of all find our way to the attic above the garage at our grandmother's house. The stairs were steep and narrow and it got hot there on hot days and cold and damp on rainy days. The roof was pitched and unfinished, without insulation, and the roofing nails stuck through the moisture-stained wood, delightfully ready under the eaves to incise anyone who stood up straight. Several generations of prized possessions had washed up there. They lingered in this neglected way station, waiting for rescue or final disposal. A garage sale all set to go.

There was a nicked-up workbench with a vise no longer very well attached to it, some battered lobster pots cast about, and frayed hunks of rope hanging on hooks; and old buoys, marked in a motley array of faded colors, had found perches on the pots or the workbench or on the unfinished pine floor. There were a couple of fenderless bikes set upside-down long ago to protect their tires that now fell flat on rusted rims. There was a trunk that held old photograph albums and a disarray of vintage clothes as tossed about as confetti, and there was a once-handsome mahogany RCA Victor wind-up Victrola as tall as I was then, with a collection of warped records that made all the singers, male or female, sound like desperately slow and sodden baritones.

We played more games there and let our imaginations loose. When we were young enough we'd dress for roles in the stories we made up and act them out and allow girls to take part. Or maybe they let us take part. Years later a Ping-Pong table appeared and the girls disappeared. If they still came it was without us. We were never together there in the same way again.

It may have been in the attic that Doug and I cooked up our code, a kind of identification system for all the human species on the planet. We took the letters C and S (why we lit on those two I no longer have any idea) and started a sequence of C.S.'s. Each was shorthand for "Certain Simpleton" or "Certifiable Snob" or "Categorically Stupid" or "Compulsive Smack," and each was assigned a number. Most were derogatory; scathing was better still. Few were positive. Very few. The S's were easier to come up with than the C's. What a wealth to choose from—"scab," "snot," "slime ball," "scumbag"—and "shit" was extended a special dispensation. It was used however many times necessary, which was a lot: "Chicken Shit," "Complete Shit," "Cool Shit."

Dragged along to endless cocktail parties, not to feel underfoot, we took refuge in our dauntless ID system. We knocked them back and forth. Doug would turn to me and say, "C.S.#4," and I'd say, "No, no, C.S.#7," and he'd say, "Right. Definitely." In the escalating melee that every evening became we eventually squeezed down to an even shorter shorthand. One would whisper, "C.S.#9," and the other wouldn't even speak. Simply a thumbs-up or a thumbs-down.

Every once in a while during these parties we'd wash cars. For a dollar a car we'd throw ourselves into the task, professionals now, whirling dervishes with soap, buckets, chamois cloths, and a hose. A way to escape mischief and make some money. Inevitably and not unintentionally, we'd manage to get each other as wet as the cars we were supposed to be cleaning. As we worked, the mix of liquor and laughter played out through the windows. Already we'd come to mock these gatherings. We vowed with all our young fervor that We would never be like Them, and yet in the rising hubbub and chatter was a comforting and familiar music we had come to know by heart, the vespers that accompanied the daily dying of the light.

WITH SEPTEMBER came the end of summer and often a storm. Nature would rear its feral head and it could be vicious and unremitting. In 1954 it was Hurricane Carol. It ripped every boat from its mooring, wrecking most, felled and up-ended trees, gutted the beach and shut down electricity for five days. Leaves torn from the trees hatched like confetti across the lawns and streets. The shapes of others, blown so hard, were stamped on the sides of houses. Chlorophyll tracings. In its destructive wake Carol left a curious hush and a scored beauty.

Other years it was simply a northeaster, a big blow. The wind would stir, the sky would build and grumble, and then the rain would come. Sometimes the first spatters took their time grading into a drenching. Others, the torrent arrived like a curtain, hissing on the pavement and exploding on the roof. Surf pounded the sand then and the tide insisted its way onto the bluff. Frequently the day after would be flawless, the sky azure, the water cobalt, and the waves still furious and turbulent and exciting to ride.

Shadows spread across the beach much earlier and more swiftly in the afternoons in these last weeks and brought sadness with them. Colors grew full and ripe. In the saturation seemed to lie an extra notch of emotion, a potency of feeling as well as the demarcation of a season. A tree would wave a freak bright bough, already turned. Last toads would hop toward safety across the soggy dirt roads and sometimes made it. The air was bracing in the morning and chilly at night. We broke out sweaters and built fires. There wasn't the heat and humidity to sniff anymore. The scents of loam and leaves supplanted them. We were full of energies and restlessness and longings. The first vestiges of autumn had arrived.

And each year came the reading of the "fractured French"

coasters. I don't know how it began. It's also impossible to explain. In high school we skinny-dipped and stole gas caps; in college we streaked and chugged beer. This was hardly that. Perhaps all families, especially large and insular ones, concoct meaningless customs that unexpectedly manage to gather up meaning. What begins by chance happens again, and in time reoccurs on purpose, and in repetition breeds ritual.

Once I witnessed two members of the Kennedy family simply saying two words to each other—"the rosebushes." They knew instantly the meaning; they shared the shorthand and laughter erupted. The laughter wasn't solely about enjoyment. At Hyannis Port rosebushes rimmed the yard where they played touch football and served as an out-of-bounds marker. In Bobby Kennedy's time that's where pass patterns took you: down and out to the rosebushes. Would you go into them without flinching or whining? If you had to, they all knew, you weren't going to come out unscathed.

We had such football games on Thanksgiving, playing first in coats and ties and later in sweats and spikes, lugging our overloaded stomachs around the yard and refusing to quit through the dusk and into the dark. No one ever admitted defeat. We turned car headlights on and taxed the batteries and drained the gas tanks until full-on night forced us into retirement.

But equally—and I can't say why—I remember the reading of the "fractured French" coasters. These coasters were of heavy foil paper, silver shiny and small, the size of compact mirrors. I never saw them used for drinks. (What's amazing is there are still sets around, up for sale on eBay.)

Each was imprinted with a bawdy and broadly drawn cartoon. Very fifties. Very *New Yorker*. A French phrase or idiom with an English translation below. Pronounce it badly, *fracture* the French, and a pun materialized. A bad pun; often a very bad pun. Drinking helped; it certainly helped.

Envision, for example, a haughty woman in riding breeches, cap, and pointed nose—a one-line sharp turn really—munching a meal off a mantel in front of a roaring fire. Her can, a very large can, a definitely exaggerated anatomical part drawn in a time and in a style that definitely and definitively could only characterize it as "can." The French is "C'est pour rire." The English is "Sore tail."

Or "Carte Blanche": a buxom Blanche spraddled about an overturned chair with great big watery eyes and heavy, dark, drowsy half-moon lids. She's been up for days or has slapped on smears of mascara like tar. She's spilling her drink on the floor. It's dangling from her hand, like a forgotten microphone. Toppling tippling. What's the English? "Take Blanche home." And the "Pièce de résistance": the baldest, chunkiest, shortest, happiest guy chasing the tallest, curviest, blondest blonde in a polka-dot bikini up the beach, hair streaming behind her. Translation: "Shy girl."

It was George who read them. It happened only once a summer, and it became ceremonial: The date wasn't specific, it wasn't locked down, but every year as dark came earlier and after it had fallen on one of the last nights of one of the last cocktail gatherings, "No, no," he would say, until not at all reluctantly he acceded by acclamation. (His favorite was "Jeanne d'Arc": a curvaceous, lurching beauty in desperate search of a light switch and a place to relieve herself, but there is "No light in the bathroom." My father loved most "S'il vous plaît:" a poor unhappy burglar yanks open a silver drawer only to discover "Not sterling.")

George called out in French. He would wait then, wait for the correct answer to be hollered back. He laughed as he spoke them and laughed harder if and when he had to produce the answer. Drinking helped; it certainly helped. As he kept on—there were twenty-some coasters—he laughed even before he started and simply didn't stop.

He had a wonderful laugh that was rich and full and contagious and lifted us out of the commonplace. Before long we would be laughing with him at the answer and then with him before he had a chance to ask the question. Doug and I were too young to drink, way too young, and it didn't matter. We sat together every year on a chaise with gutted springs and no arms. Doug had a crackle of a laugh that further got me going. The note it hit was high and startling at first, so clear and distinct and loud, but it was finally much like his father's. Our bodies bounced against each other and once we even knocked ourselves, half-playfully, off opposite sides to the floor. It was nonsense and we could not stop laughing.

No one could.

YET THE TRUE MEETING place of those summers was the tennis court, the seventy-eight-by-thirty-one-and-a-half-foot surface that stretched out beside my great-aunt's house. Over the decades since it was built in the last years of World War I, its clay had sunk into the soil or worn away, and yearly it was infused with a cinderlike substance called Standard Green that came by the ton in fifty-pound bags. Each summer's first project was to weed the court, heft the bags of Standard Green, slit them open, spread them about the surface, water the court and roll it, then do it again, and set the tapes down that marked the boundaries. Only then would the rolled-up net be retrieved from the attic, threaded with a cable, and cranked up into place.

So many scenes in our early lives played out on this rectangular swatch. For twenty years we had a tournament, and the sounds of tennis—the smack of a ball on a racket like a cork popping, or the skidding squelch of sneakers braking and then on the move again—still fill me with elation and dread, a knotty and troubled nostalgia.

We played against one another, brothers and sisters and cousins. Our parents watched and commented and often criticized, incessant small carpings that built like sediment or rust or corrosion and still lingered. They marked us; they made us. They never went away. I can remember certain wins and losses, getting sick before this or that match, even individual points with perfect recall and acutely deep, contradictory emotions. Seems odd and funny to say—as tied into the loom as the births of my children.

The truth is, tennis entered us even before we were born, when our fathers learned the game, and for as long as they could they played and played the way they wanted us to play. Near the end of his life my father talked about "watching old folks all dressed up in whites, white flannels." After they got through he and George would let down the net "because it was so much easier to get the ball back and forth without a damn net."

"Yeah, cheaters from way back," my aunt Betty laughed when she heard this tidbit.

Twice in my life I have sat down with my cousin Samantha, Doug's sister, to try to talk about him. The first time, before long we found ourselves sidetracked into these times of tennis. Up pulsed a memory: once we had played against each other and she had played badly. Terribly. She hadn't won a game, and I made some comment afterwards, probably a throwaway like "You sure were rotten today" or even "Boy, you stunk." Others might have hit me or broken down and cried. Not Samantha. Not one of us. She just tightened down and said nothing and revealed nothing until this conversation twenty-five years later. What I had been trying to say—badly, very badly myself—was how good she normally was. At least, if I'd been confronted, that would've been my rationalization. Pretty pathetic technique it is, granted, but this is the way we lived and talked and protected ourselves. We raised—or lowered—it into an art. The line between compliment and insult was razor thin or reversed or sometimes invisible. We surrounded our sentences with armature. We ironized our words.

I hadn't even been very imaginative. We weren't prone to the wonderful vulgar contortions of the English language that pop up in other quadrants of the country. "I'm going to tear off your head and shit in your neck," or "You'll be wearing that badge in your asshole," or "She could knock a rooster off a full henhouse with a veil over her face." We were creative and colloquial only in our uses of silence.

What I didn't know—had never known—was Samantha had reason to be lousy. She had been sick that day. Cramps, vomiting, diarrhea. Perhaps tension, too. She had spent the morning using every possible orifice as emergency exits. She tried to duck out, tried everything, but her father wouldn't let her forfeit the match. That was unacceptable. Still she refused. He bribed her to get her onto the court.

When we were very young, clinics began every morning at 8:30 sharp. A squadron of us lined up in shorts and shirts, regardless of gender, swinging and missing with rackets as big as we were. Those first rackets were leftovers. They spilled out of a dark damp closet in a house that had no insulation, rich with mildew, loopy-shaped wooden monsters warped from suffering through wet winters. It was years before Slazengers or Wilsons were grabbed up at the local sports store. With them came wooden presses with the lug nuts at the corners to screw down tight and prevent the dipsy-doodle bananalike curves of the originals. Metal rackets, with nylon or gut specially strung to certain weights, were next, but we were well beyond clinics by then.

There came those times then when one or two or four of us would lift our play into what we call now the zone. The when and the why of the elevation remains a mystery to me. What I do see now is how complex a weave it was of competition and family and whim and even the weather and time of day.

It could happen at noon when the sun was blasting and the heat was merciless and our shirts were stripped and we were shellacked with sweat and sets became more about stamina than skill, tests of will and acts of insanity, searching for and sometimes finding misbegotten glory before wilting into capitulation. It could happen in the deep dapple of late afternoon when the scrub pines and oaks that clotted one side made shadows that cut the court as sharply as a knife. The spreading shade in its blackness was as blinding as the midday sun. It was cool, even crisp then, and the light had an extra declension that was exhilarating.

So too could come the excitement in the rumbling imminence of a thunderstorm that shook the trees and turned the leaves onto their bellies, and the closing in of dusk that stole the ball and left only guesswork in the last twitch of light, and the surprise and laughter when you guessed right.

When we were teenagers, closing in on college, we started a mixed doubles tournament, and one summer every match seemed to stretch to three sets. Only the Newport Casino in Rhode Island used tiebreakers then, and the game count could spiral into double figures, 10–8 or 12–10, and once a single set stretched over three late afternoons to an epic 22–20. The level of play in these marathons was high and hard fought. Cutthroat. Without mercy. The weakest player, no matter the gender, was assaulted ruthlessly, yet there was a courtliness—slaps on the hands, pats on the butt, "attaboy's" and "attagirl's"—even as we took no prisoners.

Within these battles was another element. They were entwined with sexiness. We were that age, tan and fit, long-limbed and lithe, and it imbued its way into the hustle, the camaraderie, the athleticism, the victory and the defeat. It was in the air and in the sweat and in the wardrobe. That shape of wetness down the middle of your partner's back, the rhythmic flow of one haunch and then the other in fitted shorts, the pinch of pale skin glimpsed through the armhole of a sleeveless blouse.

The matches were exciting and fun and something else ineffable. I can't find the right word to convey the right emotion. Beyond description, capture. The only substitute I come up with makes no sense at first: we felt at home.

BUT IN THE YEARS long before that, when we were young, we didn't always want to play. Some of us made that a choice

that hardened into a will. One was Doug. He never got into
the game and he gave tennis up. I wonder now, knowing more
of parents and children, fathers and sons, whether his obsti-
nence hadn't to do with his father, with the stuff of their relationship; or whether his refusal was tied to dyslexia or ADD
or some visual problem no one knew to diagnose then.

There were spats along the way with all of us. My brother
was very good at throwing rackets for a very long time; I wasn't
so bad myself. But it was even before the height of adolescence, when Doug was no more than nine or ten, that he
threw his racket and at his father's insistence picked it up, and
then threw it again.

"Shit."

"Doug," his father said.

"I hate this."

"Pick up your racket, son."

"It's dumb. It's stupid."

"Your racket." The words had no lightness to them.

"I'm not going to play this game anymore," Doug said, and
started to leave the court.

"You're not going anywhere." Doug kept on going. "Come
back here. Right now." The severity of George's demand was
impossible to miss.

"No!"

"*Stop.*"

But his son didn't.

It was then that his father took after him. He made a noise
as he went, low down in his throat, a growl, that turned into
a kind of low wail: "Yes you will, yes you will, yes you will."

Doug saw him coming and ran.

Watching, I was frozen, and I wasn't alone. No one moved
except to watch the chase. They appeared and disappeared behind the trumpet vines that clung to the chicken wire along
two sides of the court, running faster and faster, full speed,
until George caught his son and dragged him back, the long-

long-legged bald smiling man dragging a redheaded nine-year-old across the lumpy grass, kicking and screaming like a writhing animal, all the way back to the tennis court.

He leaned down close to Doug then and spoke to him, spit spraying, and picked up the tennis racket and stood Doug up, held him in place, planted him on the court, and put the racket in his hand, his own great hand around it, holding it, holding Doug there and not letting him go. All the while he kept speaking.

I still cannot write this without pain. Their struggle went beyond rebellion or resistance, objection or interference. I don't remember what George said. I was close enough to hear him, must have. I was only feet away. I wish I could. I could make it up and might even come close, but the truth is I remember none of it.

Yet for thirty years it has been my profession to write in a form, the screenplay, that hangs, so it is said, on dialogue. I write scenes for a living. He said this, she said that. Long and short and spare speeches, and even a kind of silence that can speak and be loud and telling without words.

I can see that cindery Standard Green and the trail left as Doug was dragged and the scuffs and scrapes across his bare back and the dent in the clay that his racket left when he first threw it. I can see the spittle fly. I remember the smell and the rich pomegranate color of the blooming trumpet vines on the wire. I feel I can even hear the hummingbirds spinning around them. I can still feel the sun on me, and the stillness that filled and froze me.

These viscera are present and intact and extraordinarily lucid. They continue to exist with complete articulation, but amnesia has absconded with the rest. Whatever was said, however much or little, I cannot remember. Not a single word. And that silence has lasted close to fifty years, and it opened one that was to come between them.

3

THE NEXT SEVENTY-TWO HOURS in 1969 had been an odd time. Doug's arrival remained unfixed, moot. The waiting was unlike any other. You couldn't help starting to think. Mightn't there be a mistake? As the days stretched, it made the original information—awful news from such an alien place so far away via a bureaucracy consumed by the cost of coffins—seem suspect. Just part of warp.

We did not talk about this. We did not bring it up to the conversation level. We shared it in the subterranean quarters of our selves. We did not talk of Doug either. We did not share stories, anecdotes, or memories. In our family there were private places where we did not talk and where only one could enter. Here was one.

The New England winter was frozen and so was conversation, lashed even beyond its usual self into a nuclear silence. It had always been a New England goal to take taciturnity to a higher and higher level. Here was a new reason to raise the bar and perfect it further.

Friends dropped by, food overflowed the refrigerator, we played paddle tennis at the golf club, the young people went out and drank at night, and a football pool consumed my cousin George Jr. The National Football League's final week-

end was upcoming and, withdrawing into his childhood bedroom, he obsessed about the point spreads. For hours he did
not come out.

The snow that had fallen froze in place like a cap over the
earth, a slender tough core the thickness of coconut as it sits
inside its shell. New snow came and could not hold. It blew,
scattered, and seemed gone. Then it was too cold for snow. It
just looked like snow. The sky assumed that leaden yet lucent
shade. From morning to night it looked precipitous. The temperature kept dropping.

The truth is, as it always is, life went on. But it went on differently, heavy-laden and expectant. There was a shoe to drop,
the actuality, the coming of the coffin, and that would happen
soon enough; but in the waiting there was a free fall of silence,
an odd decorum, and the postponement of a free fall of emotion that could not be measured.

It swung on a tether.

——

TWICE IN OUR LIVES Doug and I were ushers in weddings
together and thought we would have nothing to do. Our
cousin Kitty's marriage was the first. The wedding took place
in Montgomery, Alabama, and we were thrown together into
that foreign country.

The welcome we received was warm and gracious, completely open and seemingly intimate. It was very seductive, a
part of what makes the South so appealing and stultifying. We
had lunch with Bear Bryant (he was eating at the same golf
club), we swirled into a roundelay of parties, we joined together in a brutal game of touch-tackle football, we heard the
casual exchange of nigger jokes, and bestowed upon us were
two girls to serve as escorts.

Chance or design had drawn Sharon and LuAnn. The rules
of such etiquette were never mentioned to us; perhaps they
can't be explained. They were charming, matched to our ages,

and bountiful with musical chatter. Water drawing across pebbles in a brook. Whatever dresses they wore each night stopped at the kneecap; every one fell precisely to mid-patella. These dresses weren't tight but in the juju of their fit they were somehow suggestive.

We were coming down from the North, where fashion was reeling. It was suddenly trendy, in flux, and ripping free. The conservative template had broken and the old guidelines given way. Hems were hiking and colors and cuts were clashing and slashing. Letting it all hang out, as was said then. Peter Max, Pucci, Carnaby Street. Language, like fashion, was a whirligig of new idioms and clichés. Seldom in civilization have so few phrases proliferated so fast and been used by so many so promiscuously. Sock it to me . . . far out . . . groovy.

Doug and I were flopping along well behind the curve. We had given up crew cuts and were letting our hair grow, but neither of us could yet get anything worthwhile to grow on our faces and we were still holding back. The insistent and fleeting instance of cachet left us suspicious. We hung on to our own brand of skepticism.

In Montgomery all this was but distant artillery. Hairstyles and makeup seemed untouched. Whether pumps or sandals, the heels these two Southern girls wore remained stalwartly traditional. They were never too low and never too high. Their closets must have lined up in perfect formations.

Both girls smoked, and not just a puff or two. They snatched cigarettes whenever they could, yet their lipstick—a shade of pink, not baby, not pale, but still definitely pink—never seemed out of place. It was a magic trick. And they still lived in a land of girdles and stockings that drew up the legs and hooked to them.

They had learned their lessons well: they knew how to flirt and how to make us join in. It was part of their birthright and an essence of the menu. Even the house specialty. We thought we were in control but before long I had my doubts. When I kissed Sharon the first night she feigned surprise and managed to marinate into her response somehow that she was both aghast and pleased:

"Why did you do that? We barely know each other."

I fell right in. "What's today?"

"What's that have to do with anything?" she asked. "It's the twenty-second of November."

"Okay, if it were the twenty-second of December would you mind?"

"No, but—"

"Why waste all that time?"

"Oh-ho," said Sharon. "Are you fast!"

"How fast is *fast*?"

"I feel like I'm in a movie."

"Is it a good movie?"

"I'm waiting for the ending," Sharon said.

"But this is just the beginning," I said.

"The way you talk!"

"The way *I* talk. I'm just a poor visitor from another planet."

"I knew it. I said to LuAnn, I told her, 'That boy's trouble.' Well, come on."

"Come on what?"

"Over here, fast boy."

She offered up her face and gave me her lips and a dancing tongue and then masterfully (and with what had to be great practice) dodged and blocked anything my hands attempted to do.

"Come up for air!" she said at last.

"But this is just the beginning, remember?"

"We'll just have to see about that."

She was a short girl with cream-colored skin, and bleached hair and a sleeveless dress both the color of butter. She chattered on a moment, shotgunning questions at me without waiting for my answers. She interrupted them. Stepping on tiptoe, she came back once more. She laid her hand this time along the back of my neck and let it drift through my hair with a sensuous nonchalance.

She stopped the kiss when she—and only she—was ready. "That was nice. Do you mind if I smoke?"

She was enjoying herself, and fully expected me to try for what she wasn't going to give me. The exact latitude and longitude of denial were subtle. She knew how to insinuate the parts of her body in endless fractionates. It had some mysterious and maddening give-and-take and then didn't. "No" always found a definite azimuth. Each time I would edge a little further; each time I would be shot down. She knew every manner of defense, the exact yanks on the leash. She was an artist at work.

THE SPLENDID TEASE aborted the night before the wedding when all the rites and rules of order fell apart.

After one party after another, a hard-core group—the wedding party minus the bride and groom and the best of the rest—found one last bar. It was a confluent spot. It sat beside a highway, like a roadhouse, and beside a golf course, like a place that harbored golfers in the bar and debutante parties in the Mussel Shoals Room.

Like Doug and me, his sister, Samantha, a bridesmaid, had an escort. His name was Jamie Lee, the brother of another bridesmaid. He was good-looking in a square, short, stout way with a crew cut and sideburns two knuckles in length. They weren't getting along. Sam had an aloofness about her, a superior air that he misunderstood. It wasn't disdain; it was discomfort and distance. She was shot through with New England and out of her element. Another alien here. Highly intelligent, driven, she was at the height of her particular beauty and yet wounded and a little shut down.

She had just broken up with a boyfriend one more time, who had the unfortunate name of Wardy or Waddy. It made him easy to mock from a distance, especially not knowing him and because mockery was our style. We lived by, in, and for mockery. Not long before, acting on my superb advice, she had popped into his dorm one night unannounced. The results were what she later caustically, self-protectively, and self-punishingly called "expected." She deeply dipped the word in our particular paint. When she walked in, the first thing she had encountered was a bare foot sticking out of the bed. It wasn't his.

For a time we had rubbed electrically about each other the way cousins can. We had spent so much time together, good and bad, and knew each other so well. Lurching into adolescence, the forbidden possibilities of our relationship ricocheted and became both harbor and catnip. They created a magnetic field, a frisson that felt chancy and very alive. We tiptoed around carnality. She had always been athletic and perfectly dimensioned; suddenly, she was a stunning young woman. I was the more-than-requisite combination of athletic, attractive, arrogant, and, lest we forget, obnoxious. And I had one other quality that I would learn could prove provocatively dangerous: I liked to look and to listen.

Once she had shown up at my school and we had spent a wonderful, silent, sexy, but unacted-upon weekend together. There were letters after it, regretting, not regretting, wondering, worrying, wandering, scrawled on a variety of stationery, blank sheets, and three-hole-punched lined paper, and I'm sure I wrote back trying and maybe overtrying to impress, be cool, or be honest. At some point I know I pronounced it was all over—whatever it was and in fact wasn't—and she called me.

"It's exactly nine p.m., Thursday, April twenty-second, 1965, here," she announced, "and would you please get off my mind so I can get some work done."

I didn't know what to say and didn't have to. She went on ahead.

"Did you mean it?" she asked.

"Mean what?"

"'The final act of this circus'?"

"Are you drunk?"

"That's what you said, your last letter said, and it killed me and it's my spirit that's calling you now."

"Hello, Spirit."

"Was that really the epilogue?"

"I thought you said 'final act.'"

"Are you going to answer the question? April tenth. That's what you said. Wrote. Did you mean that?"

"I said that?"

"You don't remember?"

"I was probably drunk."

"You were not."

"Don't believe everything I say," I said. "I get into moods."

"That's not allowed."

"You don't?"

"I want you to listen to me. I never talk around you. I'm intimidated. I'm not going to let that happen now. None of this preconceived, carefully thought-out garbage. The cult of the cool. I can't stand it. Mad, mad, mad, mad. But I want you to know what I'm really like. But I think you know me better than myself."

"Sam."

"You frighten me sometimes. The things you say. What you see. I'm not a very deep person."

"Horseshit."

"It's true. I'm tired. I just want to be happy. Maybe you don't. Maybe you like that cave you sometimes seem to crawl into, you and darkness. It's seductive and it's a drag. What's with the world? What's with people? Why do they torture each other? Why do I torture you, or do I? You torture me, or at least I let myself be tortured. Sickening."

"Can I talk now?"

"Do I want to hear it?"

"Whatever I write you, whatever I say, you know it's

Manomet, it's memories, but it's more than that. Where do you want me to start? At the top of your head or the tip of your toes. Or everywhere between, inside and out—"

"See now you're starting. And you can be so seductive. I don't want this to be a game, another game, all our games. Crazy eights, arm wrestling, not to mention—" She stopped: we both knew the blanks to be filled in. "I just don't want to talk about it anymore."

"Oh that'll stop it."

"Will it?" she said.

"I doubt it," I said.

"Of course that's what happens. The things you don't want to think about or know or remember come back to haunt you," she said. "It's so powerful and I don't want to end up hating each other."

"That's not possible," I said. "Not remotely possible."

"I don't don't don't want it to be."

We were young so there were a series of such conversations and more letters and I remember far better what she said than what I did, and how the calls would come at odd times and odd places but start the same way.

"Hello?"

"You're there?"

"Hi."

"I can't believe it. Six-forty-five p.m., Saturday, October twenty-seventh, and I'm sitting on a bed in Calhoun College at Yale."

"Of course I'm here. It's Saturday night, October twenty-seventh. Where do you expect me to be? Partying?"

"Yes."

"I wish."

"You were."

"I was what?"

"I couldn't find you."

"When?"

"Last night, the night before. I wanted you to come to the party."

"What party?"

"In New York. Never mind. It was a bad idea anyway. I wonder why I do this, call you."

"Just call me Doctor."

"My streaming thoughts I give to you."

"You've been drinking."

"I have not," she said. "I have so."

"What else is on that bed? Why are you at Yale?"

"Don't change the subject."

"Which subject?"

"Me. Glorious me. Pathetic me. Melancholy me. Bullshit black hole me. Just write me, call me. Your silence is killing me. What are we going to do?"

"I'm going to come up to Yale and sit on that bed with you, no matter whose bed it is, even if he's in it."

"You don't get it, do you? I'm going now."

And she did, and as enticing as it was, we didn't know what to do with all these things we carried, and so we did nothing.

Now Sam was trying rebellion on for size. She had set bras aside, and her white sweater buttoned up the back rather than the front. Her skirt was leagues away from pastel, a pungent pumpkin shade. Showed six inches of thigh and could've been a second skin. Its nubby fabric followed her every move.

She didn't smoke or seriously drink. To fit in she downed too many beers that she didn't like anyway. She had learned the names of some mixed drinks (rum and Coke, bourbon and 7) that sounded prissy and she didn't like anyway. She wasn't political; she carried with her that same brand of skepticism. Her testing of limits was still well within the tame and normal. She was groping about for what was next, something new, reaching out to folk music and Greenwich Village, Irish coffee and the first tentative tokes of marijuana.

Jamie Lee took her attitude as rejection and got plastered. He inhaled an astonishing amount of alcohol. Six-packs went by the board like Kleenex. Meanness appeared and she retaliated. She grew sharp and acerbic, slicing back with verbal cuts. Her mockery came out; her artistry. He asked her to dance and she declined. He insisted and they did a bad turn around what there was of a dance floor. He forced her close and she resisted. Refused. She wouldn't sink into his arms. Her dress looked forward but she remained cool and aloof and thus quietly infuriating.

Maybe he was still carrying around the football game we had played against one another like a grudge. Whoever won, it was a bruising battle and, still playing then, I had the heightened level of fitness to draw upon. I loved the fall and I loved contact. The time of the year, the bite and tang of the air, the sniff and feel of the earth, and a profound modicum of physical mayhem. The hitting. Doug was more delicate. He shied away and sidestepped such bodily contact, but he had good hands. He caught some long balls. The day was hot and dry and dusty and the ground was hard and Jamie Lee and I often ended up there. We wore no pads but the game might as well have been tackle. Jamie Lee had thought the game would be an easy win and it was anything but.

Of course football may have had nothing to do with it, and it was all the time and only about Samantha.

After they had danced she came back to Doug and together they tried to fend off Jamie Lee.

"Come on, come on," he sang, grabbing her. "Right now."

"I'm going to sit this one out."

"You've sat every one out."

"Grab your partners and do-si-do," Doug said.

"Who are you?"

"Swing your partner and do-si-do."

"What are you doing?"

"Actually, I was talking to her and actually we've been introduced—"

"She's mine."

"I don't think so."

"I'm trying to be nice. I'm asking you nice. Butt out."

"Can't."

"Can't? What does that mean, 'can't'?"

"She's my sister."

"How noble. How sweet. She's with me."

"Have a drink."

"Thank you very kindly. I believe I will, and nice try, but she's still—where'd she go?"

Where she'd gone was down to the far end of the bar, where I was waiting for another round and had been for what seemed a long time.

"Help me," said Sam.

"I could use some myself. Some service here, sir!"

"No, no," she said. "Jamie Lee—"

"I remember Mr. Lee. Your date, I believe."

"You've got to get me out of here."

"We all have dates, I believe. Look around. There are only couples here, only couples are allowed here."

"Please," she said, but it was too late. Jamie Lee had left Doug and arrived.

"Come on, doll," he said.

"'Doll,'" I said. "Did you actually say 'doll'?"

"We're trying to have a good time here. Don't start messing it up."

"You actually called her 'doll'? Why not 'doll baby'?"

"Butt out. Get lost. Catch a bus."

"Are you talking to her?"

"She's my date."

"Are you talking to me?"

"I'm talking to her and it's not going well." He was sweating and his face was blotchy, anger wrestling with befuddlement and intoxication. And they weren't mixing well. She wasn't behaving, he wasn't getting his way, and he looked like he might implode rather than explode, too many contradictory emotions drenching him at once. It was scary to see, alternately endearing and very dark.

"You're telling me," I said.

"I'm telling you, I'm telling her, I'm telling everybody."

"My friend, you have a problem. You have a date with this lady, am I right?"

"Yeah," he said suspiciously. "Where you going with this?"

"I'm going where you should've already gone. The showers, baby. This date thing, and you know this—hell, look around here, all these damn dates. You come up to bat, you swing, and sometimes you hit and sometimes you miss. A round-tripper, a four-bagger, you get to all the bases, or a dinky grounder, or a K—a strikeout. Win a few, lose a few. It's the law of averages. Ask anybody. Right place, right time—wrong place, wrong time. You gave it your best shot and I don't blame you, she's a good-looking piece, but she's from another planet where it's cold and, excuse me, the women, lovely as they can be, though not as lovely as around here, they can be cold. Take my word for it. You lost. The showers, baby."

I thought he might hit me and I didn't care, and whatever happened next—whether he cleaned my clock or not—might have changed the night and those to come, but he didn't. He hovered, swaying and rocking as if balancing on a beam. He stomped off then. Samantha went after him, but she returned alone before my eternal waiting for the next drink was complete.

"Where did all that come from?"

"All what come from?"

"You don't remember? Oh, sure. Well, thank you."

"De nada."

Neither of us said anything for a moment and the drink still didn't come. My eyes glazed over and my lids ignored my attempts to keep them open. They fell down on me. She saw it happening.

"Are you bored?"

"Cockeyed."

"Why are you cockeyed?"

"Why so, how so, me so?"

"Something like that."

"I'm having a fine time."

"Do you mean you really are pie-eyed and that whole spiel was because you were pie-eyed?"

"I'm having a fine time."

"No, really."

"I'm afraid so—yes."

"Well, I'm okay, and you can forget the whole thing."

"No, you're not," I said.

"I am so, thank you very much."

"No, you're not," I said.

"You're a damn broken record."

"Bartender, doctor, nurse, this young lady needs help here. Trach tray, IV, strong liquid, the strongest you've got, in a glass straight up."

"I can take care of myself and I have no intention of joining you."

"Cockeyed, bombed, pie-eyed, but not yet blotto."

"You're working on it though?"

"I'm working on it though."

"Who's the unhappy one here? I thought you were having a good time. I *saw* you were having a good time. Where is she?"

"It's true, it's true, I can't deny it. She's great. More than I can handle, believe me," I said. "But we don't belong here. You know that now. We both do. You said it, you asked for my help. So. So now. So now that that's settled. Let us steal away and go this night back to our own land, our own country where men are men and snow is snow and sex is sex."

"I think maybe we'd better dance," she said.

"Check," I said.

We did and I didn't feel so alone and maybe she didn't either.

"Are you sure this is such a good idea?" I asked after a while, sharing with her the drink that had finally arrived.

"Check and double check," she said.

We danced some more, our spirits rising, relieved and glad to be on our own and with each other. It wasn't close or slow dancing; it was fast and carefree, mindless and enjoyable, and very much about and within the music. We fell into its thrall.

The next thing I knew we were outside wandering the golf course and then we were lying on the fringe of a green that was cool and damp and getting wetter by the minute. The air was redolent with the scent of the grass and the smell of the soil and her. What started slowly, maybe in mere kinship, suddenly wasn't. In her gathering heat Sam made lush noises. Her skin was remarkably sensitized to touch. Everything that she felt registered on her flesh. Every fabric and texture and sniff and snuff of the green and girl was sensate. Hypnotic and galvanizing. In this moment and this place consequences were tossed away. Everything was. But.

An abrupt stir of air snapped at the flag and it shivered in the pin. It made a rattle like a rattlesnake. It broke the stillness; it ruined it, and we held up. We stopped, frozen, before coupling. A moment later, from the dark, Doug beckoned us back to what had been but was no longer the party. In our absence, after he stomped off, Jamie Lee had lurched to his car, slammed it into gear, and turned the wrong way onto the highway and head-on into a fifteen-wheeler.

His death blew out decorum. The moments of the wedding from then on held a gravity, an extra weight. The walk up the aisle, the words of the ceremony, the saying of goodbyes when they came. Every action, the days themselves, seemed precarious and more precious because we knew now how awfully and unforgivingly they could be ripped away.

Sam and I shied away from each other, awkward, embarrassed, and even ashamed, and it gathered into a silence that created a vacuum around us and between us. We've never talked about it since, the conversation at the bar and the short time on the green, she under me, where the two of us sought so briefly to meet in hunger and risk. Nor the moment afterward that is mine alone. As Sam wept, undone, and I tried to comfort her, swamped with guilt I wanted to forget and bury and could not measure or let go of then or still, I knew most of all, more than ever, I wanted her.

The whisper of death touched all of us. Doug and I knew it without ever bringing it up into words. With Sharon and LuAnn, the two of us found ourselves spending our last night in Alabama in a 1967 Bonneville, a couple in front, a couple in back. Sharon let my hands wander now, maybe further than she had planned. Under the girdle, there was a surprising heft to her haunch. In the coming years she might well turn doughy, but not yet. She had such soft skin and the springiest nest where her thighs came together. But we also stopped. We tiptoed into the wet and then backed off. Each time. We talked, we necked, we slept, and we woke in each other's arms. The last is a phrase I never thought I'd write but it's one that's appropriate. We were holding on to each other, even if we were never to see each other again.

4

WHILE WAITING FOR DOUG to come home I don't remember what we did with the days. They collapsed into one another and it always seemed to be night. Long nights, many nights, whatever the actual number.

During one of them, waking, I heard a noise. I lay in bed and listened but couldn't hear it any longer. I turned over to go back to sleep but didn't. I was restless now and the night grew loud. The cold and snow didn't snug out sound at all. Somewhere a frozen branch fretted against a window or a shingle on the side of the house. The rubbing made an eerie lament. The heartbeat of the grandfather clock downstairs worried its way into the room. I felt I could hear the rough breaths of sleep through the walls. Even the crawl of bugs through the rugs. The very air.

But none of those was what I had first heard and now heard again. Whatever it was got me up and drew me down the stairs. I listened again and couldn't hear it, but I found my uncle George in the living room. It was a while before he noticed me.

"Oh, John," he said then. "I didn't know you were there."

"Are you all right?"

"Oh, yeah. I was just looking at young George's football

pool. The NFL games. I thought I might try it. So I was making notes."

"He spent hours figuring the odds and the spreads."

"He's pretty with it, all right."

"He's probably upstairs in his room right now still at it."

"I wouldn't be surprised," he said and smiled, what seemed
an odd time and place for a smile. "But I might do all right.
I've been making notes."

"You won't catch me betting."

"Oh, it's just some fun."

"Okay, then, I think I'll go back to bed."

"I'll be up myself soon," he said. "Thanks for stopping by."

I went to the doorway and to the stairs and started up them
and stopped because I had forgotten once I had seen George
to wonder what was making the sound that I now heard again.
I turned around and went back to the living room, but
George hadn't moved and the sound was gone. Again he took
some time to realize I was there.

"I thought you'd gone."

"I had."

"I was thinking about when I first went to work at Connecticut General. It was just after the war. Actually Henry
Roberts and I arrived the same week. And Jim Torrey showed
up within a month." He had named the one man above him in
the insurance company and then one just below. "All three of
us. Odd, isn't it? Funny. We've been there for twenty-five years
and I guess we're going to be there until the end. I mean, until we retire. Which won't be that long now. Five years. It's all
changing. We've had fun. Fun." He was talking in staccato
rhythm, short sentences, half-sentences, and then stopping.
The phrases came out in brief bursts like pants of breath. "Paddle tennis tomorrow? Or today. What time is it?"

"I'm not sure."

"Is Pittsburgh any good?"

"What?"

"The Steelers."

"Not so hot. Cleveland, Minnesota, Kansas City, I think."

"And the Bears are, right?"

"How about those Bears?"

The attempted joke passed by him and he skipped on, like setting out across rocks in a river in an attempt to keep dry. "I was looking for a puzzle. I know we had it. Five hundred pieces. I could do that. Maybe there's a crossword. Maybe I'll do that. You should go back to bed."

"I could stay up with you."

"Get some rest."

"I don't mind."

"No."

The sharpness in the single word brought me up short and stopped me. In the silence I deduced he wanted to be alone and in that understanding was an agreement, a bond.

"Go to bed," he said then, and his voice was loud, insistent, hard, and reaching into shout. "Do you hear me? I said go to bed right now. Now!"

I had been wrong and the rebuke hurt and sent me back to the stairs. Only as I was on the way up them did I realize the sounds that I'd heard and were hearing now again were coming from George. A guttural utterance outside of words and beyond tears that he could barely control and could never admit and that was offering no help.

———

IF IN MY MIND this began as Doug and George's story, I realize now that—as big and ingrown as our family was— territories overlap. I am in it too, because I was a boy who had in crucial ways two fathers, my own father and my uncle.

The lore of our childhood was much about these two brothers. Over and over, we heard one way or another in one version or another of their adventures. George and Bill, Bill and George, George and Bill. These two tall lean glasses of water born in a certain time and a certain place who happened to share the same age difference as Doug and I did. Two rascals, two ruffians, two rats, as my father called them with affection or bite. It made them seem remarkably close.

For us the stories held a romantic allure. Gallant escapades, the quests of two young knights from a time gone past, like characters out of Sir Walter Scott, John Buchan, or a long-since-forgotten writer, Jeffrey Farnol, whom my father read over and over until he could read no longer. His favorite—there still is a falling-apart copy somewhere, the back of the binding peeling and broken—was called *The Broad Highway*, and this is how it ended:

> And thus it was I went forth a fool, and toiled and suffered and loved, and, in the end, got me some little wisdom.
>
> And thus did I . . . win the heart of a noble woman whose love I pray will endure, even as mine will, when we shall have journeyed to the end of this Broad Highway which is life, and into the mystery of the Beyond.

These stories we grew up with in retelling underwent subtle alterations. What happened begat story which begat fable which begat myth. They became a part of our shared memories. They were no longer literally true, but memory isn't; it's a capricious instrument. We like to think it's a camera, a tape recorder, but it is no such thing. We experience and then we double back and double back again to make sense of memory, and in some way the sense we want or need. It's ongoing and the years only deepen the version we ask ourselves to believe.

When they were at school together in the thirties "the boys," as they were called, would return home by train. They loved cars and longed to drive, but trains were in their heyday and ran through their lives. Club cars, dining cars, bar cars, a whole busy well-appointed man's world fixed with newspapers and drinks and cigars and fedoras finding purchase on the racks that lived above their heads.

Within two miles of the train station in Buzzards Bay was the Blue Moon. The name alone conjures. As a child, picking my father up at the same station, falling asleep in the backseat at night, I'd catch a glimpse of its sign: the shapely slice of neon blue it bestowed upon the night. It was a place back then with great bands (if not Glenn Miller, then Glen Gray), great dancing, a long wide deck outside in back, and a driving range next door.

On Labor Day there was the Midnight Frolic. Massachusetts's blue laws forbade dancing on the Sabbath then and liquor couldn't be sold or served on Sundays either. So the party began at 12:01 a.m. Monday morning and continued all night. One year my father and my uncle ran right from the train to the Frolic and that night became a favorite tale that someone would raise at one of the last cocktail parties of the summer, before George would take over the story:

"So some of us tramps would go over and hit golf balls and the girls still wanted to dance. Some of them were pretty cute, maybe we were making headway, maybe not, and it was pretty good fun. But anyway, Bill and I and our friend Eddie Buttner finally left the girls and never really went to sleep. By nine we're going down to the Plymouth Country Club to tee off and Bill was having a little problem with the ball. The ball was sort of moving around."

"Sort of fuzzy," my mother interrupted.

"Kind of using a club to stand up," George continued. "Started out and he got a nice seven. And of course I got a three. It didn't affect me, the night, the whatever, and the second hole he got an eight—it was a par five at the time—and so on the third he steps up with a two wood and knocks it right in the hole. A hole in one."

"Two hundred and twenty yards," my father said, speaking for the first and last time.

"One hundred and seventy-three," George said. "Whatever."

"And George never had one," Betty said.

"And Bill's had several," my mother said.

"Two," George corrected her, and laughed as if the exact number meant nothing, lying of course. "And to finish—we never went to the Blue Moon again."

"The Blue Moon may still be there," Betty said.

"I think a Frolic starts at twelve-oh-one tonight," I said, though I knew and somewhere they must have known by the time of this telling it was long gone.

My father was the silent one, the numbers man, and George was the salesman. This was a bit of a misnomer. Digging deep enough, I came upon versions that said my dad had been mischievous, a hellion, and the wilder of the two when they were very young. Only somewhere along the way something had happened. I didn't think a lot about it then, what it might have been, but as the years have passed, both of us getting older, it worried its way in pursuit of me.

One summer when he couldn't have been more than six or seven, my uncle remembered lying on the floor gazing at a map on the front page of the newspaper. The map charted the lines of battle along the Western Front. Little tanks served as symbols of the strength of the forces and measured their advances and retreats, sometimes a matter of yards, like the flowchart for a football game. He had no idea of the human cost or context. For the boy it was just interesting and fun to look at. This was his sole recollection of World War I.

A war later, George was stationed in Washington, D.C. A trained actuary by then, it became his job to make those charts and maps he had seen in the newspaper on the floor as a boy twenty-five years earlier. Before the war was over—and this was true for D-day—he headed a team that studied troop strengths, estimated how quickly and effectively they could be moved to a possible point of attack, like Normandy, and then gauged casualties. They were factored into every battle plan, a real and genuine concern, yet still paper figures thousands of miles from the men who would so soon live and die in a withering struggle to make their way off the beach and onto solid ground and across France.

My father hadn't served. He was granted an exemption because he worked for a utility and had a son. He stayed home and yet he never was at home. Church meetings, community service, the blood bank, the boys' club, the board of education. He was absent and then he was in shadow, his brother's and the one he made for himself; and somewhere about then, both before and after I was born, he began to turn inward and to alcohol and never became as successful as his taller, older, more smiling brother.

The two of them, my father and my uncle, were two of ten children. Two of the others had died young, but by the middle nineties it seemed as if the eight who'd survived would live forever. When news came that Percy, the oldest brother, had cancer, it was a tough moment but somehow not to be truly worried about. These Yankees would carry on, survive. Even if Percy happened to go, they wouldn't.

Percy had a benign, rumpled countenance. He was also bald and had very pale skin, like a baked potato before butter, and wore thick glasses he often forgot to put on and then forgot why it was he couldn't see. As a boy, bending over, going backwards, he had drawn train tracks along the large smooth sand plots on the beach. A station at each end, single-lane tracks, passing tracks. He had traced a whole network of them. Once in a while he even convinced one of his brothers to participate in the creation.

The three hundredth anniversary of the landing of the *Mayflower* had cinched his love of trains. For one time only, a specially outfitted, celebratory train had chugged out beyond its normal final destination at Brockton through Duxbury all the way to Plymouth. Percy got to ride it, and trains became his passion.

He knew timetables across the world by heart. For years his hobby had been checking out new routes, searching for different lines and then, often alone, riding them. At sixty-five, it became his vocation; that was how he spent his retirement. Until recently, he could successfully claim there wasn't a single outstanding line or route, new or old, here or abroad, that he hadn't traveled.

This summer he came home for the first time in a generation. Clearly sick, clearly diminished, he wanted to talk. I'm not sure how he let this be known, since nothing in our family is directly stated. At his choice, we settled him in an Adirondack chair at the edge of the bluff overlooking Cape Cod Bay, and taped him as he talked. He got cold easily and he dressed up for the occasion in a seersucker coat, a V-neck sweater and a deep-blue polo shirt with narrow horizontal stripes, and a porkpie hat with a wobbly brim. His long, slack, liver-spotted fingers (between but not on the knuckles) were lively.

Percy had been an officer on a 172-foot sub chaser that escorted convoys during the Second World War, at first in the Caribbean and then in the Pacific. As children we seldom saw him or thought about him. He wasn't much in our lives. He never stepped onto the tennis court that I remember. He seemed mild, meek, and unathletic. Not so. He had earned a varsity letter in track in college and his war had been a lacerating one.

He had been in battle and seen the aftermath of more. This day he recalled a dark joke. They had come upon the cruiser *Pittsburgh* and it had broken up. It was completely separated into two parts and someone said, "I've just discovered a suburb of *Pittsburgh*." Around it—the shallows of the sea were strewn with bodies. In the Solomon Islands he had witnessed a murderous typhoon, and when an ammo ship docked nearby his own blew up, he saw many more die. His binoculars became helplessly full of people screaming. It was night and they were lit by the flames that were killing them. Oil had spilled along the surface of the sea. Hoping to escape, they leapt into the slick and like lit matches set it ablaze also.

In August 1945 he had been in Tokyo Harbor. His ship was moored less than a mile from the *Missouri*. He saw the Japanese officers presenting themselves in formal dress and top hats while Douglas MacArthur sat in shirtsleeves. Through binoculars again, he was witness to a momentous event, the surrender that ended the war.

Still, his own war wasn't over. Before he was mustered out, in San Francisco, he had been court-martialed when sailors on leave under his command went on a celebratory binge. They wreaked havoc. One was killed. The verdict was overturned, he was exonerated, but it changed and sobered him in a new other way. The heft and hurt of responsibility led him further into his already solitary self. Always sensitive, he withdrew and grew quieter and more private still. He never looked at events the same way again.

None of these events had I known. My sense of him had been mistaken; maybe it's often so. We are quick with preconception and to judge from what little we may know. Percy was digging back, surprised himself perhaps as well as us at the moments that cropped up and demanded to be relived. And it's true that those incidents that hang in memory tend to change in middle and old age, to both calcify and expand. Up finally come kernels of the deep past that seem new and in fact have been long and well forgotten.

That fall and winter fifty years later he took to looking at the half-inch tape we made from the camcorder footage, watching it often, watching it after he could no longer read, watching it after he couldn't really hear and maybe couldn't even see, and it was one of the last things he did.

———

ONLY THREE YEARS LATER my brother called because my father was in the hospital.

By then he had had a small stroke, quit drinking, and was quietly lucid for a time. It was a wonder after all he had done to himself that he had any organs left—after the ounces and quarts and gallons and tons of alcohol that he had mercilessly consumed. "Living without alcohol after fifty years of living with alcohol—try that on your piano," someone once said. "Now that's comedy. Now that's tragedy."

My father's short-term memory was now very short-term. He asked me once for a book to read.

"What would you like?"

"It doesn't matter."

"Fiction, nonfiction, biography, mystery—"

"A mystery would be fine."

I brought him a selection, including a couple by Charles McCarry.

"Where is that book you gave me?" he asked me the next morning.

"Which one?"

"I don't remember the title of it."

"What was it about?"

"I don't remember."

"What was the dust jacket like?"

"I don't—"

"What *do* you remember?"

"I liked it."

Even when I showed him the books he was unsure. Yet he was surprisingly peaceful and sometimes downright perky before he started having trouble walking and breathing.

From the hospital Mason put him on the line. "Where are you?" he asked me.

"California."

"Oh . . . where's that?"

"I'm coming to Plymouth."

"Have anything going?"

"Not—" I stopped, confused. "I'm coming there."

"They've got me all rigged up."

"But you're okay?"

"It's a bad place."

"What is?"

"Where I am." And then he asked Mason, "Where am I?"

"The hospital," I could hear my brother say.

"The hospital," my father said. "They got me all rigged up."

I knew he wasn't well and the hospital was only a temporary solution. Being at home wasn't one; my mother could no longer take care of him, not alone, and he didn't want anyone else. I flew back and took my son, Jake, along. I wanted him to have a chance to see his grandfather and I wanted him with me. I knew, too, what I couldn't tell him: Jake was now the age I had been when my father and I had confronted each other every night.

In his sobriety, decades earlier, after he had been elected the head of the Junior Chamber of Commerce, my father was interviewed on the radio. I still remember it. I got to crawl into my parents' bed to listen. It was a local station, a Saturday morning, but that didn't matter. My dad was on the radio. He was never around, always gone to meetings or playing golf, and yet here he was. His voice at least, that deep voice, slow and lulling then.

On the boards where he served he was known for having a laid-back ability to listen and sort through opinions, however lunatic, smart, or hysterical, before casting his own. He had an arbiter's calm and a measured sagacity. I was too little to understand what it meant when I heard my relatives say, "Let's talk to Bill about it," or outside the family, "Let's see what Bill Young has to say." What I did hear was something in the tone, a deference and respect that enlarged him even in his absence.

But by the time I was Jake's age that had changed, whittled away and all but forgotten, and he was home nights and he was drinking. When he drank alone he didn't talk; not at first. He would sit and move change around in his pocket, an irregular ongoing jiggle. For the rest of my life I will be able to call up the sniggery sound of the coins playing through his fingers. He would move his glass on and off a coaster or a napkin, adjust the one and then the other. He didn't slug the booze down. Closer to sips. He just kept at it. After a while the grunts would start. He'd make noises, clearing his throat. Soon enough they would turn into dark phrases. They started under the breath and, growing louder, degenerated. "You just don't understand." "You don't get it, do you?" "What's the matter with you?" "What's wrong with you?" "How can you be so stupid? Stupid." "Dumb bastards, just don't get it."

It was a process of hours, worse when it was gin, not bourbon, and worse still as he got older. Quickened then. Unchanged, in need of fresh paint, the kitchen where he usually situated himself aged around him. The walls yellowed and grew waxy until they were the shade of fly strips: twenty years of grease from frying pans and smoke from Chesterfields. His system had to be sodden. Major organs drowned. Liquor sloshing around in his blood like antifreeze, invading even the smallest tissue.

He did all this often without moving from his chair. In the kitchen his chair was a rickety, off-kilter thing. He didn't notice, or didn't care to notice. The same with the living room: he always sat in the same chair and it was an uncomfortable one.

As it stirred and grew, his bile found a destination: my mother. He would chip away at her. The patience and quality of judgment he had been known for washed away in the liquor. What came up then were corrosive emotions and accusations. My mother played into it and the two locked into a struggle, sometimes loud, sometimes muttered. He sniped and she perfected not noticing. The obliviousness fed his dynamic and shaped his bitterness. He assailed a missing target. She hid in a performance that became both cause and effect.

By my adolescence it happened every night. The dynamic was the same, always the same. I knew not to wander onto his radar screen. If I didn't steer clear I'd be included. But I found myself, despite myself, defending my mother. I would ignore what I only too well knew and join the fray. I couldn't stop myself. For a time it was an attempt to make peace. The consequences of these futile efforts rumbled through therapy and my experience with Adult Children of Alcoholics. But after that time came another. Purposely, I fell within his range. It was insane behavior. I knew it and couldn't stop it. I asked for trouble, got it, and gave it back. I stirred it up, and it wasn't hard. I made war as well as peace.

It could start with him saying to me, "Hold your head up," or "Why don't you get a haircut?" or "What's the matter with you?" It could be in response to something I said or as likely something he said and not necessarily waited for an answer to recite his own. Recycle it from the night before, a hundred nights before. My father in his chair, my mother at the stove or at the dishwasher or on the phone or not in the room at all. Me in the living room, ignoring the incremental small-arms fire for as long as I could before yelling or coming in, always finally coming in.

"Peggy, how come you don't get it?" he was saying by then.

"Dad!"

"You just don't get it."

"How's the bottom of the glass, Dad? The view from there."

"Don't you know anything?"

"Hey, Dad, cut it out."

"What do I have to do? Paint a picture? What are you, stupid? Goddamn stupid coward—"

"Dad, leave Mom alone."

"What?" For the first time answering me, maybe even aware of me.

"You want to talk like that? You talk to me."

"Johnny," my mother said, "don't try and get a rise out of your father."

"He isn't going to talk to you like that."

"He doesn't mean it."

"It doesn't matter whether he means it."

"Just ignore him. That's what I do."

But she'd been drinking too, and maybe crying, and I turned to him: "You want to have a conversation? Let's have a conversation. Just you and me. Leave her out of it."

"You could learn a few things."

"Well then, teach me, Father," I said, lacing in the sarcasm.

"What's the point? You won't listen."

"I'm listening."

"Sure you are," he said, lacing it right back.

"I am." Even closing in on being ready to—which didn't last long:

"But what do you hear? What's the matter with you? You hear anything?"

"I heard you loud and clear all the way from the living room."

"They're all liars."

"Who is?"

"You know who I mean. Read your history. Do you know history?"

"You mean—let's see—Nebuchadnezzar, Al Capone, FDR—"

"He ruined the damn country."

"Or the Kennedys."

"The whole damn country."

"How about William Brennan?"

"I don't know what happened to him. I knew him. I don't understand. They got to him."

"Brainwashed probably."

"What's the matter with you?"

"I've got a boil on my ass."

"Read Jefferson. Why don't you read Jefferson? What do you read anyway?"

"Karl Marx, *Mein Kampf*, Henry Miller, Harold Robbins."

"Who? What's that? Some trash? Democracy. You know what it means? You don't know."

"You've told me often enough."

"The crowd. The masses. *Demos*. You know your Greek, your Latin? Not the people. That's what Jefferson wrote. This isn't a democracy. It's a republic. A republic."

"And it's going to hell."

"You laugh, you sit there—"

"You want to talk about *who's* sitting—"

"You don't get it, do you? How come you don't get it?"

"Because you're full of shit."

"What'd you say?"

"You heard me."

"I could throw you out the window."

"You want to try it?"

"It's not even worth it."

That stood me up, if I wasn't already. "Come on."

"Look at you," he said, his fists clenching, and struggling to his feet. "What do I have to do? Paint a picture? Look at you. Why don't you grow up? Goddamn coward."

Our words weren't new, and there were buttons to push, like FDR, that were always good for a rise, purposely lacerating and provocative, and Supreme Court Justice Brennan, which was more personal and wounding; but we had no idea and couldn't see how close to humor, to "Who's on first?" we were as the words and sentences circled and recycled and grew uglier and more lost and reached to the same place and the same words that my father had rained on my mother, the vituperation accelerating until every night he determined again it was time to throw me out the window and every night he would gesture or get up to do so. We would line up chin to chin in furious intimacy, screaming, spitting, as seconds elongated into minutes and never seemed to end.

What I don't know and seldom and don't want to think

about is what damage he did to me and I to him. There is horror in how in my own way then I became like him.

Our family talked of an intervention, but it never happened. My mother wouldn't sign on. She wouldn't fully admit his condition or her own. Even if it was mostly wine, she was knocking the liquor back equally well, and who could blame her. The enabling ran very deep.

Once I tried. It had been a long bad night and my father came down to breakfast late. It was a dark house with brown wallboard patterned with rain stains from leaky roofs, like Japanese prints scrawled over a period of fifty years. Sunlight and a long wooden table filled the dining room in the morning. The windows were old enough that the panes weren't flat. The glass had mars and stipples that brightened or bent the light, the way it shimmies through leaves or underwater. My father didn't come to his place in the dining room. He went into the living room and sat there out of sight.

I don't remember why I had decided to confront him that day, whether there was something particularly awful the night before. In the summer with gin and humidity and the gathering of family the effects of the drinking could mount. Worsen. I got up and went around the corner into the living room. It had the same shade walls and didn't get the morning light and was very dark. There seemed to be a thickening and heaviness to the air as there is in deserted rooms.

The chair my father had picked was bamboo with faded cushions, a porch piece that had landed somehow among the crowded flotsam here. He wasn't at his biggest. The alcohol that had bloated him had now started to ravage him. Still the chair was too small for him. The newspaper was on the coffee table, but he wasn't reading it. He was just sitting in reeking humility. He didn't have his glasses on. At some drunken point he had taken them off and I had found them on the floor. The lenses were smudged and scratched, the degree to which made it hard to imagine they were worth wearing. I carried them to him, but he didn't take them. Without them his eyes loomed large.

I picked up a wooden stool and set it down close to him and sat at his feet. He didn't look at me. I thought I would wait him out, could. I was wrong. His hands were shaking and I could smell him, but he refused to look at me. I got up as if to go but didn't. I set the stool back where it had come from and pulled a chair over even closer. We were face-to-face now. Now when he tried to look away I moved my head into his field of vision whichever way he turned, and I got closer still. I was going to coax or force an admission. I invaded his space. His hands shook worse and his breath was deathly.

"Dad, I want to talk to you."

He didn't answer.

"Dad, can you hear me?"

"What?"

"Can you hear me?" I was six inches away; of course he could. "You've got to stop it."

"What?" His "What?" was the same "What?" as his first one, noncomprehending. He was blocking the conversation out.

"You heard me."

"What are you up to?"

"The drinking, Dad. It's killing you and it's killing Mom and it's killing us. It's got to stop. And if you can't, we can help—"

I stopped. He wasn't looking away, he wasn't looking through me, and he wasn't looking at me. He wasn't looking at anything. He was trapped inside himself and what I saw wasn't anything I had expected. Girding myself, getting up my gumption, I had tried to play out what might happen in my head. Would he hit me, fly into a rage, stomp off, shut down? This was none of these. It was fear. He was naked and haunted in there and he was terrified.

I lost my anger and my righteous certainty. I was suddenly as scared as he was that I was only hurting him. I had pushed into some tender point. A tear started down his right cheek. I could not tell whether it was from hangover or fresh pain. I could not tell anything. His anguish was acute and mainlined to me. I couldn't look at him now. I had the heart-wrenching recognition that I had as tough a time as he did in the tender places. I could only watch the slow progress of the unscraped-away tear as it made its way out from under his eye and down across his face.

I left him in the dim, brown-stained room, and although countless more times at night the two of us played and re-played the same useless scalding argument in the same useless scalding words when he was drunk, we never again spoke in the light of day about his drinking. That scene was left forever regretted and unfinished, and I could only wonder about the power of pain, how it blocks us, burns and cauterizes, yet makes you feel alive even while wishing you weren't, and how close it can fall in its torqued and twisted way to love.

It was in those years that I came home one night and found him stretched out on the floor. He was on his back, laid out in the dark like a cadaver. The sight was shocking: I thought he was dead. He looked and felt stiff and I couldn't find his heart-beat through his clothes at first. A wheezing exhalation can-celed my panic and readiness to call an ambulance. He was alive. Still I couldn't get him to move or respond; I couldn't rouse him. I tried whispering and shaking him and calling out and they all failed. I covered him with an afghan finally and left him to live or die.

When morning came he wasn't there and there was no sign he had been. He was already up, showered, and off to work.

The next time it happened I was still afraid, but it turned in time as it kept occurring into the darkest of comedies. Never knowing when, I would come in and find my father on his back on the floor in a similar position and a similar place. We might as well have been actors given a situation and improvis-ing behavior take after take.

Once when I shook him his eyes snapped open and he smiled and he said "Hi" innocently, even sweetly, like a boy caught in a prank hoping he still might get away with it. Another time he struggled with me and swung his arm and cuffed me in the head. Another time he pursed his lips as if for a kiss. Another time we actually had a conversation.

"Thirsty," he said, opening his mouth and moving his tongue around. His lips were dry and his teeth were not good, yellow and crooked and stunted with fillings, and his tongue was coated and looked very large. Dry white spittle stuck at the corners of his mouth.

"I'll get some water."

"What?"

"Water."

He looked directly at me as he seldom did, his eyes narrowing, seeming sober and sharp: "Fish fuck in water."

He closed his eyes and left consciousness again, and it was the only time I ever heard my father say the word "fuck."

Another time, looking for a pulse, I found my hands around his throat. I wondered if he could feel them, tightening them as an experiment to see when I would get a reaction, any reaction. I didn't get one. I squeezed. I didn't. Nothing happened. Only then, my hands digging deep into his creping neck, did I realize I was strangling him.

I left him then and again in the morning he was gone and I have no idea whether he had a memory of my hands, or any of the other instances. Maybe I was alone in them.

5

THERE ARE A FEW THINGS in my life that I'm undeniably proud of—my children, certain pieces of work, and a stand or two well against the grain—and there are no small number of which I'm not. In the long weekend of the second wedding Doug and I were ushers together lay both.

Only two years after Montgomery it was his sister, Samantha, who was getting married. It happened very quickly. After college Sam had moved—escaped, she once told me—to San Francisco, and hadn't wasted any time. She met someone and that was that. And so for the first time I went to California.

In the busy years since, going back and forth, the flights from east to west or west to east have become a frequent and regular part of my life. It's easy to forget that such trips, even then, were far more unusual. It still felt like an adventure. I got off the plane dazed and wide-eyed and ready to see a New World.

The first thing I encountered was a tram that sauntered people along automatically, like a treadmill. Commonplace now, they were foreign to me then. I had never seen one before. It took me flowing past a long mural with maps and fields and avocados on its vast length the size of Volkswagens. Fallbrook, California (wherever that was), it seemed, was "the Avocado Capital of the World."

That same year, the movie *The Graduate* opened carrying Dustin Hoffman riding on exactly such an apparatus. The film was blessed by timing, arriving simultaneously with the largest graduating class in college history, the peak of the baby boom, and became a huge hit. So many sharing the same dilemma: the lust and torpor and dislocation it portrayed in the marrow of those troubled years. At its core, though, it was old-fashioned with a new tweak. Boy meets girl; boy meets girl's mother. Just in the wrong order.

That girl's first moment on screen brought a gasp when I first saw it in a sold-out theatre of four or five hundred boy-men. Her image, larger than life, twenty feet high in a dark room at what was then an all-male school. "Gasp" is an insufficient term, an inadequate description. The sound was less than that and more unique, a low widespread sucking in of the breath, a shared inhalation. It was tied to sex and to our dreams. She was stunning and virginal and seemed holy, but without any fancy or religious wrappings. Pure freshness. Much what Sam carried for me.

In truth Katharine Ross, the actress who played the part, isn't and wasn't the image that appeared. What we ourselves brought into that theatre—our ardency and longing—intersected with what Hollywood does. Wardrobe, hair, makeup, story, and felicity, as well as youth and beauty, created the fiction. Even so, I once stood in her kitchen in Trancas, north of Malibu, trying to explain the impact she had had. That moment. Tiny, with a fine chamois beauty now, Katharine's reaction wasn't what I anticipated; it wasn't at all simple. She teared up, but it seemed as much from pain as from pleasure. She had been—and had to know it—such a cynosure, and here was someone remarking on it as if it were yesterday. Perhaps that was the rub. It wasn't, and for us all, especially actors, time is fleeting and vanity is so close at hand.

I heard the voices in the airport before I saw them: "Is that him?"

"No, it looks like it, but it isn't," laughed Samantha. "He doesn't look like a Young and he's got a big neck."

Her voice was disembodied and loose in the air. The direction it came from was impossible to pin down in the airport hubbub. It was clearly recognizable, its tone and intonation, its cadence and music, one that I'd known all my life, and I knew my feelings about her were still darned up.

There was Samantha then. Her hair had changed its cut and her dress seemed to bounce on her as she walked. It never got close to her knees. She looked new, released, free, and aglow. Light seemed to incandesce off of her very hide. She was headed the opposite way, holding her fiancé's hand. They were by me by then without seeing me and I let them go. We didn't hook up until the baggage claim.

"How's the northeast?" she asked me then.

"Oh, the northeast is the northeast," I said.

"Oh, John, why do you always have to be so sarcastic?"

She had changed and I hadn't, and the man she had fallen in love with was an illustration. His name was George and his father's name was George. The wedding was stuffed with Georges. Seemed funny, so many of them, surrounded by them, and marrying someone that shared the name of her father and her second brother. This bridegroom-to-be George wasn't tall. He was the same height as Samantha was, and when he met her he hadn't gone through any of the elaborate and awkward, laid-back, don't-say-it-and-barely-do-it antics of a New England mating dance. He had vectored in. Once she was in his sights he became a testosterone missile. Few things are more flattering than utter attention. The totality swept aside her inhibitions. She had no chance to back into any protective immolation. She had gone to San Francisco to get away, and wasn't this it?

The three of us sat in the front seat of George's car. This George talked. He liked to engage, to argue, and his opinions were deeply planted. Discussion was discourse, not dialectic. He was studying for the bar and in the thrall of the writers of the moment, Hesse and Vonnegut, and two Thomases he had read earlier, Mann and Wolfe. His gush was saved by his intelligence and the energy of his enthusiasm. As he talked Sam's hand fell onto his thigh and found its way higher until it slid into the final cleft. Found a deep fit there.

Doug was already at the Plantation Inn, where we were staying. The name seemed such a long shot—so far from Plymouth and the Pilgrims and yet the name was the same as a bar and a hotel back there. It suited our de rigueur sense of bleak irony. When I arrived the two of us threw in with each other and set out looking for adventure.

This was the spring of 1968, and San Francisco was breaking loose. The city was jumping. It made the East seem like the South had seemed when we had been in Montgomery together. It was easy to fall for. The air was brisk and bracing and a wind whipped the bay up. The sun latched onto the sharp hills, warming them, and dyed the water deep and set Alcatraz and the Golden Gate up in rugged and red relief. The steep streets were clean and alive with eye-catching women in edgy wear, whether hippie or high end, men with their arms around each other, and fishermen of all races and persuasions leisurely festooned wharves and piers and the marina. One such, a black man, buttonholed us.

"Once he sees that sun, he just goes crazy," he said, holding up a string of fish proudly. "Here, take my picture." He produced a Brownie Hawkeye camera and posed. It seemed to have film in it and the shutter snapped, but it looked as if it had tumbled down the length of Lombard Street. I had my doubts whether it worked. The man kept talking as he displayed his catch as if they were big game. "This is the place. I got my spot and when that sun comes out I got him and I am a rich man. Those other days, all those other days, we won't talk about. Just won't talk about. Not today. Ain't no way then. Ain't no way. But today—today anything is possible."

The Plantation Inn was the last place we wanted to be. We

didn't want to go back, but the first of the wedding's events, a rehearsal dinner, was looming. When we got there Doug flopped down on his bed.

"This is where I live when I'm at home," he said. "When I get up and go downstairs I don't know what to do, which way to turn, so I go back to bed."

"Well, not here, Douglazio," I said, falling back on an old nickname.

"I rub my magic ring twice and I'm still where I am," he said. "But maybe that's better than most."

"Zounds, man, cease and desist."

"Let's toss this place."

"What?"

"Toss it."

"What is this 'Toss it' stuff? And the accent? The pathetic English accent?" He was quoting from a movie I hadn't seen and I had no idea what he meant.

"Okay," he said, more seriously. "What are we going to do?"

"There's a wedding, maestro. Remember? Your sister. This George guy. The carnations in the lapels. The dinners. The drinks. The family."

"Oh, God."

"I know, but today—today anything is possible."

"You bought that?"

"We could go for a swim in the exciting Plantation Inn pool."

"That sounds exciting all right."

"It's empty, it's waiting."

"I guess it's something to do."

The Plantation Inn was four stories high and each floor had a balcony that the rooms opened onto. The pool, heated during the day, sat like a central courtyard and was a bright pastel blue, a Hockney shade. Cars lined up around it. The balconies loomed over it. We had to look straight up to find the sky and then we looked at each other. A thought dawned.

What made us think it was a good idea? The truth is Doug and I were looking for trouble and the pool was inviting. We looked up and saw the potential. A dive. A high dive. A mite dangerous and a mite forbidden. We didn't do it, there were way too many people, and we didn't really know if we ever would do it. The possibility glimmered and went away.

It was hours later—after the rehearsal dinner at the Empress of China and after sojourns in a series of other establishments, Rascals and Blues and a place aptly called the Twilight Zone, and finally the scarfing up of a Hippoburger—we returned to find the pool empty. It was lit, and it lit the rising tiers of rooms. The effect was lackadaisical and undulating and played out across all the floors. It was pleasing, hypnotizing, and mischievous. It made it impossible to resist contemplating what the light would look like in the wake of a leap or two. The effect of splash. What would be, of course, entirely a visual experiment and exercise.

The distance now between the thought and the deed was miraculously short. We weren't *complete* idiots—we made sure no one was in the pool or standing next to it and we didn't scream or laugh too much and we actually hesitated before doing it. Not very long. But we did. It was the conception— it just seemed a necessity. And, after all, we didn't jump the first time and then dive the second and then, oh whoops, cannonball from the fourth level. Only from the second. Okay, okay, the cannonball splashed some cars and maybe even a guest or two. Oh yeah, and the manager was not a happy camper when he came out to yell at us.

It wasn't long before my uncle George arrived at our room. He stood over us, his towering self, but whatever he felt underneath, it wasn't fury he showed. Closer to a disconsolate bewilderment. "Did you do it?" he asked.

I dissembled instinctively: "Do what?"

"Did you?"

"Yes," Doug said simply.

"You guys. What am I going to do with you guys? What do you expect me to do?"

"What do you mean?" I asked.

"The man who came out and caught you. He's not only the manager, it seems, he's the owner of the Plantation Inn."

"That's not so good?" I asked.

"That's not so good," answered Doug before his father could.

"Not only did you do something wrong, something obviously wrong, by violating the apparently *posted* rules, you upset other guests. They complained. Their cars got dirty. Even the police got called. Not only is he angry—'pissed' might be a better word—at you, he's pissed about possibly losing business, he's pissed about possible damage to the pool, he's pissed about possibly being cited by the police for safety violations, he's pissed about possible lawsuits and losing his insurance. So what do you want me to do?"

We were breathtakingly without ideas.

"I did what I could," George said. "It's up to you now."

"What do you mean?"

"It's your turn. You go talk to him. Explain yourselves. Or, maybe, if you have it in you, apologize. Maybe then he won't bring charges. Maybe then he won't kick us out of here."

"He can do that?"

"He can do whatever he wants."

"Us maybe. But not the rest of you!"

"All of us. That's what he said," George said. "It's up to you."

"You already said that," Doug said.

"I could, Doug," George said to his son, "say a lot of other things."

Not for the first time and not for the last I saw the dynamic that had come between them start to play out once more.

What I had missed and would never fully know were all its chapters and verses. I interrupted before it could get fully rolling.

"Okay," I said.

"I'm not going," Doug said.

"Let's get it over with."

"I'm not—"

"You're coming."

This time I wasn't only interrupting him. I dragged him out of the room, past the pool, to the office and knocked on the door.

In my misadventures, I had learned a curious and valuable, if tricky, truth. When you step into it, let denial go and save guilt for later. Get out in front. Take the offensive. Whatever is required, deliver it in person, directly and straightforwardly. Even, if you will, right between the eyes. It was striking the impact it could have. How it could help defuse the stickiest of situations. Still, knocking on that Plantation Inn door wasn't the favorite thing I'd ever done.

The manager, whose name was Abe Fostermann, answered. He was smaller than either of us, maybe fifty, and he had wound what hair he had around his head. A combover—the first I had ever seen. One more California offering. He wore a white shirt over a white T-shirt and had a mole on his nose. He looked at us and didn't say anything. He didn't let us in and he didn't relent his gaze.

"We've come to apologize," I said. "We're sorry about the pool. We hope there's no damage. We won't do it again. We promise." I kept on going when it was likely I should have stopped. "We weren't trying to do any harm. It was just a joke, a prank, something to do."

"Just a joke? A prank? Something to do?"

"We're sorry," I said again and quickly.

"It's a little late for that, don't you think? For your little joke. Do you know what you've put me through? Any idea? You could be in jail. *Should* be in jail. And what about *you*?"

He had turned to the silent one of the two of us.

"He's sorry too. He is."

"Can't he speak for himself?"

Doug said, "Let's toss this place."

"What did he say?"

I looked at Doug, worried about what he next might or might not say, and improvised. "Actually, he's deaf. The jump injured his ears. We've called a doctor. We don't know the damage yet, how serious, how permanent. But for now he can't hear a thing."

Abe Fostermann couldn't have believed me for a second. Nevertheless, it threw and disconcerted him, and offered the contradictory lesson to the one that first propelled me to the door. A cop once said to me—one of my first jobs was interviewing cops for a television series, *Police Story*, more than a hundred of them—"Tell the truth, always tell the truth, but if you're backed into a corner and there are walls all around you and no escape, lie. Lie like a motherfucker."

It was Doug who spoke. "What?" he said in a croaky voice. "I can't hear you."

"I said we're sorry."

"Sorry," he said. "What?"

"Sorry!" I was yelling now.

"So am I," he said, yelling right back. "So am I!"

We were both screaming now, and at each other. We were crowding up Abe Fostermann's doorway and he'd had enough of us in any number of ways. "Just don't do it again," he yelled, screaming too, all three of us screaming. "You hear me!" And he slammed shut the door.

The wedding was small—it had come together quickly—and was held in a chapel across the bay in Sausalito. In Montgomery the wedding had been large and formal. Black tie. This one was not. Doug and I were the only ushers, and a girl named Joan Holcomb was the sole bridesmaid slash maid of honor. She was tiny with a quick, sweet-and-sour tongue. She wore a short sleeveless lichen-green sheath and kept canting her head to peer at us and saying, "You two don't say much, do you?"

She did, though, and it was Joan, sipping champagne after the ceremony, who rattled off what we hadn't known, the degree to which George had interceded for us. He had stepped in far more than he had told us, far more than he ever would. He had fended the police off when they came. He had talked Fostermann down. The manager-owner was insistent on evicting us and charging us with malicious mischief and vandalism. George refused to accept it. Using rawboned charm, a salesman's savvy persistence, a father's protective strength and promised tough discipline, and even his size—that great implicitly intimidating height of his—he had hammered out a deal with Fostermann before we got to the door. If we came and apologized, the matter would be dropped.

Even when we got back to our room where he had been waiting he never told us.

There wasn't only the wedding while we were in San Francisco. Randal Robinson, the groom from Montgomery, came through on his way to Vietnam. A commercial flight through Atlanta brought him in for a layover before he crossed the bay to Oakland and Travis Air Force Base, and we went out to see him.

I didn't want to drive and Doug didn't want to come. He didn't and I didn't, but I went. I think back and wonder why we were so busy striking an attitude. We were resolute in our muleness, and trying on mischief like we thought it was manhood. We hadn't much rudder within us yet and we were fighting what rudder had been enforced on us. The rage of our childhood was trying to find a voice, and it was easy for us to confuse bravery and foolishness. The ache to prove ourselves worthy could be very misbegotten.

Perhaps we were also trying to do something that was impossible: replicate the seductive lassitude and immense intensity of the first wedding we had been to, the one in Montgomery. We were in a very different place and already a different time, and one that was changing very fast. It would be only days later, on my way back from the wedding, on a television in a bar in the TWA terminal at Kennedy Airport, that I would catch Lyndon Johnson announcing he would not seek re-election. Two days after that, Eugene McCarthy took 57 percent of the vote in the Wisconsin Democratic primary, and four days later Martin Luther King was assassinated in Memphis.

By the time Doug and I met again in Los Angeles only a year and a half later both the world and we would be very different.

SO WITHOUT DOUG, George and I went to the airport. There was a third person with us, my great-aunt Doff. She hadn't been to Alabama but she wasn't going to miss this one. Her real name was Dorothy, which no one ever called her, and she was ninety years old and not done yet. On her way to a remarkable hundred and five. Born in England, raised in a sod house in Nebraska, she had graduated from Smith, taught school for two generations, climbed mountains for three, run with the artists in Taos and Tucson in the twenties, and stepped away from her Republican family and voted passionately for FDR in the thirties. Never married, she lived the final fifty years of her life with another woman, first in New York, then in Baltimore; and a couple of years before this she had packed up and driven across country in a 1958 Chrysler with huge tail fins to Seattle.

Her hair was winter-white, her skin creased and crumpled, and her hands shook. I would watch her take a cup of tea, sure it would never make it to her lips without spilling. The shaking wasn't slight; it was eye-catching. I was always wrong. It never did. She told me that she had had arthritis in her seventies and eighties and had given it up. She had a catastrophic hook of a nose that in more minor form had passed down to my father and my uncle. As a kid Aunt Doff must have felt saddled with it. She wore it now as part of her distinction. She was a ruthlessly energetic and emancipated woman, always vivid and vitally alive. The ferocity of her spirit kept her young. Like few her age, she was still in her heyday.

Even ten days before she died, though she had been in and out of the hospital and her eyesight and hearing were suddenly failing, she was mushing around among her flowers, using a magnifying glass to read, and looking forward to voting against Ronald Reagan a second time. She kept coming downstairs until the effort was monumental. Too much. At last, then, she took to the window in her bedroom. With help she sat herself there, set up station. She looked out through the glass at the world she had been such an indefatigable part of. When even that became too much and only her bed was left, she fought against it and cried "No" and called out "Help me. Help. Please," and then she stopped. She stopped talking and she stopped eating. After so long and glorious a life, she waited for dusk on a fall night and took a big breath and reached her arm up above her head, a salutation, a blessing, hail and farewell, and went.

It wasn't only her character that led her to the airport. A crucial event in her life insisted. During World War I, close to forty, she had taken a sabbatical from teaching math and had gone to France. She joined a volunteer ambulance unit, not as a nurse but as a driver. For the last year of the war she drove one. The lumbering vehicle handled like a boat—sometimes in the rain and slathering mud it might as well have been one—and the sights she saw stayed with her. They burned into her core.

Coming from Paris after the brutal battle at Château-Thierry, the volunteers reached the village of Vaux and found it gone, not a wall still standing. Only remnants of families picking through rubble of what had been their homes and their lives.

That first night at Château-Thierry Doff slept in a garden only to discover a German corpse in the morning in the moat behind the garden, and then eighteen American graves across it. The Red Cross had set up quarters at a bombed-out train station. Six hundred wounded men were there, the two hundred worst on stretchers. Most had been gassed and many wouldn't make it. More kept coming. The flies were the greatest trouble. They had been in the rubble and in the garden and along the moat but they were worst at the train station. Along with the smells, they were terrible and sickening to see. That day a thousand wounded were loaded onto trains and evacuated to real hospitals. She never learned what number survived.

The trains couldn't hold them all and they commandeered two barges. The barges had to be refitted in a hurry. In the hold—using any manpower they could muster—bunks were hammered together along the hull to carry forty patients, the worst of the wounded. In between they set seats and stationed benches on deck. The French captain lived in the bow and had to take the coal they used as fuel into his cabin.

When the barges were ready they were loaded in the dark and without lights so they wouldn't be marked as targets. The stretcher bearers couldn't help but occasionally stumble, lose control of the men they carried, sometimes fall. The doctors realized some of the men were not fit to be moved but there was no choice. There were no nurses available and Doff volunteered to help.

On her first watch she soon found she wasn't the only one awake. Many of the men couldn't sleep and called out to her. She put soda and water on gassed men's eyes, and dished out the black coffee the French captain had brewed. It was a cold night and a French lieutenant hemorrhaged. The doctors discovered the supplies they had been promised didn't exist. They took two wooden horses and put a ladder across them for a table. While one doctor operated, Doff covered the lieutenant's eyes. But the hardest time came later. There was a man whose left jaw had been shot away, his tongue gone, and he had a hole in his throat. He couldn't talk but he refused to lie down and insisted on writing his name for their records. He wanted coffee and Doff tried to use a tube to get some down but he couldn't manage it. She was sure he would pull through, he had such spunk, she said, "but he couldn't manage it."

The ride up the Marne along the canal and onto the Seine was slow, and it was a wonderful day when they reached a town and were able to get supplies and cook a square meal for the 107 men aboard. They even found a phonograph. It didn't play quite at speed and the men sang off-key, but it didn't matter.

She made the trip eight or ten times during August 1918, and the carnage Aunt Doff saw remained unforgotten and toughened her and livened her and, all these years later, brought her with us to see Randal. She had lived in such changing times, ones we could only be astonished at and long for, and she knew how lonely the wounded boys had been, whether dying or not, and how much it meant to see a familiar face, an American face, and hear a voice, an American voice.

Before we reached the airport I knew why I hadn't wanted to drive. It wasn't a pretty realization: I wasn't up to Randal. By ducking responsibility, I made a pre-emptive strike to clear that up fast and up front. It was puny of me and an embarrassment I wanted to get rid of and I went on ahead to find him.

Randal saw me before I saw him, at a gate that was downstairs on the tarmac level, with a bunch of others in uniform, including a sergeant twice our age.

"John, you didn't have to come all the way out here."

"Of course I came," I said, as if it had been nothing.

"Sergeant, this is my cousin-in-law John. The sergeant here's a career man."

"Twenty-seven years," the sergeant said.

"Look at his confetti collection." Randal meant his ribbons. "The Army won't have anything left to throw at him. He's on his way back to Vietnam for a second tour."

"You in the Army?" the sergeant asked me.

"No, sir."

"Where are you?"

"I'm in college, sir, right now." I was caustically, even bitterly, amused at myself for snapping so into line. "George and Aunt Doff are waiting upstairs in the restaurant."

"Excuse me, sergeant. Catch up with you later. My family's waiting."

"Yes, sir," the sergeant said.

We began to walk away from the cluster of men waiting for flights at the far-flung gate and down the otherwise barren corridor.

"We're all trying to hitch rides to Travis Air Force Base. I've got to get out there before eleven. We're all on assigned flights. One of the men back there's going at ten, another at midnight. They're leaving every hour tonight."

He had an assurance and an ease I hadn't remembered. It wasn't simple and it was hard won. He was in controlled stoke, his fear and adrenaline tamped down. He was going where there was no father or uncle to save him or indemnify him or for him to fight against. His manhood was in place.

In the restaurant, with civilians, with family, it was harder to hold on to. The conversation grew desultory. Randal brought up another cousin who was "getting into interesting things in Sarasota," flying jets and landing on aircraft carriers. That kept talk afloat a while. Even George struggled. He couldn't find a comfortable place and, flustered, he swung awkwardly about trying to find things to say. It was a clumsiness I hadn't witnessed before and let out a vulnerability he didn't want to show and I didn't want to admit I'd seen.

It didn't occur to me then how much freight he must have been toting. His only daughter had sprung her marriage on him. One son couldn't even come and the other, Doug, was

giving him trouble, and not just jumping off of balconies. He
was meeting his son-in-law and his son-in-law's family for the
first time. He didn't know San Francisco well; it wasn't his city,
his state, or his side of the country. His wallet and credit cards
had to be at the ready every way he turned. His prescribed
role, the happy host, had to chafe. It couldn't have been easy
to play. For that matter, he may not have wanted to be at the
airport either; and I don't know if he ever thought back to
that night when Doug left for Vietnam.

Only Aunt Doff managed to be unaffected. She plowed
through the thick clots of feeling that lay around Randal's few
minutes with us and were so difficult to cut through. She had
a remarkable knack of asking questions that didn't seem to
pry, but that came from a rich vein of a word that's easy to
denigrate and was a reason she was so alive—interest.

Soon enough, I was back in the corridors with Randal. He
was relieved, I think. At Aunt Doff's insistence, he had ordered
two pieces of toast and a Michelob draft, and he had them with
him. "You must eat and take care of yourself," she said, but he
couldn't eat and they ended up in the trash. We walked down
halls of varying lengths and widths searching for transporta-
tion for him. All were blazingly lit. The fluorescence was eye-
squinching. His polished shoes rang on the polished floors. I
walked with him, glad now I was there, and I think he was too.

As we kept going, journeying further and further out to
the extremities of the airport, Randal said, "John, this was the
toughest decision I've ever had to make. Leaving Kitty and
the baby. I didn't think I could for a while. It's not a happy
night in Montgomery, Alabama."

CLOSE TO TWENTY YEARS LATER Kitty talked to me about
the days before his departure. We were in her living room on
a Sunday morning in Charleston, South Carolina, where they
had lived since the war. Her four daughters, now teenagers,

were still asleep. Randal was with his National Guard unit; he would rise to the rank of brigadier general before retiring. He had made it back alive. During his year he had done his job, flown his chopper, looked out for his men, and adopted a dog named Irving he found in Long Binh. Randal ran missions into Cambodia and Laos he still didn't talk about.

That Sunday was a rare span of peace and quiet. Slowly, Kitty and I were drawn back to that time and before we were done Kitty was crying. It wasn't sadness. Quite another emotion reigned. In the day-to-day of life, in the many years that had come and gone, she had forgotten the gravity of then, how dire it had been, how important it had been, how precarious it had been, and what came close this Sunday morning to sacramental.

When they knew for sure that Randal was going to Vietnam they had moved back to Montgomery, where Kitty was going to stay. His orders were due any day. They were ready, they thought, but the orders did not come. They wanted to get the year started, get it under way, get it out of the way, but the orders did not come. Suddenly they were living day to day, waiting, not knowing. They were stuck in limbo, a kind of hell, and still the orders did not come. The delays worked on their nerves, festering like a tumor, a secret that lay between them that they both knew and could do nothing about. Their lovingness started to fray. The longer they had to wait the worse it became, and still the orders did not come.

When they finally did arrive they felt like a letdown and too late. They had run, they thought, out of emotions. They were wrong. They discovered to their pain that there was a whole other reservoir. Leonard, Kitty's father, drove them to the airport. They were sitting in the backseat and couldn't talk. Leonard tried—he was a great Southern stem-winder—but he soon dried up. He tried talking about his own time in the Navy, when he was in Pearl Harbor on December 7, which he had never talked about before. But that was too close to the bone. He tried a story or two, but they seemed way beside the point. He tried some jokes, but they fell flat.

Kitty and Randal could not touch each other enough. Kitty kept squeezing his hand and at the airport she found she couldn't speak. Literally. Her mouth would open and nothing would come out. They had said everything in the night when they hadn't been able to sleep and in the days and weeks before while waiting, but it was hard. It was still just very hard. And if he had to go—if he finally and at last and truly was going to go—she wanted him gone. All the way gone. She wanted the year to begin because only then could it end.

After the plane, when they got back home, her mother insisted upon spring cleaning. It was a well-orchestrated maneuver, a put-up job, to give Kitty something to do. They turned the house upside down. They vacuumed, dusted and oiled, tore curtains down, and even pulled up the rugs. In yanking up the one in the living room they came upon rose petals still left from the wedding two years earlier.

Kitty wrote to Randal every day. It was a conscious decision. Every night before bed she sat down and did it. Every night she found something to say, a little news about the family, about the day, about their new baby, a dollop of love. Every night, and she numbered them.

If the baby awoke, she would put the letter downstairs after feeding her, and if not she would wake up on her own and set it on the table by the door. It'd be gone when she got up again. Her father mailed it on his way to work.

Kitty never doubted Randal's return. She had a conviction, and held on to it with a certainty the letters were very much a part of. One after the other, they built a chain and if she didn't break it—somehow he would be safe. In this deep pretending she found her will and an oasis. They became the fabric of her belief and acts of faith.

Oddly, the nights were the best times. During the day she was aware of the dragging hours and she missed him, and doubts would wiggle in. She could feel fear ready to leap in the door and she couldn't let it. At night she knew this: when she woke up another eight or ten hours would be gone. Another day had passed. Randal was that much closer to coming home.

The more letters Kitty wrote, the more she loved writing them and the more important they became. The numbers on the letters—100, 200, and 300—became mileposts. She didn't talk about it, carefully she didn't, but there was an aura about her and even about them. She found sanctuary in them. The postman, a fellow named Freeman Bozeman, picked up on it. He saw the numbers, and he became, as was said then, part of the program. He carefully took the letters when her father was away or wasn't working, and whenever there was a letter back Freeman Bozeman rang the doorbell.

Once during the year Kitty was supposed to go to Texas for a long weekend. Three days. She couldn't do it. The chain, she realized, wasn't only about writing letters; it was also about receiving them. What if she missed one—wouldn't the chain be broken? She got as far as the airport. That alone was unbearable. There were so many soldiers and so many people saying goodbye. She turned around and went back home. The three days went by without a letter coming, but it didn't matter. She knew she was right. The chain was intact.

For Randal the letters were a source of kidding at first. This ongoing avalanche arriving in bunches. Clearly, he was pussy-whipped. But that changed as they kept on coming, first to respect and then to awe. No one else got so much or so many or with such consistency. No one else got mail with those damn numbers on them. Eventually, they didn't call out his name when the next arrived. They called out the number. "Hey, Robinson, 312 today." And if, say, 311 hadn't come, as could happen—they didn't always arrive in correct sequence—the crew of his chopper and the other pilots worried about it until it did. The letters grew beyond Randal into a part of the lives of the men around him. What had begun as kidding and envy transformed into pride. They became juju, an ingredient in their superstition and their luck that kept them alive. It was as if these numbered letters were addressed to all of them.

———

WHEN WE GOT BACK from the airport Doug was waiting. He was tired of sitting, tired of waiting, and tired of himself. The trip to the airport, whether we went or not, changed our demeanors. It sobered us up and we knew it and tried to shuffle it off. We had talked about topless joints, asked around, passed a couple—they weren't hard to find—but hadn't gone. We did the same now, talked and didn't go. We hitched a streetcar up to Nob Hill and walked the circumference of it and then descended to the Red Garter. It was packed. After a beer or two we found ourselves at the Fillmore. Steppenwolf, the Electronic Groovies, and Country Joe were playing. The strobe lights were psychedelic and never stayed still. The whirling gels were hallucinatory. It was packed. We drank another beer or two and moved on. We walked more and moved on more. We were sightseers, and didn't want to be.

It was very late—or very early—when we got back to the Plantation Inn. It was quiet now. The office was dark, so were most of the rooms, and the balconies were bare. The pool was dark and lay at rest. The water scarcely fluttered. With the lights off it wasn't a Hockney anymore. The life of San Francisco echoed its way into the silent courtyard like the roar of the ocean inside a shell.

We went into our room and without speaking to each other stripped and put on our bathing suits. No towels, no shoes, no shirts. We walked out of the room and climbed the balconies, this time to the third story.

"One more?" I asked.

"That would be showing off," Doug said.

It already looked a long way down to the dark pool. The merest glimmers on its obsidian surface.

"We could miss from up here."

"That wouldn't be good," Doug said.

"This is going to take bravery and accuracy and audacity."

"That would be good," Doug said.

"Technique and know-how."

"That too," Doug said.

This was alcohol and bravado and stupidity talking and we both knew it, and I copped to it: "This is crazy."

"That's true," Doug said.

I took another look down. The distance was vertigo inspiring. "Seriously, we could kill ourselves."

"That's true," Doug said.

"Maybe we'd better rethink the whole idea."

"I'm just following the leader," Doug said.

We retreated from the rail, backing up, and leaned against the stucco wall for some deep thinking until we were both shivering.

"Are you still up for this?" I asked then.

"I could be persuaded," Doug said.

"We could be in some deep shit. More deep shit."

"Shit happens," Doug said. "I'm over it already."

"Oh, God."

I was rooted to the spot and then I wasn't. I was mounting the railing, still sure I was going to stop and go back and forget the whole thing, and I was jumping. I was falling and I was laughing. I was striking the water and it was no longer still or serene. The wet surface scalded and ripped at my skin and swallowed me up. I was underwater in the roiled dark and I was laughing.

We had found for one last time our adolescent substitute for where Randal was going and for where—though we didn't know it then—Doug would follow.

And he was ahead of me the whole way.

6

IN SOME WAY, decades later, my father knew that if he went to the hospital he wouldn't come back alive. It didn't seem so at first. They stuck him with an IV, put him on Lasix, and drained the fluid buildup in his lower body. He got better and they didn't hold him long. Hospitals don't anymore; they unload people as fast as they can. He was sent off to rehab and physical therapy at a nursing facility. Medicare covers the first one hundred days at such places. That was my father's next stop, and it turned out to be his last.

It was well after dark on a hot June night when Jake and I arrived straight from the airport to see him. In the six months since I had glimpsed him last he had become a bird. He was in a hospital bed, the back propped up, his long limbs scratching about under the sheets. He was half-asleep under a crumpled porkpie hat. It was so worn and faded that even the insignia of the golf club it carried was illegible. I was soon to discover he wore it all the time. The hat had become a part of him. He would pat it, take it off and adjust it; he would tuck it down tight so he wouldn't have to see and couldn't be seen when he had enough of people, doctors and nurses, all the bodies that came and went and poked and prodded and wouldn't leave him alone. He pulled it down until it sat like the tiny blue cap Jake had had in the hospital nursery after he was born.

If my father's hat had to be off, he held on to it with his hand. He wouldn't let it go, and I came to wonder what it meant to him. Did he wear it out of habit or for privacy or protection? Or to keep his crown warm because his skin and scalp were cold where he was nearly hairless now? Because his brain felt like it was leaking out and somehow the hat could stanch it, like a bandage can stop blood? And I came to realize even if any of these were true there was something simpler and more elemental about the wearing of it. He felt naked and vulnerable, and this miserable duffer's hat was his marker, his rebellion, and his life preserver. It was what he could control, the piece of his life he had left. *His.*

"What're you doing here?" he asked that first night, coming out of his doze.

"We came to see you," I said.

"It's good to see you too."

"I brought Jake with me."

"The young man. I hear about you. So you're a Tiger now. I know about you."

"Hello, Grandaddie."

"You don't look so big. I thought you were big. How tall are you?" But he didn't give Jake a chance to answer. "There are some rascals around here. Where are they?"

"Who?" I asked.

"You know," he said.

"What?" I asked, confused.

"This is a total disaster. I'm not staying here."

"Just until you get better."

"Once they got you here . . . they never let you out. It's rampant."

"Dad, it can't be that bad."

"You sound like one of those rascals. The doctors, those rascals, know nothing. Not a damn thing. Got me in here.

Peggy!" He shouted my mother's name suddenly, without warning and to no avail. She wasn't there. "Where is she? Bathroom, bathroom, bathroom."

"What is it, Dad?"

"Peggy! I gotta go."

I understood now and helped him up as Jake watched and looked away and undoubtedly wondered why he had been forced to come and wishing he were somewhere else. I lowered the bar at the side of the bed, got my father's feet into slippers, which he didn't want to wait for. With my support, he was walking then. Hurrying. The toilet was hospital height and there was a rail to hold on to. It didn't help him. His fingers were fumbling. He couldn't get his pants undone.

"I can't make it," he yelled. "Can't hold it back. It's coming. It's too late." His face was suddenly rubicund and turning a tortured red. I fumbled too, my fingers struggling besides his. "Help me," he said. It wasn't anger anymore. It was strictly need, urgent and unrelenting, cut with embarrassment and humiliation, and a situation that would repeat and intensify over the next days. Soon enough there wouldn't be time to get him out of bed. We would have to use a paper cup to catch the urine, sometimes successfully and sometimes not. And it wasn't so long before even that wasn't enough and didn't matter. This time, though, working together, we made it, and I learned what I hadn't ever known. My father was uncircumcised.

When we were done he was better for a while. He started talking to Jake about a bridge hand he once had. He exactly remembered the bidding, one no trump, and the play of the cards. How he'd taken every trick, all thirteen, and made a grand slam. He talked about football, which Jake had played and my father hadn't but thought he had. Or thought he knew about. It was a little unclear. His mind could wander, go in and out of focus. "So you're a Tiger now," he said to Jake again, and asked about Princeton, where he had gone and Jake was about to. Certain familiar subjects, the ones most tried-

and-true, the ones I had long since tired of but that serendipitously connected him to Jake, helped him focus for a while. His memory would stir up and make sense.

Across the years my father had never talked much with me about his childhood. Never talked much about himself. Only once did he ever bring up my writing, an instance that both surprised and touched me. When my first novel was published, despite the reviews, my mother disowned the book. The men in it weren't pretty; they lived on the outs, wildly and then sadly. Too rough for her. "They're disgusting," she said. "I can't talk about it or recommend it to my friends!"

Not long afterward, knowing what she had said, my father "happened" to mention it in passing while we were watching television. "Your book," he said, and cleared his throat and wiggled the change in his pocket, and cleared his throat again and went on with all that he would ever say: "I know what you're talking about. I knew guys like that." He wiggled his change and cleared his throat one final time and that was that.

The man wasn't a talker. I saw so little of him as a young boy, and then I was a teenager and we were battling and I wasn't listening a lot anyway, only three stories have stayed with me. There must have been others that I don't remember, and I don't know why I remember these three. Only one came from when he was drinking. Two he told me on summer afternoons after lunch when it was quiet and most everybody had gone to the beach. One was about a skunk, one was about a bow and arrows, and one was about risk.

The skunk, he said, was one of his first memories. "George and I saw this thing," he said. "We were little characters and scared of the scent of this skunk, not that we'd admit it, and we were big on tennis, but we decided not to come over to the tennis court and get in the way of this skunk, and we went to the beach instead."

"Mother and baby skunks, I thought," my mother said, passing through.

"We didn't make a mistake then and we haven't made any mistakes since," my father said.

"With skunks, you mean," my mother said.

"But you've known plenty of them," I said.

"Right," my father said, and smiled.

That was that. Such a small thing, so why did it take hold and still does? Where was the pratfall? Where was the danger or death or melodrama?

The second one was more understandable.

In 1920, upon the occasion of that big three hundredth anniversary celebration of the landing of the *Mayflower*, my father had purchased a bow with all the money he could muster together. Four arrows came with it. While everyone else went to Plymouth he marched off alone after adventure. He hadn't had a bow before, or ever fired one, but he was confident. There was a big tree on what were then woods to him, a big empty lot. The perfect target, and not a difficult one for the young marksman. He aimed up into the sky and let fly. The first arrow missed. So did the second and the third. All four did. That was okay. He would gather them up and fire them again. He searched for them and couldn't find them. It was impossible but true. Not a single one. He lost every one. By the time he told me the story they were archeological stumps or long since fertilizer. It's the image of the boy I hold on to, the boy pretending, the boy tramping, the boy searching about the territory that he would someday walk as an old man, not so much with his children but with his grandchildren. Between bouts of drinking then, or after he'd had his stroke, he led the very young, including Jake, in search of mushrooms like an aged and gentle Pied Piper. He knew mushrooms from toadstools and every mushroom one from another.

I like to think it was soon after the tennis court incident with George and Doug that my dad collared Doug and me—commandeered us somehow successfully against our will—on one of his tours. The exact chronology long since escapes me and I don't know, only that we must have been young. What is true is that for many years after he stopped playing tennis much, and then at all, my father turned a dining-room chair around and sat and watched the tennis through the window there. You couldn't see him because it was so dark inside and there was an old, heavy screen. But we felt him, and knew later he'd have things to say, sometimes over and over, about how we had played.

Where we went that day was to Rabbit Pond, one of the smallest of the 365 in the county. The route my father took was through the woods, tangles of soft wood sumac, awkward clusters of pine—tall and fallen—and thickets of bull briar. They made it impenetrable, but he found a path where there were none. The ground along this narrow way was a mattress of fallen and long-since-fallen leaves, the ones underneath mulching but those on top still dry and loose and fun to kick up into the air. "See that?" he warned. "Don't step there. Those leaves, the ones in threes." He wasn't talking about mushrooms. He meant the sprouting clusters of green leaves with a three-leaf design that looked lightly seasoned with powdered sugar. Poison ivy.

We went up a hill, along a narrow ridge, and suddenly down a ravine where the gouged earth was raw and the exposed roots served like broken and irregular steps. Without warning then, we arrived on the dirt road that encircled the pond.

Rabbit Pond was tiny and shrouded by undergrowth. The glimpses we had of it were like sightings of stained glass, but my father found a way to the water. For a few feet along the shore there was a clearing. The pond was pretty to look across. A wind riffled the water, flawed its polished surface. It was tamer and warmer than the ocean, and close up, looking down, it was murky, a nutmeg brown. Doug and I stepped into the shallows. The bottom was gushy with mud. It squished through our toes and, when we wiggled our feet, sucked us in up to our ankles.

As Doug excavated his foot to wander in further, my father reached out and grabbed him, stopped him in his tracks. "It drops off," he said, and it did. One step was knee deep, the next up to our necks, and a third was over our heads. "Be quiet," my father said then, and we grew still. Slowly the pond came alive, frogs around the lily pads, Baltimore orioles in the trees, and a hawk up high.

"Are there snakes?" Doug asked.

"I wouldn't say no," my father said, "though it never stopped your old man and I. But no water moccasins, not around here. Are you ready?"

"Ready for what?" I asked.

And he gave Doug a shove and in Doug went, spluttering. A second later I was following him and the two of us swam as my father watched, holding our shirts.

I would like to say we had more conversation. If I were writing the scene we would, something said that would come back to ring and reverberate with further meaning. A telltale nugget. But that's not what happened. In the haiku of our lives its significance was in and of itself. That's what there was. He took us, he warned us, he shoved us in, we swam awhile, enjoying ourselves, and my father said then, "All right, you characters, enough of that. Here, use your shirts and dry off and take a shower when we get back. Use soap. You've heard of it, haven't you? Soap? This water isn't the ocean. Not so clean, not to mention the ivy."

On the way back he said little or nothing, except when he stopped now and then to pluck up mushrooms, showing us the underbellies of the ones that were edible and that he was going to cook.

When I took walks with Jake when he was little the woods were gone. We still went one pond to another, or along the beach, climbing the stone jetties and checking out the boats pulled up above the tide. We saw cans to pick up and rocks to skip, sidestepped the helmetlike husks of horseshoe crabs, listened to the calls of the foraging seagulls, and sucked in the smell of brine, and what did we say? Very little too.

The third story my father told me was one that I wrote down and forgot about and discovered years later and then couldn't forget. I realized it may have changed his life. My father was still drinking and we were having a useless argument about nuclear power at one in the morning. It was a grinding, degenerating round. He was saying over and over how safe it was and he knew something about it; he had spent his entire career at a utility company. His opinion also was weighted with their bias. I was saying over and over again that he didn't know what he was talking about. He said, rightfully, what did I know? I said, finally, even if it was sort of safe, kind of safe, even really safe, it didn't matter. It only took one incident, one Chernobyl, one Three Mile Island, one meltdown. It was too risky.

He turned on me with a savagery I had never seen before: "You want to know about risk? I'll tell you about risk."

For a minute then he didn't say anything and neither did I, and when he did he had made a late-night transition. The rancor was gone and the bluster disappeared. So did the stubbornness. The effect of the alcohol evaporated. He was suddenly quiet and vulnerable.

When he was about fourteen, my father had gone sailing in an eighteen-foot dory. His cousin Miriam begged to come along. He didn't particularly like her and didn't want to take her. Reluctantly and churlishly, he agreed. He showed off and treated her badly. Foolishly, he went way out beyond the points and the three-mile buoy—and they capsized.

The dory was a heavy boat and he couldn't right it again. His cousin Miriam was younger than he was and could barely swim. There was no way she was going to make it to shore. It was up to him. "Stay here and hold on," he told her. "Hold on and I'll swim to shore." She didn't want him to go and he tried again to right the boat and failed. "Hold on," he said to her, but she held on to him and wouldn't let go. "Okay," he said, already tired. "Hold on, hold on to me then." He started to swim and he was a strong swimmer, but it was a long way. He swam until he was too tired and then he turned over and floated on his back with her beside him. Then with her on his back he did the crawl again and then he tried the breaststroke and then he had to rest again. He was too tired finally to do anything but sidestroke. At first choking him, Miriam held on around his neck. When he had to rest again he looked back to see how far they had come and ahead to see how far they had to go. The boat was small and distant. He had come a long way, too far to go back, and yet the shore looked farther away still, and he was very afraid he wasn't going to make it.

He started again, knowing this. Exhausted, he kept going, trying not to think, trying not to and unable not to, feeling the increasing tonnage of fatigue in his arms and legs and along his back and neck, and he never saw or heard the man in the powerboat coming at full speed until the boat was right there on top of them. From the top of the bluff the man had spotted them through binoculars by chance and rushed out to save them. By complete chance.

I don't know what tumblers unlocked to loose such a deep, wounded memory this particular night. It never happened again. What would have happened if the man hadn't appeared? Would they have made it? It was an incident full of questions that had no more answers now for him than then. It was unchained by prejudice or entrenched belief like nuclear power, and out it suddenly had come, so personal and still sore years later, unsolved and hung upon.

"That was risk," he said.

7

DURING THOSE DECEMBER DAYS and nights in 1969 I saw
little of Doug's brother George—behind his door poring over
his football pool—and when we were kids Doug and I had
seen little of him as well. He had been enough older to lead a
separate existence. He must have played paddle tennis with us
on the frozen wooden courts, the snow set into the corners
and along the sides like caulking around a bathtub, the sand-
papery surface crackling underfoot, and the stiff wire strum-
ming like a guitar as the ball ricocheted, but I don't recall.

George Jr. rose quickly in business, was a good golfer, an
excellent tennis player with a perilous twisting left-handed
serve, and for a spell in his thirties ranked in squash in the state
of Maine. For all that his father was better, taller, more successful. At least that was the perception we had and he was
saddled with. Every summer when George Jr. was in his teens
the two of them would play singles against one another. It was
like an assignation; it would happen only once. Deep into August the encounter would come. For several years, even as he
grew decisively better, George Jr. still couldn't beat his father.
He would implode during the match—and then, oddly, once
he did win they seldom if ever played again.

In 1972, early in the fall after our grandmother died, three years after Doug's death, the two of us found ourselves staying in the Big House while waiting for our parents to adjudicate its fate. I had gone to California and failed and come back home, uncertain what to do next, whether to try again. George Jr. was working in Boston, commuting by bus, and saving his shined-up secondhand Mercedes for the weekends. He was jut-boned, leaned out to the point of asceticism, and in his successful years. He was moving up quickly then at John Hancock, in the same business—insurance—if not the same company as his father was. His salary doubled between 1967 and 1971 from twelve thousand to twenty-four thousand, an amount that well outdistanced the inflation rate and seemed a lot of money then.

A September storm showed up. It had a hurricane name, Carrie, but it never achieved full hurricane status. Still it brought a pelting rain in the night driving across the screen porch. The porch was fifteen feet wide and completely soaked and the downfall pinged against the windows. Its slant was dramatic, virtually sideways.

The rain made plain the house's distress and disrepair. By mid-morning pots and baskets buoyed the floor from the profuse drip. On the second floor on the ocean side there was little distinction between outdoors and in-. The house had no insulation then and no wallboard. One closet wall was slimy from falling water. It softened and stained the wood, turned it gray and cadaverous. Along the windows were wet lines around the locks, a liquid ledge. Beyond them groused and rumbled the angry ocean. At high tide it would be on the bluff, stealing vegetated chunks. Hurricane or not, Carrie was on its way to delivering nine and three-quarters inches of rain, the largest amount ever measured within twenty-four hours in the Plymouth watershed.

We woke to watch the Olympics in Munich, not knowing the Israeli athletes had been taken hostage, nor their fate, and before we found out we were on the beach rescuing boats in the animate gloom of the gale winds and thrusting rain. It was something we had done before; it was part of beach living, a coming together to help. Alone, no matter how strong, one can't handle or turn or tip or drag more than a swamped dinghy. For what felt forever, Doug and I had been too young and too short to help. A certain male rite was stitched to grabbing a place along a gunwale, hefting together the weight of one boat after another, feet churning through the sand, and hiking them to safety on the bluff. Manhood wasn't complete without it.

By 1972 we didn't wear sou'westers anymore. We had ponchos with hoods but our faces were exposed and strafed by the rain. Below the waist the waves drenched us. The saltwater felt warmer than the rain until we were out of it and the wind had a chance to work. Sand coated our legs and gathered in the crotch of our bathing suits from the swirl of the breakers. Our hands and faces were red and raw. It was cold. We were windblown. We grew colder. It didn't matter.

After the boats were up, we climbed the steps from the beach, shucked our clothes, took showers, built a fire, and made coffee. Thawed out. Warmth came slowly and with it a sweet, shared contentment.

As the rain still fell, George said, "I am messed up."

"Hey, what's new?" I said in jest.

"No, I can't stop," he said.

"Stop what?"

"I just want to ball every chick."

"Is that bad?"

"I don't know. Especially young ones. But once I know I can get it I don't want it. I lose interest."

"I'll be the first to admit Carrie's addled my brain, but I thought the other day you were saying how—pick a word—smitten you were by the girl you met on the bus."

"You're right."

"You're tired of her?"

"No, I guess not."

"She looks pretty fine to me."

"She is."

"But?"

"No, no."

Her name was Didi and she was a tall, breathtakingly young woman, snug in her skin. It pulled tight around her body and she moved with the long-legged, lithe gait of a dancer. She looked sensational in slacks yet oddly less so in a bathing suit: too short-waisted. The one time I had met her then, and the times I would see her again, she seemed to completely adore him. The stars still in her eyes.

At the top of the hundred steps that led down to the beach then there was a landing. A place you could sit. A wooden bench we several times burned our initials into using the sun's power and a magnifying glass. Once Doug and I had come down the windy path upon his brother and a girl necking. We froze in the shadows, voyeurs for a moment. We were young, itching to have the syllable "teen" coupled to our ages, and it seemed racy, adult, and extremely provocative. In fact all their clothes were in place, their hands in check, just their mouths joined.

We were riveted and then embarrassed. We snuck away silently without being seen, giggling only when it was safe, dismissing what we wouldn't forget, tied up still hopelessly in our own innocence. Maybe George Jr. was too.

"I met this other girl," he said then as the rain continued to fall.

"What girl?"

"Barbara."

"I haven't heard about her."

"I met her at a wedding and I've been thinking a lot about her lately, thinking back on her. Maybe I made a mistake. I told you I was messed up."

His tone was baleful. He wanted me to believe it despite everything he had, and had always had; and maybe messed up he was, especially as I think back on it. But I knew then it was also useful, a flavor of aphrodisiac. Women read the pain, felt the sexual imperative. They saw his success, his Mercedes, his tight stomach and jutting jaw, his prowess, and were enticed. He seemed innocent of it and that only heightened it.

"That's not it," he said then.

I took a guess. "There's another one."

"I told you," he said, and laughed at himself.

He told me then of his affair with a married woman that had suddenly ended six months before. The husband traveled a lot. George would drive out to her house and move in for several days. He'd leave his car in the driveway. The two of them were that irrational. The woman had no children; she couldn't. She'd been born without a vagina, a freak thing. An operation had given her one, including labia. Yes, she could orgasm. That had been the best sex, the one time he didn't lose interest. The woman's husband's father had gotten sick and been expected to die. But unexpectedly it had been his mother who did, and it was only that tragedy that stopped them.

I thought then it might be Doug's death that set his course, but before 1972, before 1969, George Jr. had been married and divorced. He had eloped to the other side of the country, to Seattle, and applied for a job at an insurance company there. Only hours later his father knew—the industry that small, his father's stature that significant. He had sought to break out through distance, even through self-destruction, and had failed. The marriage hadn't lasted, and neither would the one that would come to the breathtaking girl on the bus.

Years later, my own marriage in trouble, I had called him in search of advice or answers and asked him what had happened with Didi, who had seemed so in love with him, what had gone wrong.

"She didn't love me enough," he said.

I was astonished, but no more astonished than when I looked inside myself and found a not dissimilar such scary hole.

I realized it wasn't Doug's fate that had unseated him. It was planted like a harpoon long before in his primal struggle with his father. He was his mother's favorite and his father's fitful hope and full-time competition and it bounced him between the poles of ambition and mornings like those when he pulled his car into the driveway and left it for all the neighbors to see.

While Big George was turning suddenly, shockingly ill, George Jr. left for Europe. When I asked him whether he regretted going, missing the last days, he didn't say, "He knew I loved him, and I told him I loved him, and I knew he loved me." He didn't say, "We had said all there was to say." All he said to me was, "We had nothing left to say."

Doug is still with me—our time together and what it meant—but my memories of young George are difficult to draw back. They have fallen away, hidden or gone, like he drew behind his door while we waited that Christmas. If I ever did, I don't know him anymore. He stays in Maine now, seldom comes down.

But perhaps all three of us were attempting a similar thing—to escape. George Jr. in that futile flight to Seattle and what came after; my path into movies, television, and California; and Doug's journey into the Marines and Vietnam.

———

THERE WAS A NIGHT during my father's final illness when we gathered at my brother's house. The summer was young and it was still light out and maybe because we didn't want to talk about anything serious, maybe because it was hot and the june bugs were insistent and the mosquitoes were in love with us, we made a batch of martinis.

George and Betty had brought Smirnoff and I had found in the freezer an untapped bottle of Absolut. It was a big bottle, 1040 milliliters, and as soon as it was spotted the Smirnoff went to the side of the road and took a rest. George used his thumb to doctor in vermouth, just a smidgen, even less, a smidge, and we served the martinis in sherry glasses. The portions were small, the refills were frequent, the pace was ongoing. George called them Bombs. Betty called them Bombs. This was a new usage to me but before very long, in quite short order, in fact very quickly we all joined in. We were all calling them Bombs.

At some point there was talk of reading the fabled Fractured French coasters, but we were in the wrong house. They were in the tennis court house and it was too early in the evening and too early in the season. It wasn't September. The drinks made me want to forget and to remember and I grew nostalgic and I wanted to ask about the times of the Blue Moon. I didn't have to. It was George who took us back to that time, if not to that place. He launched into a George-and-Bill story that I'd never heard before.

It was about a night they'd been riding around in a car and gone out to Manomet Point where there was a hotel then, a big, sprawling, and for a generation bustling and quite posh resort hotel that was long gone now. The goal was to find girls and they had encountered some.

"We thought these girls were pretty cute," George said. "Waitresses from the Cape and from Boston or wherever, and we drove by and talked to them, or tried to, didn't make much headway, and drove back to Buttner's house."

"Oh my God, not Eddie Buttner," Betty said. "It's always Eddie Buttner."

"He wasn't so bad."

"Oh yeah. We know all about Eddie Buttner."

"*Anyway*," said George, "we had a few more drinks, maybe, and these guys, the busboys, or whatever, they didn't think it had been very nice, us talking to the girls—"

"I don't think it was either," said Betty.

"They were right," my mother said.

"*Anywaaayyy*," said George, "they came over to Buttner's and started tearing the house apart." He stopped as if the story was at an end.

"That's it?" I said. "That's the story?"

"Your dad needs to tell the rest."

"If he were here . . ."

"Well," George said, "I guess I'll have to be the one."

He hadn't gone to see my father that day; he seldom had. The one time I had been there when he had come he didn't stay in the room. He sat outside in a lawn chair and my father, still walking then, came out and sat beside him in a second lawn chair. George mentioned his garden and the rabbits that threatened it and my father said something about tomatoes and started wondering about mushrooms. They didn't talk about the old days. They didn't talk about the news, worldwide or local. They didn't talk about much, and the conversation died away.

In the longtime New York Yankee Frank Crosetti's obituary not so long ago, there was a story about a reporter, John Mahon, sitting in the lobby of the Hotel Chase in St. Louis in the summer of 1936. He found himself within hailing distance of Joe DiMaggio and his two Yankee teammates Tony Lazzeri and Crosetti. It occurred to Mahon that the three ballplayers had not said a word to each other in some time. "Just for fun, I timed them to see how long they would maintain their silence," Mahon remembered. "They didn't speak for an hour and twenty minutes. At the end of that time DiMaggio cleared his throat. Crosetti looked at him and said, 'What did he say?' And Lazzeri said: 'Shut up. He didn't say nothing.' They lapsed into silence, and at the end of ten more minutes I got up and left. I couldn't take it anymore."

This was the way my father and uncle were, except that day it wasn't an easy nonconversation, a content silence. George was uncomfortable. He couldn't sit still. My father, glad to see him at first, slowly withdrew inside himself, whether from his medicines or from fatigue or habit. There was an increasing awkwardness; less and less was said. The two grew especially, even architectonically laconic. It could have been funny. Wasn't. The lengthening lulls were telltale and desolate.

We were near the front door and before the two of them badly retreated into their Quiet, my father graciously said hello to the first few oldsters who came and went. Then he didn't. Then he started talking about getting out of there. Whatever he said then, that was what he said. He had to get out.

George only returned once after that. He refused to go with Betty, and it was Mason's wife, Beth, who accompanied him.

"So when they came," George went on, "Bill was half-asleep and he tried to get up and this guy tried to take a swing at him. Bill was still dressed. It may have been near morning, but we had never gotten our clothes off. He tried to get a hand out of this old raincoat he was still wearing and it ripped. The guy gave him a pretty good whack.

"And the next day we went out to play touch football and these same guys were there." He laughed. "And we beat the dirt out of them."

The memory was a good one, whatever its exact veracity, and we all laughed. And I knew even through the Bombs there was a familiar ring to it. I might have heard a version before and forgotten. It may have been part of the goulash of some other of these gatherings over the years. I felt I could even hear my father in it, who lay now fighting for life—or was it fighting to let go of life? I could hear his voice in the ripped pocket of the raincoat and the "pretty good whack" and it was a pleasing thing.

"What did Grandfather think?" I asked. "Say to you guys?"

"What?" asked George. "About what?"

"About tramps and whatnot and girls and whatnot and what happened and whatnot?"

"Oh, I don't know."

"He said nothing?!"

"Not so far as I know."

"You mean your father didn't have a viewpoint about the behavior of his male offspring?"

"Come to think of it," George said, and looked at me directly for once and keenly, "he said, 'Take your back swing a little slower.'"

And here was golf again.

"Did Grandfather play golf?" my brother, Mason, asked, laughing again. This was also news to me, but my grandfather had died when I was four and I didn't remember him.

He had come over from England at sixteen and then brought first his brothers and then his mother and his sisters after him. In his success and until he died, he had sent each of his sisters a check every month to help support them. No one had a bad thing to say about him. He, perhaps justifiably, had moved through myth and into distancing legend.

There were foibles. Within the family he was celebrated for his steel trap of a mind yet his extraordinary lack of ability to recall names. At the dinner table, unable to come up with his own children's names, he would resort to calling out the chronological list of them until he got to the right one, the one he wanted to address. It could take a while with ten of them. When his children started to marry and he had to introduce them he was known to resort to "This is my son-in-law," and then, pointing to his daughter and unable to dredge up her name either, "and this is my son-in-law's wife."

"He was ecstatic about breaking a hundred," my aunt Sally said. Kitty's mother, she was the youngest of the siblings and had married Leonard while both were in the service during World War II.

"I get ecstatic about breaking a hundred now," said George.

"No, really," I said. "I know there is golf and there is life and there is life and there is golf. Golf. Life. You with me so far? There used to be golf and God and God and golf, but not anymore. God got lost. He went out of bounds somewhere into the deep rough or the water hazard and never was found. Now there is golf and life."

"Better bring out the net," my brother said.

"It was only a moment. A mo," I said then. "It's passed, it's gone, it's over, it's history."

There was a silence and they let it go, whatever I had said, whatever I was talking about, whatever it had meant, and George said, "For a long time there was a score card in the bureau drawer, in Father's bureau drawer, which we inherited, and it was still there after he died. And there was this duffer on it, a Pilgrim—"

"A Pilgrim duffer?" my brother, Mason, asked.

"With a hat on," George said. "And Father had an eighty-eight that day."

Sally said, "You know Leonard's story?" He had died not so long before. It was a rhetorical question and she didn't wait for an answer: "He always called Father Mr. Young, and we were living here for several months and it was January or February and Leonard came down to breakfast one freezing Saturday morning and Father said politely to this poor Southern rube from Montgomery, 'How about it? You want to play golf today?' 'Ah, uh, Mr. Young,' Leonard said, 'should we? How can we . . . ?' 'Yes, let's go play some,' Father said. So they did. They wrapped up, they had to wrap up, and if you remember, the second hole then was a water hole—"

"The fourth," George corrected her.

"And they hit their drives and they walked across the ice!"

We all were laughing again. "We had this black dog," said George. "This terrific black Lab, Smoky, and he'd go anywhere, and he saw that water hazard and then just ran to take a dive in and he just landed on the ice and skidded halfway across."

"I'd love to have seen that," Mason said.

"So Smoky played golf," I said.

"Well, we let him come along in the winter."

"Did he carry his own bag?" I asked.

Everyone laughed and Sally said, "Of course there was no one else crazy enough to be out there."

"Now can we have an interruption from all these tall tales of fun and frolic and get a drink?" George said. "Bombs away!"

Some of that evening, however lot or little he was mentioned, was about my father. Under the drinking, through the drinking, we were aware of him and thinking of him, and as the Bombs dropped he joined us in his own way for the night.

When George and Betty left, he had trouble managing the steps down from the kitchen to the patio. He almost lost his balance. I thought it must be the martinis. What I hadn't noticed before and still didn't when he was sitting down was suddenly sobering and undeniable. He had changed. He walked differently now because it was going dark and the steps were steep. He walked differently because his hips had been operated on a second time after the first time hadn't worked. He walked differently because he was eighty-eight. He, too, had gotten old.

AFTER THEY'D GONE, after everyone had, Mason and I sat alone. He was a good cook and we ate dinner. During, and even more after, we talked as we seldom ever had and never had since we were young. My brother's hair had silvered and so had his beard. He had large hands and enormous thumbs. Their last knuckles were double in size, the nails wide and broad and flattened like squashed half-moons. He was tan and strong, but certain body parts ached and at times this one or that one would decide not to work for a while. Old injuries, mostly from athletics, long since healed, had come back after decades to haunt him. Plus the vicissitudes of life thereafter. He had gained weight and a gut and he had drunk too much this night. We both had.

Years younger and years leaner, we both had fit on his Triumph 500 when he lived for a year in Mississippi. I flew down to see him in Jackson, where he was working for an oil company, and we crossed to Vicksburg National Battlefield on the motorcycle. Unlike Grant's first frontal assault at the Great Redoubt, we didn't fail and fall back, or have to lay siege like the Union had a hundred years before, ringing the city, packing the populace inside and underground, "black and white like sardines in a box" and reduced to eating mule meat.

We mounted our charge, overlooking the Mississippi from where cannons had sunk the ironclad *Cincinnati*, and lit out across the rolling and rugged terrain, lifting off the bike as we leapt the gullies, me hanging on to his jacket, his waist, whatever I could clutch, dodging fallen cannons, some recently repainted, and rumbled along the hard-packed mud of Thayer's tunnel, which the Union had dug, and wheeled through the remnants of the fifty-foot-wide crater they had made by exploding 2,200 pounds of powder that had blown a breach under the Third Louisiana Redan, and circled the worn and mottled stone shaft that marked where Lieutenant-General Pemberton of the Confederacy had surrendered.

The rush and excitement of the ride set aside the grumbling graphite and gray day and Mason's serious state of disenfranchisement. He was alone and unhappy in Mississippi. He would quit his job and his first profession before the year was out. That day, though, we didn't know we were tired or cold until we were on our way back and had to make a stop at the Admiral Benbow Inn, where Judy Moon was appearing. Her hair was hived and lacquered atop her head and she called out when a couple dared to depart during her set, "I'd play 'Exodus' but I don't think you're Jewish." We ate like we were famished and drank as if dehydrated and took up for a while an expression from the name of the place: to be "benbowed," as in, "Let's go get benbowed."

Mason turned to the times he had spent with our father. Fishing and playing football and caddying for him, sometimes when Big George and the old man had played together. He remembered being treated in the clubhouse after a round to a Purple Cow—sarsaparilla and vanilla ice cream. Mason had an image that I didn't: our father, so much younger, lean and fleet of foot, unhinging his limbs and flashing across the yard. Still amazed at the memory of his speed. In it was the hint of what we had heard about our dad when he was young. How he had once been swift, carefree, and fun. How he had a temper but also a cool composure. How in college, for example, he had picked up a javelin and given it a throw and broken the school record and not bothered to throw it again. How he had loved and was so good at finding mussels beneath the hanks of seaweed in the niches of the rocks at the lowest tides. How he cooked and marinated and served and ate them in his own special secret concoction.

But Mason's recollections had splinters. They weren't all benign. As we sat together in the dark, sobering up slowly, waiting for the time that I'd go back to be with our father through the night, he called up another incident: way back no more than five or six walking on the beach. It was after a storm and good to be out and great to be with his dad, but Mason couldn't keep up. The tall man had long strides. Mason tried and failed and our father didn't slacken his pace and Mason stubbed his toe. It bled. Our father hadn't bothered to bend over to take a closer look. He had no sympathy; he was scathing. "That was a pretty stupid thing to do," he said.

The comment still angered and hurt all these years and drinks later ("Tee many martoonies," as our parents said in the fifties). The bruise was unhealed, the sting and bitterness unchecked. Only two years apart, we hadn't had the same childhood. Other than the trek to Rabbit Pond I had few, if any, such recollections. A part of me was jealous. Even bad memories must have some good in them. At least they were time spent together. They had an existence.

———

BY THE FOURTH NIGHT of waiting for Doug to come home in December 1969 we were stir-crazy. Connecticut was still frozen. We didn't know what to do with ourselves. After due consideration, George took us out to the side yard that ran down a hill to a still-empty lot and then to the street. He made us all come; demurring was not an option. We loaded on the warmest clothes possible. All to no avail. He had brought with him a couple of things—a front doormat, a seven iron and a nine iron, and a bucket of golf balls.

"Here," he said to Mason, handing him some tees. "Try these."

My brother bent to set one in the ground. It was not possible. Mason got out a knife. All to no avail. The hardened ground rejected the jab of the blade and then snapped it off.

"I thought so," George said. "That's why I brought this." He unrolled the flat rubber front doormat from underneath his arm and set it on the edge of the slope. "We can hit off of this."

Somehow I was chosen to be first up and couldn't come up with an escape. I was no golfer, and the added bulk of the winter clothes, hat, mittens and gloves made me a Michelin man. Swinging while hogtied by the clothes, I was confronted by an ugly possible fate. If I whiffed, an endless and merciless family replay awaited me. There was only one thing to do, however carefully, pathetically, and badly: at least hit the ball.

"Fore!" George laughed, and Mason said, "Nice swack," as my interminably slow and cautious swing still barely topped the ball and it dribbled down the hill "Your grip's all wrong to start with. Interlace your fingers." He illustrated, using the seven iron.

This time the ball went screaming off to the right.

"Nice slice," he said, laughing again.

Everyone was laughing now, for the first time in several days.

"Who's next?" I called out in an attempt to escape further embarrassment.

"No such luck," George said. "Here, watch this. I'll hit one."

He stepped up, spread his long legs and set his feet, and

somehow still looked thin in his overcoat and scarf. He hadn't bothered with a hat and his bald head seemed illuminated and must have been freezing. He gave a little waggle and, looking completely loose and free, swung the club. The ball began a high and perfect journey, sizzling off into the sky, and we all gazed after it and he laughed once more and handed the club to Samantha. "You'll be next after this victim."

So each of us took a turn whacking the ball and listening to his advice: "Head down, keep your head down, and follow through before looking up." "Use the torque of the back-swing and the first part of the downstroke and the follow-through to power the ball." "The rest, let stay sweet. Swing it easy." "Not like baseball. This is not baseball. The club is not a bat. More like scything grass."

Well hit, a ball made a crack in the cold and the dryness like a rifle firing, and then it seemed to sing, glowing and leaving a trail of sound like a comet leaves a tail. Off it flew into what had turned the blackest of nights. All the colors ever used to describe such darkness came to mind—pitch, ebony, fresh blacktop—and all fell short.

But we forgot we were cold and it was crazy and we kept hitting golf balls into the night until the bucket was empty and there were no more left.

Two

8

ON A SATURDAY AFTERNOON I came to see my father in the nursing home and couldn't find him. His room was empty. It was confounding and worrisome. Had there been a sudden relapse? Could he be gone? There was no one at the nursing station. I went up and down the hallways looking for him and couldn't find him. There was no one in the office. I went upstairs to physical therapy and couldn't find him. I went past the lunchroom, looking in, and didn't see him at first and almost not at all.

In a wheelchair, leaning on the straps that held him in, my father was turned away from the door, his face hidden, his head down, his hat on. His body was pitched forward like a drooping crane. It was a forlorn sight.

He wasn't alone in the room. It was crowded and it smelled. From the moment you walked in the front door of the nursing home it was in the air. An odor, a stench, a stink. There was no escaping it, and it wasn't only in the lunchroom and it wasn't alike every day. The degree differed and the brew changed—this or that cafeteria food, strong medicines and stronger disinfectants, and the penetrating, acidic whiff of urine. It was always there.

A woman in an overcoat played the piano. She thumped the

keys but her selection was limited. There were four men settled at a table as if for bridge, except there were no cards and
no conversation. There were several men and women who
weren't moving or doing anything. There was a woman
hooked up to an IV who was dancing. Sometimes she thought
the IV stand was her partner. Sometimes she knew she was
dancing alone. There was a woman who didn't stop talking
and one who moaned and one who was convinced her spoon
was ruining the taste of her melted ice cream. She had a pain
in her stomach. She was "in pain. In pain. *Pain.*"

Before I got to him my father reacted to my coming and
looked up. "Thank God somebody came," he said. "I'm an
orphan."

"It's okay now, Dad," I said.

"Is it?"

"I'll take you out of here."

"You will?"

"Come on."

I wheeled him out of the lunchroom back to his room,
where I discovered as he talked that the "rascals" had become
"knuckleheads." He had to go to the bathroom. Again it came
with terrifying suddenness. I cleaned him up, put him back on
the bed, and took off his Bass white bucks and put them under the bed. I turned on the television and he would get lost
in it or wherever he went and then come back and look at me
expectantly and with what appeared to be a scathing eagle eye
and ask, "What's your game?" At first I thought he might mean
tennis, because Wimbledon had begun and Jana Novotna,
who had a reputation for losing, was winning. But he kept
asking, and using that word of his "rampant." "Insanity was rampant," he said, or "Inanity was rampant." I couldn't tell which.
The words slurred as he kept repeating them.

He kept feeling his face and he needed a shave. His razor
was on a side table and I plugged it in and shaved him. The

flesh was slack across his jaw and the skin was bristly. It took a while and he let it. He let it happen patiently and even seemed to enjoy it. He felt his face over and over with his hand when I was done. "Nice bit," he said, and I looked at him for translation or elaboration. "Nice bit," he said, with great precision and deliberateness. "Nice bit." I realized it was a compliment and not a small one, and as much as he could muster in sickness and more than he could in health.

We were quiet awhile and then he looked at me and said, "They won't let me out of here." The tone wasn't woebegone. It was worse—it was dead.

This then was the afternoon I managed to get a pale blue cardigan sweater onto him, buttoned it up, and wheeled him outside for one last time. He adjusted his hat. In a rumpled way he looked almost dapper. The air was fresh and exciting. A wind was coming up and rain wasn't far away. He was very aware of the flowers and the grass that was being cut. He was very sensitive to temperature and I wrapped him in a blanket. His hearing was extraordinarily acute, if misguided. He thought the hum of the air conditioner was a car coming and then that the cars were from the twenties and thirties. A Franklin, a Phaeton, a Packard. He seemed suddenly alert, as if measuring the wind and listening for the rain. It was a while before I realized it was about the cars. He thought they were all cars, and he was waiting to be picked up.

"George is coming," he said then. "George is going to save me. George's coming to get me and I'm going to run away and go to the Big House and sit on the porch and look at that bay and have a drink, a drink, a drink of soda, and that's where Peggy will find me. I'll be there."

But George didn't come and I didn't take him there and when the rain began to fall we went back inside. He was completely tired suddenly and he looked around his room and said in the saddest words I'll ever hear: "So this is it. This is my home."

———

UNLIKE MY MOTHER, my brother's wife, Beth, was very good with my father. It wasn't that my mother didn't visit him. She came every day. That was a given, a duty, but she didn't like to be there. Her visits were short and she took to bringing something to do. Needlepoint. A crossword puzzle. She was very good at one and a wizard at the other, and they offered distraction, a place to escape from him while with him.

With others who were ill it hadn't always been so. Years before on a Halloween night, my mother, Jenny, and I had gone to see Florence St. Clair, the woman who had hosted the Christmas party I had interrupted in 1969. Her son Stevie's suicide had been only the kickoff of a calamitous collection of events for the St. Clairs. All of our lives are fragile nets that tragedy tears at as it sets loose a danger—the impact on the survivors and their relationships. Check the divorce rates of couples who have lost a child; they're heartbreakingly sky high. The nets can mend in time, the lives imperfectly spun back together; but once in a while the fates violate reason, belie randomness, and download an amount of tragedy that defies explanation. It comes to visit too often, as if with design. Such was the case for the St. Clairs.

After Stevie's death, his father's liver turned bad. He died quickly and miserably and there are few more awful ways to die. The remaining son divorced and remarried and moved to California. After one unsuccessful business venture after another, he somehow won the Republican nomination for Congress from a district north of San Francisco before he too was struck down, this time by brain cancer. The last one left, Florence began moving from one house to another when she wasn't in Florida, and took to hanging out with the captain of what had been their new boat. He was devoted to her and soon needed to be. Cancer struck her too and stripped and skinnied her without mercy.

The previous July I had seen Florence, still heavy, wading in a swimming pool using the short skirt of her suit to wet herself. It was a childlike image except for her nicotine-stained teeth and the cobalt burns on her chest. Now at the end of October she was carved out as only pain can do, and nearly unrecognizable. She wasn't ugly; she looked old and young at once. Her face seemed smooth until you looked closely and many fine lines appeared. There was a row of tiny perpendicular pleats on her upper lip. The only things untouched were her hands. They looked young and firm and cared for. I couldn't see any liver spots. The nails were smooth with a clear polish. Her hair, too, almost looked the same. It was freshly coiffed and colored and pulled back. One roller set in front. She had leaned too far over in the bath, she said, and had gotten it wet.

Several times a day now her captain (as she called him) gave her shots. His name was Charley and he counted on his fingers the hours since the last one. He was small, but his hands were fair-sized and looked well used. On the first knuckle of each finger he had a tattoo, letters that I couldn't read, but that he said spelled LOVE on one hand and HATE on the other. He was fifteen years younger than Florence, not yet fifty, and he wore an elaborate stainless-steel waterproof watch with lots of dials. Its face was the size of a twenty-dollar gold piece. He was drunk. He called Jenny "Miss Priss." He eyed her. He eyed Florence. He got her a glass of ice water and sat in front of a heater, aghast at that day's morning temperature of thirty-nine degrees.

Charley was an ex-Navy seaman who, besides the tattoos, had bad teeth, a smashed flat honker of a nose, and the burned-in tan of years on the water. His skin looked like deep-dyed wood in need of a varnish. His face was weathered and he had an upturned grin like a person with false uppers, and deep long lines that pulled and stretched his face when he smiled or laughed. The laugh was hoarse, quite blue; it had heard and told many salty stories.

He and Florence bickered. He mostly—she was too tired. She tucked her head now and again and closed her eyes. In some way he had won her. He might have been her husband—he was taking complete care of her—but there was little to savor. It was a bitter victory. It took her dying to do it, and she was dying. It left him embattled, rude, jealous, and anxious. Her battle was beyond temper. It was with a greater pain and knowledge. Her brash voice and brash laugh were quelled. She was listening for the running-down clock that was herself. Listening, listening, not wanting to hear what she could feel.

Charley went to answer the door and hand out candy. Florence explained tersely that his grandchild was also in the hospital. He was torn whether to go or stay. He returned and said the kids were getting bigger—they were now bigger than he was. Florence smiled before she withdrew. Her eyes turned in. There was a purity about her. In the wan lamp she looked beautiful, and at what a cost.

She still smoked. So did Charley and my mother then. Three people in a small room lighting up. Stubs crammed the ashtrays. Charley dumped one into a wastebasket. We all moved too quickly to help with anything. We chattered, especially my mother. Charley was drunk, occasionally obscene. I was quiet. Florence tucked her head. We left.

In the car I wanted to talk about what we had seen. The two women didn't and wouldn't. Death's approach made me angry, and I wanted to rage at it and rag on it. Beat it back somehow. Fight the futility. It was a young man's reaction, and one I would come to know better. An anger against the helplessness of the dead and against my own helplessness.

The women carried what they felt inside, complexly and

emotionally, the way a baby kicks during pregnancy. That basic, that seminal. It wasn't without fury or anguish and yet a certain acceptance. It wasn't going away. They knew that and there was nothing else to know. Other times and other places they could talk a storm, but this Halloween night words were fruitless and beside the point.

I gave up finally and we drove through the rainy streets that were flooding with falling leaves. The trees had picked this night to shake loose and empty in a lazy blizzard. Curled leaves, like lemon twists and collops of orange rind, puttered around us along the wet asphalt. The rain wasn't heavy, little more than a drizzle, but it wet the air and garnished all it touched. The tread marks of the tires from the last few cars lay like wrinkles on the shiny road. The streetlights had halos. When we stopped we were silent but the night wasn't. The plangent rain and the dance of the leaves encircled us.

My mother could remember Florence's sixth birthday party when Florence's cat had disappeared. They had known each other that long. They were two smart girls—my mother spoke or could read eight languages and Florence was swiftly competent at anything she tried, whether it was geometry or waterskiing—and both had set their gifts aside to become wives and mothers the same year. It was Florence who told my mother there was a house for sale on the same street. The house I grew up in. In those first few years of marriage before their paths separated they talked every day. In truth they were very different. Florence was much more sophisticated and had far more means; she was very strong and sometimes cruel and her life had turned tragic and pathetic, variations on Lady Macbeth. And yet there was a spark between them, an enduring durability. They had shared so much so young their bond never broke, and my mother went regularly to see her that last fall and brought her bright energy. She carried the conversation, chatted about this and that, mostly small and inconsequential things even after Florence's ravaged beauty was gone and her bones loomed and jutted like in concentration-camp pictures. Her head stayed tucked then in its pain. She moved into the pale and my mother became the only person she allowed to come. In my mother's childlike faith and belief that death was benign, in that unspoken certainty, Florence found a way to keep herself going a while longer. Or let herself go a little sooner.

Now, years later, it was an essence my mother could not bring to my father. Every day he would wait for her arrival. He would repeatedly wonder where she was, and then for a short bad while reverted to harping at her. His behavior became like the last years he was drinking. It wasn't pretty, and because of their history it had a nasty and corrosive echo.

Mason didn't like being there either. He reacted as if the room was claustrophobic. If he wasn't good at being in the same small space with his angry fading father, he had ample excuse. For the last years, living so close, he had become the caretaker. The one who opened and closed houses for the summer and winter, who cut lawns, fixed whatever was broken, fielded phone calls, took over finances, and drove to doctors and hospitals. The frequency made him the equivalent of an outcall ambulance service. I think it granted him a place in the world he hadn't expected and a sense of completion. It was also exhausting.

Beth's first husband had died of cancer when both of them were very young. She had seen plenty of hospitals and had acquired a gracious gravity. She was a big, warm, natural woman, not without opinions, and my father and George liked all of that. She was also blessed by coming along late enough in their lives and our own to not be plagued by so much of the family baggage.

In her time with my father she witnessed his increasing befuddlement. He was often mixed up and he knew it and hated it. "This rigmarole," as he called it, "this whole rigmarole." And "rigmarole" became the word that replaced "rampant" and that he relied on for a while. I thought he meant the doctors, the place, what he saw as his incarceration. It never occurred to me until later that he might have been putting a larger meaning into it.

His language started to break down. What he said could seem brilliant, tantalizing, and it could be incoherent. He had never spoken much and now phrases or insights popped out that were startling or elliptical or even eloquent. He said in one of these moments, with some humor, that he was now "living out here on the edge of recollection."

He would fixate on things. His watch was one. He'd worn it for years and it needed winding, which he forgot to do now. His arm was so skinny and flaccid the watch slid right down to his elbow. The skin hung like laundry on a line on a windless day. But he took to studying the watch's beaten-up face. "See," he said, "the pieces of light?"

"What?"

"See the pieces of light. Look at them."

"Where?" I asked.

"You see them. Right there. They're moving. Damn pieces of light."

"Let me wind it."

"What time of the land? Let me guess."

"Dad," I said, not understanding.

"Tenby land."

"It's two-thirty, Dad."

"One-quarters," he said, not understanding my not understanding. "It's so bright."

I didn't know what to say; I didn't say anything.

"You have a hand, don't you? A pretty fair game going. I think you're available. It's going to break up, plenty of rocks, or some such damn thing. Mason does able that guy. I think he's got the gear. Whatever the hell he is? Do you remember where he plays? Seven no trump or something . . . I have a lot of difficulty, though . . . I'm not quite out of the woods yet.

Look at this thing." He was back to the watch, or maybe in some way he'd never left it. "You ever see such a thing. It's the crystal. Look. The pieces of light. I can't read them worth a damn." He descended then into gibberish.

That night he had a very bad night. He was very restless and gunk struggled up from his lungs and gathered in his mouth. It was my turn to stay with him and I swabbed big gobs of it out with big pink hospital-sized Q-Tips. He sucked on them for a while like lollipops. His teeth were bad and perhaps they hurt. One that hadn't yellowed had a hole next to it, a tooth gone, and he rolled his tongue and the swab around there. At about five in the morning they knocked him out and at last he was quiet.

The next night in the roller coaster of illness he was better. He didn't want to eat with the regular inmates. Our term. Down the hall there was "fine dining," a room with better food for those who were in better shape. I wheeled him there and found a table and served him dinner. He ate all his carrots and strawberries, but wasn't much interested in the casserole.

"I'm not really very hungry," he said.

"Just another bite or two."

"What's that?"

"What's what?"

"Look at those shoes. Look at those feet. Look at them. Look at them move." We had put on his Bass white bucks with the easy-to-tie stretch laces and he was delighted with the sight in a mirror that filled and blocked the opening to a fireplace, of all places. "Aren't they something? Whose are they?"

"Yours."

"Oh, right."

They were far more interesting to him than his food. He grew quiet and I tried to make conversation:

"Tell me, Dad. What was the best round of golf you ever had?"

"I could never beat him."

His answer took me aback and confounded me. "Who?"

"I never got better, I don't know why. He was always better." He was bewildered and vulnerable, as if the wondering and defeat of it were still brand-new. "I could never beat George."

"But you got the holes in one."

"He was always better."

The sense of loss and defeat was profound, so I changed the subject. I asked a different question:

"Tell me about when you worked in Maine. In Waterville. You've never talked about living there. I do remember once hearing about you skating on black ice."

"Right. Black as tar."

"Were you a good skater?"

"Right."

"What do you remember most?"

"Right."

I was afraid I was losing him and tried to key his memory: "Were there dances there? Did you dance?"

He looked at me right in the eye and laughed: "I guess you could call it that."

"What would you call it?"

"You know what I'm talking about."

"I'm not sure."

"I was sort of guilty."

"Guilty?"

"She got me into trouble all right."

Again he surprised me. More than that, startled me. "Back up a minute."

"Her father was a nice guy, I guess. He was my boss. What else could he do, I guess."

"Who was this girl?"

For once he took off his hat. It seemed a courtly yet unprotected gesture. His face had fallen into fascinating ruin. His eyes under the thick lenses of his glasses looked as vulnerable and wet as open oysters. "If I'm allowed to say it, she was really active."

"Did you like her?"

"Really active."

I was a caboose barely hanging on to a fleeting train. "I'm a little lost here."

"She was making me." His hat went back on and he pulled it down so his eyes disappeared. "She was into some game."

"So I guess you're not talking about dancing exactly."

"I guess you could call it that," my father said. "I'm not really hungry anymore."

Later, after I put him to bed, he begged me not to go. I stayed a while longer but when I started to leave again he begged me not to go. Again I lingered but he sensed and then he knew I wasn't really going to stay, not forever, or not for long enough, and his emotions went away. He withdrew. He gave up. His farewells were distant, cursory, throwaway. "Good luck," he said. "Don't get lost."

I went to a tiny neighborhood restaurant and had two Ketel One martinis, a slab of prime rib and garlic mashed potatoes, and watched the Phillies play the Red Sox. The food was basic and cheap and I thought I was hungry and then wasn't. I couldn't shut my mind down. Still reeling, I ended up walking on the beach. The sky was suffused with stars and a northeasterly scent of the sea. The firmament was alive and so was the beach. The last embering flames and shouts and laughter from a cookout down the shoreline. I sat in the sand and knew dawn would come with its salmon crease of light along the horizon across the Cape long before I would calm down or absorb what I had heard and I shivered despite myself.

I had wondered, especially in these last few weeks, about my father's life and what had happened to him. There must have been a telltale incident, I had thought, a turning or breaking point where a young, antic, mischievous young man had so lost or buried those qualities. Perhaps it was because he had stayed at home during the war with a young child while his siblings were all in the service. Perhaps because he never left the job he had first been successful at and then stifled in. Perhaps because it was at a company where his father had been so much greater a success. Perhaps because he had turned down an offer to join another family's pharmaceutical company as treasurer. Perhaps because he had passed up an opportunity to move to California with a different utility company. Perhaps, of course, because of alcohol.

This night I had asked a couple of simple questions and had stepped into the very deep end. I knew of such stories, especially about men who'd been to war, and I had a friend whose father had suddenly broken silence about his experience in World War II. At Thanksgiving dinner, without preamble, he started talking about a fellow GI next to him, laughing one minute and blown to pieces the next. Filaments of his brain floating around like bloody dandelion fluff. For fifty-five years it had been locked up and sealed off, festering inside, and for fifty-five years the man had been trying to make sense of it and couldn't. Out it had come—exploded—like the buddy beside him.

This night my father's answers shook the foundations of everything I knew or thought. About the brother he loved so much. About a girl I had never heard of. His answers only raised questions I would never have thought to ask and never would have answers to. Were there other important nooks and altering crannies to what I had always heard of George and Bill and Bill and George? Had my father slept with the girl, had he loved her, had he lost her? Had he, maybe, even gotten her pregnant? And what had it done to him?

9

AFTER DARK ON THE FIFTH DAY of waiting in that December, Doug finally made it home.

A Marine, a casualty assistance officer, has to escort each fallen member of the Corps to burial and with Doug, knocking at the door, came Sergeant Don Nalley. "I'm here with Corporal Douglas W. Young," he said. "He has arrived safely and is at Ahern Funeral Home." He said it quickly, right away, to Samantha, who had answered the door and then remained in place standing on the steps until George joined her. Then he said it again.

"Thank you for coming," George said, and as Don Nalley lingered still: "Do you want to come in?"

"I can do that," Don Nalley said and did.

He settled stiffly down in the living room in an armchair and his posture remained erect. He was a small, short, balding soldier with marbles for eyes, round and multifaceted and impenetrable. His hair was all shades of rusty, dark and rusty on the sides and lighter and rusty where it was thinning on top. His beard was a third shade of rusty, almost carrot, and even freshly shaved he wore its hue in five o'clock shadow. His wrists and hands were tiny and he wore a signet ring that looked outsized because they were so diminutive.

We loosely gathered around him, waiting to hear we didn't know what, but he said nothing and we didn't know what to say back. It was an awkward situation.

We had just finished dinner and George asked, "Can we offer you something to eat?"

"No, I fortified myself with McDonald's before coming over and knocking on your door. Two orders of fries. They're good." He patted his belly. It showed now that he was sitting down, as did a double chin. "Plenty of salt. The way I like them."

"Something to drink then?"

"A Coke would be fine. I had a giant-sized one, but I'm not going to turn down another."

His bright spirits set us back and offered another awkward silence, but George kept trying: "We have real drinks if you want one. Name your poison."

"I'm a beer man. I can chug down the suds all night long and a slosh of bourbon's not bad either. But can't do it. Not while I'm on duty."

"Anything else we can get you?"

"Lemon with that Coke and lots of ice. Lots and lots of ice. I chew it. I hope you don't mind. Can't help it."

"Your duty," Samantha asked. "What do you have to do exactly?"

"My orders from fifty-seven fox trot are to make sure the Marine arrives safely home and to stay with the Marine until he is safely interred and finally rested."

"That means a couple of days."

"Whatever it takes." He cracked a grin. "I get to see the country and meet a lot of people. Do you mind if I smoke?"

We wanted contact with him yet we resented him. He was visible proof of what we had started almost not to believe. This is what he did and he had to be aware of how strong and shaky and mixed our emotions were, but he wasn't helping. He seemed oblivious to the difficult spot he and we all were in.

"Do you need a place to stay? We could put you up here."

"No, sometimes actually I bunk in at the funeral parlor. It's not so bad," he said, as he lit up and looked around for an ash-tray without getting up until Samantha brought him one. "But this time the Marines popped for a local motel. It's all arranged. I checked in before McDonald's and before I came over. It's got a vibrating bed and free coffee. Just perfect."

George kept on trying: "Where are you from?"

"Wheeling, West Virginia, but now I'm stationed at Marine Corps HQ in D.C."

Samantha asked then, "Have you been to Vietnam?"

"Oh no, and I have no intention of going. I think I can swing it, too, so I don't have to."

The ramifications of what he said flew right by him and brought one more silence. We ricocheted into a kind of dis-belief that made us ask what we weren't at all sure any longer we wanted to ask, another question. It was Mason's turn:

"How often do you have to do this?"

"Oh, it's not so bad, and it's getting better and busier and we know how to handle it now."

"How did you get the assignment?"

"I volunteered."

"Why?"

"This is what I want to do."

"Want to do what?"

"Become a mortician, and this is a way to get some practice and learn how."

I couldn't help myself: "This is what you *want* to do?"

"Oh yes, it's great. I get to see how it all works. Everything. It's an exciting field and a great opportunity," Don Nalley said. "When I get out of the Marines I'm going to be able to jump right in."

In smoking and talking and drinking his Coke, Don Nalley had become more comfortable and grown downright chatty. His posture relaxed and his belly let itself stick further out. He was ready to stay awhile and, through his unasked-for and un-realized twistedness, add to the nightmare.

———

THERE IS AN INCOHERENCE in illness and in dying. We want to know why and how to thwart it. We want some answers and seldom get them. Often doctors aren't much help. They've seen so much of it they've developed the manner—been there, done that—especially around a nursing home.

I had been in and out of hospitals with some frequency as a visitor, as a parent, and researching scripts—the Mayo Clinic, this and that ER, even animal hospitals—and had seen enough to realize what may be obvious but we like to ignore:

1. An operation, whatever the supposed risk, is an attack on the body. Shit can happen.
2. Anesthesia is an art and a science. The practitioner better be capable of both.
3. Anesthesia preempts one of the body's major defense systems. Pain. Unbelievably helpful, but whoever threw together our bodies put pain there for a reason.
4. The more we know the less we know. New developments and discoveries mean more tests and more opinions and more maybes as well as more answers, and uncertainty takes a heavy toll on patients.
5. The language of medicine is a fabulous jargon, which tends to turn into a headache-inducing mumbo jumbo to the average Joe. Its technicality is bewildering. It explains little, clarifies nothing, and makes you feel stupid. The one thing it successfully does is separate only further the doctor and the patient.
6. For better or worse, except in ICUs, they're giving up on sterilization. Staph infections are abundant (the studies are frightening) and often deadly.

The bottom line it's easy to come up with is simply this: never go into a hospital when you are sick.

My father's doctor, whom everyone liked, was young and in a hurry. His bedside manner was speedy. He would come and go with astonishing swiftness. His arrival was never quite when his office said it would be. His departure was moments later. He never was with my dad long enough to soft-boil an egg. It was difficult to catch him.

The Pimpernel aspect irritated me. I lay in wait for him early one morning and cornered him in the hallway before he could escape. I had talked to him on the phone, one more anonymous voice from a large family, but I had not met him. I started to grill him with questions about what was wrong and what might happen. He was little help and had little to offer. The medical part of the conversation was unsatisfying, useless. I was angry with him and embarrassed for him. He was hurried, a little frayed and disheveled, and ready to get on. I learned this wasn't his first call of the day; in our different roles we both had been up through the night. His pace was partly cover for his own exhaustion and distress.

When it came to him I was that son, the one from California—from Hollywood—the tables turned. He became the inquisitor. He had a story to tell, a good story he was sure, and he wondered how to sell it. Would I be interested? Could I help? I was appalled and amused and a little bored. Just as mine must have been for him, I had heard these same questions plenty of times before. Even here in backwater Massachusetts I was buttonholed. He sailed into a talking jag. He wanted to tell me the story now. If not now, how long before I went back to California? He was about to go on vacation, fishing the lakes on the other side of the Canadian border. Maybe when he returned.

He realized, suddenly, that we had been in the corridor for longer than he had expected or was used to. He stopped himself and got very to-the-point. He said: "Your father is dying.

It's all breaking down. I don't really know why he's still alive. His heart is very strong. There's not much I can do for him and I just don't know how long it will be."

The unusual directness was a weapon to end the conversation, to take me aback and to assist his escape. We both knew it and it worked. After lingering only a moment longer, he got himself into gear and was on his way. I never saw him again.

THERE WAS A DAY not long afterward when I read to my father and he seemed to listen. He had moved beyond language now. I would ask him how he was and he would struggle to answer, scratch out a hoarse "Right" or an "Okay," but there were no sentences left. "Is there anything you wish to say?" I asked him once and he held my eyes with his hand to his throat and tried to talk, as if both asking for something and trying to say something. He tried very hard. The only word forthcoming was "Well . . ." and then "Well . . ." again and then "Well . . ." once more.

There seemed much there, but my father could not get any more out. He was a difficult man, who was loving and had difficulty loving, and he had never been able to express himself in response to such questions anyway. He used head nods or hand signals now, thumbs up or down, or a waver of his palm, "Comme ci, comme ça." He would also wink. In his winking there seemed extraordinary emotional variations, an equivalent of a greeting or a smile or pain or "Okay, let's move on to something else." There was such a range of them, and they knocked me out because he still seemed glad to see me, whoever it was who came in. Somehow it was moving and hopeful.

But one by one things were going. He wasn't eating any longer, and they poked away at his right forearm with IVs, glucose and potassium, to get some nourishment into him. They had trouble finding veins and there were purple and blue outbursts on what was left of his forearm even bigger than the liver spots. An oxygen tube was clipped up his nose now and all his nights were fitful and he slept the mornings through, his hand holding to the rail of the hospital bed, his head canted to one side, his mouth ajar, and his hat set back and askew on his forehead now.

I read a section from one of the Jeffrey Farnol books he loved and some from Philip Roth's *American Pastoral* about Newark, where my father had lived for a while and then worked like his father before him. He bent toward me as I read and I leaned in, almost whispering in his ear, and his eyes seemed to gleam, as if listening close and avidly interested. His eyes were lustrous, and it wasn't until later that I recalled such a sheen was often the look of the blind.

One of those nights an alarm went off on one of the machines in a neighboring room. I went to get a nurse and had trouble finding anybody and it wouldn't stop. It went on for an hour and it was the next day before I learned that unexpectedly a man had died. He had been as feisty as always only hours before and then was gone in his sleep. Within another day a woman also died. The staff, good and bad, all talked about how deaths came in threes.

And my father was fading and somnolent. Even asleep, under layers of blankets, he seemed to be diminishing, descending, disappearing. When I said his name he barely croaked open a papery left eyelid. The iris seemed blank and yellow. And then he looked away from me and wouldn't look back. He stared across the room or into space or into nothingness or into himself. I could not tell. He made an alarming noise when I started to read. A grunt of unhappiness. He did not want to be read to now.

The fluids he was being fed weren't processing. They stopped up inside him. His arm would bloat; so would his belly or his legs. His chest was congested and the antibiotic wasn't solving it. For the first time he was having trouble breathing. His breaths came slower and were noisy, wheezes, and he was hooked up to a nebulizer. He was started on morphine. His features became clearer, his thin upper lip, his bushy right eyebrow, and his beak of a nose.

His right arm, we realized then, was dead. It lay completely limp and unmoving. He had had another stroke and nobody had realized it. It was the arm the IV had made a pincushion of and he looked at what was left of it. His left hand came out from under the covers and felt it, picked it up and played with it and dropped it, then did a slow, stretching, finger-counting dance of its own. That night in the dark another alarm sounded and the hand he had left came out, sensed an object, and grabbed it. It was my hand standing close by and he held on, one last shake.

The next night his hat wasn't on when I came in. It wasn't on his head and it wasn't on the bed and it wasn't behind the bed. I couldn't find it. It wasn't under the covers and it wasn't in the closet and it wasn't under the bed. I couldn't find it. I turned the room upside down and I was crying before I located it where it had somehow fallen behind the television. I didn't know why it was off or how it had gotten across the room, and I didn't want to be crying. Over a hat; it was ludicrous. But I put it back on. I set it and reset it until I thought it right.

My father didn't know about my search. My father didn't know about my starting to break down. My father didn't know about my placing it back on. Other than to breathe, he didn't move or know or care any longer. There was a new and final wall between our existences. He was going away into the Mystery.

On one of those nights when I had to return to Los Angeles my brother sat with him, making a kind of peace, moving beyond his frustration and anger and exhaustion, and writing a poem that he called "Sitting with My Dad." Beth sent it to me later and part of it read:

> *As I listen to you breathe, rasping for life,*
> *I think where we've been and what we've become*
> *Years of difference that no longer matter*
> *Things that you've taught us, not knowing how,*
> *Only by being the person you are . . .*
> *Quietly now the breathing keeps on,*
> *An opening eye to see who's around.*
> *A nod tells me you know it is I.*
> *Sitting and thinking of who you are.*
> *Dad.*

The last morning of his life my father awoke. Beth was with him and she said, "You look one hundred percent better. Are you feeling better?" And he started to talk. It was gobbledygook and he looked confused, as if surprised he was awake or even alive. The nursing home staff swung into action. They set up more IVs and called the hospital and prepped him to go where they would insert a feeding tube into his stomach. My father kept looking over to the IVs and his confusion turned to fright, as if he might be poked and prodded and stuck again and have to deal with worry and pain and one more invasion of his already birdshot-to-shit sense of privacy. He had come to his own exhaustion. Beth saw it and put a stop to it. "No, Bill," she said. "There's going to be no more IVs." She felt as if he understood and he closed his eyes and went downhill fast after that.

He died before midnight.

A WEEK OR TWO LATER, still in Massachusetts, I drove down to the Cape and across the Sagamore Bridge to get away for a day. I went as far as Chatham and parked and came upon a Cape Cod League baseball game. I stayed for the first few innings as the light fell and then wandered away and back along Main Street, restless still, and happened into the Yellow Umbrella, a bookstore. I lost myself in the shelves until I realized I was staring at an author's name and a book, *The Way Beyond*, the sequel to *The Broad Highway*, by Jeffrey Farnol.

The copy was a cheap Depression or wartime Triangle Books edition. It had a dust jacket in plastic wrap but under it the front binding was buckled and the book was worn and somewhere it had gotten wet and the pages wouldn't lie flat. Along the spine they were moisture stained and had discolored to a cheesy papyrus shade. I started to leaf through it and discovered to my further disbelief writing on the inside, an inscription in fountain pen:

> The reading of this book brought to me pleasant memories of *The Broad Highway* by the same author.
>
> I remember the real pleasure my Dad derived from the reading and the many zestful discussions of *The Broad Highway*. Many times we reviewed the characters and certain incidents in the book.
>
> I realize, now, how Dad enjoyed a good book, how he could live with the characters and understand their problems, their joys and their sorrows.
>
> To him a good book was surcease from the cares and worries of the day—a comfort when he had reached his haven of rest in the easy chair at home.
>
> To him, and to me, a good book was counted a true and lasting friend.
>
> February 20th 1942

I bought the book and found myself pulling over on the way home to read the inscription again—struck and desolate and breaking down yet consoled somehow—and then once more, after dark in the headlights of passing cars, retrieving briefly all the lost light and bringing back the maples and pines along Route 6 in ghostly shapes of weathered copper.

And I read it still.

BUT BEFORE THEN, on the night prior to my father's funeral service, there was a gathering on the screen porch at the Big House that had been my grandparents' and now was George's. It sat on the highest rise between two points, Manomet and Indian Hill. The porch—the one the storm Carrie had soaked—circled the house and lorded over Cape Cod Bay. This July night was full summer. It was hot, humid, and sticky, and there seemed no movement in the air, but the porch caught a breeze. It always seemed cool there.

As I left, night had all but drawn down. The grass had shed its color. Only the rim of the horizon and the mackerel sky held a lingering glow. George had to switch his martini glass to shake hands and say goodbye.

I said, "You should be speaking tomorrow."

"No, no," said George.

"You're too modest," I said, thinking of all the youthful tales of the two of them, and all my father had said for as long as he could, right to the end.

George looked away and looked back to me. "I never really knew him. I mean, years ago when we were young we had fun together. He was a great guy."

"No, no, the way he talked about you, you two. You were closest to him," I said again, both insistent and confused.

"Not really."

"But all the stories . . ."

"Oh, those," he said, and waved his long lanky fingers at the end of his long lanky arm. "We had good times."

I must have been staring by now and he must have seen it.

"Your brother says your dad had a drinking problem. I

never knew that." He was looking down at the darkness gathering in the grass. "He was a good guy."

IN CALIFORNIA SOMETIMES when I had to explain my family people were often not a little mystified. The way it traced back to the *Mayflower*. Thirteen relatives arriving on it, or seventeen—the number seemed to change now and again. Twenty-two first cousins. Tennis and golf, golf and tennis. Touch football games on Thanksgiving that might as well have been tackle.

That my father didn't write letters; I had never gotten one from him. That the only time I saw his signature was on a check where my mother had filled in the amount. That for years he didn't answer the phone. That things never got talked about; you never got the complete story. That this was a New England trait. That complete silence might well offer Nirvana.

"Maybe ten percent of what we say to each other is with words, and words conceal as easily as they reveal," the writer John D. MacDonald said. "The rest is body language, our cants, tilts, postures, textures." So it had been with my father and his last weeks had epitomized his own and our own Morse code; and as I spoke at his service, partly because I was telling Bill-and-George and George-and-Bill tales and partly because he was sitting right below me, I found myself looking at my uncle. But he wasn't looking at me. He made no eye contact. I tried to determine where he was looking and couldn't, and perhaps it wasn't to any certain spot. I had watched my dad turn inward and I wondered if that was what George was doing now, blocking the emotions I would have thought had to be there, whether he was a master of denial or not.

I should have known better.

10

WHEN DOUG AND I were teenagers we pulled some lobster pots. We sold the lobsters we caught, some to the local fish store and many to members of the family. Licenses were easy and cheap then and we didn't use winches or haulers to pull what are usually called traps now. The few we had were inherited from Doug's brother, George Jr., and we never took the task as seriously as he had. We may have been at an age where we took nothing seriously; or more accurately we had decided life was too serious to take seriously. I was always in and out of good deeds and trouble. Doug was quieter. His modus operandi was slower, less showy, less obvious, but perhaps deeper. His rebellion was more resistance than rebellion.

That summer we were especially unenthusiastic. It hadn't always been so. As early as eight or nine, we loved going out with a man named John Martin. Few men who lobstered did it as their primary employment. They had other jobs, as contractors, carpenters, truck drivers, gas station attendants, or, in John Martin's case, as a Congregational minister.

John Martin was Massachusetts through and through. It shot through his voice, in his accent and the cadence of his words, even in the creases in his skin and the set of his thick graying hair. He was equipped with a sly humor and four daughters. Increasingly, one to the next, older to younger, they strayed from the straight and narrow. I dated the third daughter, Martha, called Marty by everyone. She had a lush figure and a lot of teeth. She was a warm girl looking like so many of us to be wild in ways that were largely safe, only to be treated badly by a sequence of my cousins, and me. Once in college she came to visit and I gave her a horrible time. I was smitten by appearances then and embarrassed by how she carried herself, the way she dressed and talked and the way of her gums and teeth suddenly seemed overwhelming.

It was a time then when women's bathing suits were first becoming two-piece. If bikinis existed in other places they weren't here, not by any means, not yet. Such things as string bikinis were still years away. These two-piece suits had bottoms like short shorts and the tops were underwired and well covering. Marty had a brown plaid one with a white belt at the waist that cinched together with a buckle like a military uniform might. It seemed tremendously provocative.

Stories of the first time abound. But for me, and maybe for many of us then, the earlier bases—first and certainly second and maybe third—were equally charged and as specifically tactile. Marty and I never slept together, we never went all the way (as was said then); but I can call back that bathing suit and the sight and feel of her breasts in and out of it. They were full and heavy to hold and tremendously taut with nipples that grew large and tight. The sensation of their touch I can still retrieve and feel on my fingers and it brings an excitement and a longing and a regret that I can't equally call back and change my behavior. It is way too late now and probably a memory she doesn't carry and a remedy she long since doesn't want or need.

I called her just now to ask her about her father and to say something about then—to apologize. "What do you remember?" I asked. "I remember it was exciting and then you were an—" She hesitated a microsecond and I joined in with her:

"an asshole." (The difference was she said "ahs-hole"—she works at Harvard now—and I said, "ass-hole.")

John Martin told us stories, often tall tales, leg-pulling tales. He kidded us and played tennis well. His play couldn't match the competitive fiends in our family but he was canny and un-orthodox on the court. We called him "the Reverend" or "the Rev," but he was decidedly unecclesiastical. His faith was secure, low-key and largely unstated; we never saw it on dis-play. His dress around us was secular. We only saw him in shorts, dressed to lobster, or in a casual open shirt when we went to Fenway. I only saw him in church once.

The person John Martin most often took lobstering was Dick Goddard, a neighbor who had the face of a seaman and the mind of a child. Dick loved to swim and he loved to drink beer. Year after year, long after they had faded, he wore the same plaid trunks, with a Life Saving badge sewed on one leg. For two generations he lived with his sister and earned money cutting lawns, though he'd rather be paid with beer, a can or two or, God willing, a six-pack.

When they came our kids were leery of Dick and he was leery of them. He couldn't remember their names and called them "the little girl" or "the little boy." Cautionary lessons may have been drummed into his head. Inevitably, rumors si-dled about that he might be dangerous; the odor of molesta-tion wafted without any concrete basis. We never saw any such hint. Which wasn't to say Dick wasn't strange. He always wore an old, tweed, remarkably chewed-up English driving cap pulled down low. It gave him a look out of *The Wind in the Willows.* He didn't drive and he walked the streets, low to the ground and pitched forward, moving quickly, a gait like a stumpy Groucho Marx.

His drinking was a sight to behold. He would take a beer and study it, turn it over in his thick hands, like a raccoon checks out its food with its paws. He wasn't supposed to drink. He told me this repeatedly and conspiratorially, almost as often as he asked for one. Then he would open the beer. He would look to me as if for approval and he'd smile (he had very bad teeth) and thank me. He always used my name, with his flat Boston twang, and then, whether bottle or can, it would be to his mouth upside down and it would be empty. The draining was incredibly swift. Excepting the leap of his Adam's apple, it seemed effortless and instantaneous. He would thank me again by name and then ask for another. I would say no and he would ask again and I would say no and he would thank me again and then he would start to go. But calling me by name once more, he'd wave me over. I could hide a beer under the toolshed, he said. Just under the corner where the shingle was coming loose. No one would know. He'd never tell. And he would come by for it. So sometimes I did. And he would. After Dick was killed, hit by a car as he walked along the street in winter's dusk, I found one somehow missed and forgotten in the hiding place under the by now tattered and rotting shingle.

That was the one time I saw the Reverend in church. He came out from Melrose, where his parish was by then, to conduct the service. He had a quiver full of stories about Dick but he chose only one: how when they went lobstering he had Dick sit in the bow of the boat as lookout and he told Dick to pray for a good catch. "Say 'crustacean' three times, Dick . . . Say it three more . . . Now chant it, Dick." Dick fell in love with the word. Mispronouncing it, he invoked it as often as he did my name. The futility he didn't retain. He only remembered when the prayer worked and so for him it always did. It was successful—and in that the Rev located a lesson of faith.

For the rest of the service, like his vestments, John Martin gathered again around himself his regularly assigned role as a Congregational minister. The occasion warranted it, but I missed the ordinarily so wry and idiosyncratically funny man who could make me believe it didn't have to be a heavy thing to believe.

When we lobstered with the Reverend we got wet. It was from spray as the boat slapped over the waves; it was from the liquid peel off the line as we pulled a pot in. The water settled in the bottom of the boat under the floorboards until sometimes they started to float. It wet the seats and our bathing suits when we sat on them. Before we were done the damp lining of the suits bit into our flesh. Our asses got sore.

At first we pulled the pots with our bare hands to show our strength and prove our rough-toughness. There was something in the feel of the rope, pulling it hand over hand, the saltwater peeling, and the gathering weight on the arms and shoulders of the pot coming up. As it grew near it came faster and expectation rose. Every time the hope that it wouldn't be empty. Eighty to ninety percent of the time the pots were; and when there were lobsters, fifty percent weren't big enough to be keepers. The state issued a brass gauge, like a chunky school compass with a tooth set at each end that measured the catch from eye socket to carapace. The lobsters had to be that big or back they went. We hitched the gauges around our waist to keep them handy and quickly they lost their sheen and dulled to a dun shade. We also had to throw back berried ones, lobsters with eggs.

There were many days of nothingness. There were the normal days, lots of them, where a couple of lobsters would arrive among the twenty to thirty pots, and maybe once a season there would be a bounty—two or three keepers in a single pot. We would peg their claws—they use thick, wide rubber bands now—the wooden pegs jammed into the joint so the lobster couldn't snap them. Otherwise they could be dangerous.

Often other sea life came up. Crabs were frequent interlopers. They got tossed back. On a bad day in frustration we hurled them high and they seemed to sit in the sky. Occasionally a cod or cunner or even an eel wandered in. A skate too, though it was a mystery how a monstrosity of such a shape got through the hole webbed into the netting. And once there was the blowfish. He wasn't happy at all. He'd puffed himself up to the maximum. His sharp gills, normally like big wings, flapped but his body overwhelmed them. He'd become a balloon, a dirigible. However he got in, there was no way out.

Soon we got smarter. Smells and sharp objects put us into rubber smocks and rubber gloves. The strongest stench came from the bait we hooked into the pots: tautog, or flounder stripped of all its fillets. Only a head and a tail and a translucent slice of backbone were left. They could get very ripe and the smell could get all over and seemingly inside of you. The first chore back was a shower, sometimes a preliminary dousing outdoors before a second scrubbing inside.

Such smells were virulent, nasty, but others were a reason to be there. In the scent of the early morning of the wind and of the salt, in the smell and sound of the Johnson or Evinrude outboard motor, in the wake of the boat and the singing slither of the rope coming up hand over hand, there was a sweet earned rush. Lobstering was work and it could be boring and fruitless and it paid little money. None of them were the point. What it offered was the company of the sea and a joy of accomplishment that was for a time unalloyed.

THE LAST SUMMER we lobstered Doug and I were supposed to repaint a fourteen-foot skiff, marine blue on the inside and white out, touch up some of the buoys in orange, black, and white, and recondition some of the pots. It was early in the season, still June, still chilly in the mornings, and we could see our breath the first hour or two. We were older now. Some work was getting done but not a lot. We were fooling around in my grandmother's garage, downstairs from where we had played on rainy days when we were younger, and had discovered we could flick paint across the room or at each other with our brushes. Thin the paint, get a good snap of the wrist going, and we were suddenly making Jackson Pollacks on the far wall.

Doug's father stepped into the trajectory of one beautiful fling and broke up the creativity, and we were in trouble. George got splashed. His reaction was surprisingly swift—his hand shot up and parried most of the damage exactly the way he moved at net on the tennis court.

There George was very much Big George, a towering presence. For tennis we even had a special nickname for him, "the Spider." He had a gangly grace and was surprisingly quick for such a big man. His long limbs had enormous reach. We never could pass him down the alley and he loved to poach across the court. He was voracious and nearly impregnable. He was too tall for us to aim at his head; unless it hit him the ball was on its way out. The only hope, slim at that, was to assault his midsection.

It was infuriating and so was his demeanor. He gritted together into his play an unwavering concentration and a ferocious competitiveness that was like a fit or a controlled rage that didn't reveal itself. It never showed its hand—he never lost his temper. After a point or a match, win or lose, his winning smile would come out. It would rise; it would blossom. His manners were impeccable and unbreakable. Equally infuriating.

"Well, what's going on here?" he said now. The question seemed neutral and innocent enough and of course wasn't. The fuse was lit.

"We're painting," his son answered.

"I can see that."

"Looks pretty good, don't you think?"

"Looks pretty stupid, I think."

He was smiling what wasn't really a smile. It had been my flick of the brush that he'd encountered but I said nothing.

"We'll get the boat done, Dad."

"But when? This year?"

"That's funny."

"What did you say?"

"I said—"

"I was the one who did it," I interrupted now. They both

turned and looked at me, and in George's look there was blame and there was irrelevance.

In his last years George came to count on my brother. By then Mason lived catty-corner across the road from the Big House my grandfather had originally built and George now owned. They talked most every day. They kicked around the weather, the progress of the gardens, the wear and tear on the bluff and beach and, implicitly, the rather fallen state of the world.

What George thought of me I never knew. At times I suspect he found me entertaining, but long and lean I was not. I chewed up the tennis court. I fell, and it wasn't always, if ever, pretty. I was a collision waiting to happen and it often did— into the net or into the ground or into other people in the sports I was better at, football and hockey. In high school I carried an anger that was suited for hitting people just short or just not short of rule violations. In college I blew past two hundred pounds and moved on the court like a surprisingly agile buffalo, but finally still exactly that, a buffalo.

Long after this I bought a house down the street from where we were standing, the first of my generation to do so. This intrigued George. We exchanged letters about zoning restrictions and membership to the group that had built the stairs that led to the beach. When he retired I wrote him a letter and he wrote me back. I forgot about it until after he died and Samantha found a copy and sent it to me.

But this was about the two of them and not me. They turned back to each other and I might as well not have been there.

"Well, what are you going to do for an encore?"

"Don't worry, Dad. We'll come up with something."

"What's the matter with you?"

"I give up, Dad. What's the matter with me?"

"I just don't get it."

"You don't have to get it."

"That's unacceptable."

"Too late, Dad. Too late."

I knew the exact meaning of what was going on wasn't in the words, but I was still leagues behind. There was a ton of history I hadn't been party to.

"What are you going to do? Nothing? Hack around? Not play real sports? Not get good grades? Not apply yourself?"

"Sounds about right."

"You're going to straighten out and fly right."

It was then that Doug attacked his father with garden shears.

I had no idea where they had come from. That wasn't literally true; the garage was only rough-framed inside and they sat with some other loose tools along one of the crosspieces of two-by-four that braced the vertical studs. What I hadn't seen was how they got into his hand. How he had reached such a state. He swung them with complete savagery—the sharp points—at his father's face.

There is something about violence and there is no mistaking it. You can feel it. It charges the air itself with a dangerous valence, usually before, certainly during, and always afterward it leaves a trail. It vests the moment even as it screws coherent sensation beyond a point. But the coming of it this time carried no warning.

George blocked the blow and caught Doug's hand and wrestled the shears from him. The struggle was ferocious and ugly and swift. Their faces rent and distorted, and then George had them away from his son. His face was an eggplant shade and in rictus. His features anatomized. He looked as if he was going to strike back and kill Doug. The rage sucked the air and all else out of the garage. The instant felt like forever.

And then he laughed. There was no transition. The change wasn't natural and it wasn't pretty. He willed the laugh into being, as if that could erase the fury, stitch a peaceful reality seamlessly back into place, his own and his son's. Complete and compress an almost Doppler effect.

"That's good work," he said. "Maybe I better keep ahold of these until you're done. They need cleaning and sharpening anyway. Just how about putting a little paint into the boat."

His high-beam smile regained, he patted his son on the shoulder and left us as if the moment had never happened.

———

AFTER THE SERVICE for my father was over there was a party and the next day, a hot day, we buried him, only to move him later down the way to a quieter spot on the side of a hill. He had been cremated, his hat along with him, and his ashes weren't much. We laid him in the ground in a small hole that seemed odd because it was so small. Julia, my younger daughter, took the ceremony very seriously. She found a leaf she liked and laid it on top of the little box, and there it sat along with an acorn she also found and a mushroom, one of the things my father had loved and known so well, until he, or what was left of him, was covered over.

My father had gone to nothing, or to a place we could not visit, but perhaps not at all for the first time. We talk now in our age of psychobabble and meds, of alcohol and depression, the connection between the two, and it may be true. The possible genetic roots of depression seem to be beyond controversy, and often tied to an early death or an early trauma. With them can come an incomplete mourning that wades through a life, dammed up—rage and hurt and sorrow—only to become a source of self-destruction.

Whatever the cause and whatever the link, even beyond my father's anger and my own, even beyond our struggle for love, there was a place that alcohol took him, a very dark place that nobody should visit and that neither I nor any of us could know or share or understand. It was very black and, like his last possession, his hat, it was his and his alone, and the terror there and the toll it took I would never never never know.

11

WHEN I WAS SEVEN YEARS OLD my father offered me a bribe. This was in 1954 and the sum he held out in his hand, a quarter, twenty-five cents, was a big deal. On the face of it his act was a simple inducement to stop me from seeing a movie. He looked on them as a waste of time and it was a Sunday. Sunday was golf, Sunday was yard work, Sunday was the papers, and Sunday was church. It didn't mean it was exactly the Lord's Day—it certainly wasn't a day without alcohol—but to go to the movies on the Sabbath tipped the venture into decadence and toward sin.

It's always possible he also knew or may well have guessed the particular one in question, *The Atomic Kid*, wasn't much of a movie. It quickly abandoned reality. The character Mickey Rooney plays in the film happens to wander his way onto a nuclear test sight at the time the bomb detonates, lurching away afterward, babbling, looking like a coal miner or a chimney sweep, his lunch—a peanut-butter-and-jelly sandwich—toasted, but otherwise he's unscathed. Without any lasting negative effects whatsoever.

First the offer, and then the actual silver appeared in my father's outstretched palm, but I turned him down. I went anyway. Whatever drove me held firm. Even then beyond a quotient of stubbornness an interest had lodged inside me. Its birth may not have an exact moment, such a simple epiphany. It may reach into or even through DNA, but years later it found a subject when I began to write about Vietnam.

When I landed the assignment of writing the first American miniseries to be made about the war, as significant as it was, it seemed to me a beginning, not an ending. I started a novel about the war, wrote a screenplay about the war, dug into a second, much larger miniseries about the war, but each of them in turn stalled or failed. None of them got published or made.

In the twist of those disappointments, I happened to meet William Broyles Jr. Tall, lean, delicately handsome but by no means delicate, Bill had already sported through several careers as a writer and editor of magazines, as well as publishing a book, and in his restless nature was casting about for yet another. He had been a Rhodes scholar and an officer in Vietnam, and in coming west to California to reinvent his life once more, wondered about movies and television and whether there might be a series about the war.

The two of us sniffed and snorted about each other, scrutinized each other's work, and discovered we were wildly different and yet well matched. In our ways he was swift and I was slow, how we wrote and how we lived. His initial drafts of scripts flew onto paper. If a mess, at least they existed and his true work could begin. On the other hand, I wrote and rewrote in my head, tooling and retooling sentences, whether description or dialogue, in the hope, however foolish, that the first draft would have a perfect birth and emerge whole and complete and ready to shoot.

Bill had thoughts of a comedy, a half-hour show perhaps set in a Saigon hotel, people coming and going, soldiers and journalists and USO performers, a crazy hodgepodge in a crazy place. He had held on to the moments of music and laughter from Vietnam—remembering how deeply they were needed by the men—while what excited me was a drama that might strike after the bone, and in my digging into the dark and his holding on to the light we found a complementary kinship that began a search together for a fresh way to look at the war and that time.

The idea we came to—what would later be described as "a women's steam bath in the middle of this vast men's locker room"—was simple and what we both had been seeking. Women would serve as our way in. The sixties had turned upside down all our lives but perhaps women's most of all. With all they had to wrestle with, let them be the mainstays, the eye of the hurricane. Set them into the crucible of a real place, China Beach, near Da Nang, where a triage hospital and an R and R center had clustered. Surround them with sun and surf and the storm rumbling just out of sight. The war just over the hill, the war beyond Monkey Mountain. This huge, inescapable, offscreen character. Surround them with the young men seeking to escape it for a day or two, surround them with the helicopters that came with the wounded and that never stopped coming. And shake and stir.

It was an untold story, and after much research and many interviews I went to my office on a Sunday morning and sat down, and in one of those rare instances that defied my reckless optimism wrote what began and was never to change:

FADE IN

A WOMAN

sets up a rickety chair on a beach and settles into it. She picks aviator sunglasses, a beat-up Thermos, and a dog-eared paperback, *The End of the Affair*, out of a ditty bag.

Her name is COLLEEN MCMURPHY and she's a strawberry blonde, one part flax, one part autumn leaf. She wears no make up, has done nothing special with her hair; she could care less about such things.

Her body doesn't get special attention either and doesn't need it—it's American, athletic, resourceful, resilient. It carries her youth and exhaustion without a seeming dent.

THE BEACH
is like McMurphy, no nonsense, yet something to look at. The arc of the coast, a lifeguard stand, long, leisurely dunes, and a cobalt sea shuffling up surf.

CLOSER
It's so hot McMurphy drags her things toward the water. The lifeguard miraculously appears to help her. His name is BOONIE LANIER.

MCMURPHY
Hey, Boonie. Thanks, Boonie.

BOONIE
That's affirm, McMurphy.

He's casual, handsome, there and gone. Colleen settles down a second time, sticks her toes in the water.

Pretty close to heaven.

The WAVES break with a BOOM a little like artillery, and chatter and die around her in a whisper, ssss. Boom–sssss.

It's quiet but for the waves; you almost feel you can hear the sand talk. Whisper, whisper. It's beautiful. Yet.

There's another SOUND now, distant and deep and now deeper and ONCOMING.

McMurphy's head falls forward and

THE BEACH
McMurphy walks up the dunes and a song starts, "Stay" by Maurice Williams and the Zodiacs, and the beach is no longer pristine, empty, sandbags appear and now concertina wire and men running and the deepening sound clear now.

It's a helicopter.

510TH EVAC HOSPITAL
Without stopping, MUSIC rising McMurphy walks into a hunk of metal shaped like a tin can sliced in half and plunked on its side.

Here there is no quiet. The place is aroar with hustling personnel and the raw notes of an emergency room.

Fresh wounded are arriving.

Without peeling her bathing suit, McMurphy dons nurse's garb. Fine flesh disappears and busted flesh rolls in the broken, unrepaired, double doors from the chopper pad.

This is not Malibu, Hawaii, Tahiti, this is not 1987. This is China Beach, Da Nang, Vietnam, 1967.

These first pages became the two-hour movie that initiated the series *China Beach*, and as these things happen I fell in love with the actress who played the lead. It took a year for Dana Delany and me to realize it and act on it, and three more years to realize what else was there, the fatal booby traps in our perilous pathologies waiting to doom the relationship. That we lasted so long in what was so misbegotten speaks to her forbearance and to the powerful force that good, timely, meaningful work can provide.

It would be a whole other story and not the object of this one to plumb the hows and whys of our failure. (I remember a woman taxi driver once told me that the word "plumbing" came from the Latin for lead, that the chemical symbol for it was Pb, and somehow she connected these to Nero fiddling while Rome burned.) The relationship had dragged in Pygmalion, my father, her father, her mother, my wife, her drinking, my lying, my second childhood and third child, a lot of good and bad sex, and probably Hamlet, Lear, and Medusa too. Did I leave anything out?

It was intense, melodramatic, wonderful but not right, and I was clearly no small part in fucking it up. Mistakes were legion. One I made was to read her journal twice. The first time I found a portrait of myself that was so much less than I hoped for, including such an evisceration of my sexual prowess that I was destroyed. Literally turned impotent until a slow-fueling, burning rage won out and hardened me again. The second time I read it I found a note addressed to me. "Fuck you if you're reading this, John," it said. "Fuck you."

At the end of working together we were exhausted and struggling. As a prize, and in search of healing, we took it upon ourselves to travel to Vietnam. In 1969 I had followed Doug to California and now many years later I followed him again to where he had gone next and last and I still had never been.

IT WASN'T MY FIRST attempt to get there. In the late seventies I had tried, when it was next to impossible to get in. By then I had missed the war itself but I had witnessed—sometimes up close—the domestic strife it had caused and the haunting and the hurt that were still echoing through my generation and myself. It was still true in the nineties. It's still true now.

In 1977 I ended up stranded in Bali, waiting, trying to pull strings, hanging out in a hut not so far down the beach from one of the few hotels. Bali was a very different place then. Very little tourism, no resorts and no bombings. The country still felt raw and not completely invaded by tourists or Westerners. Smells were pungent. They flavored and sometimes saturated the air: the sweet ripe fruits, the cigarettes made out of banana leaves, the stench of garbage and the acrid smoke as it was incinerated.

I may have been the only one trying to get into Vietnam, but I came upon a colony of men who had served from the U.S. and from Australia and had ended up on the beach in Bali. They had fallen out rather than return home and had let their hair grow and their skin burn dark and they painted or built furniture or did nothing at all. They lived in a lulling world of drugs and surfing and women who sold batik across makeshift counters in the makeshift booths that popped up along the shore in the day and disappeared at night. These women made their living by bargaining, knowing little or no English except the denominations of dollar bills, and when a deal was struck they would often unwrap your purchase from around their bodies, leaving themselves topless in the blue blue of last light.

Bargaining was fun. It was an enjoyable game and a way to communicate when there was no other language. But the high it gave had little resonance and lugged along an illusion. The sense of this is how I knew the people. That *fab*-ulous temple and that little Balinese *gal* I talked down to fifteen hundred rupiahs. The landscape was changing. The invasion had begun. Already the battle against tourism was becoming a losing one.

There was a dark-dark-skinned character that hung out on the beach. He had long Christlike hair and hair on his face halfway between a goatee and a beard. He had offers to make: "Lay-dink. Thai stick. Coke-kane." He was around. I'd turn and he'd be there. At night he lurked. He'd waft out from a shadow of a tree and reiterate with sinister knowingness his list of invitations: "Lay-dink. Thai stick. Coke-kane."

I rented a rackety old Chevy Impala and drove upland in search of where Margaret Mead once had lived some four or five decades before. Amulets and charms jangled from car mirrors for luck, and offerings woven of fruit and beads and bamboo, the size of small pies or pizzas, sat on the dashboards under the windshields to appease the gods and ward off evil spirits. There were no sewers yet, but I passed workers digging out the Iung River. They loaded the sand on the bank and then shoveled it into baskets and carried it on their heads to the road and set it there and then shoveled it into a truck. The workers were all women. They shed their clothes as they worked, changing from sarongs to dresses depending on whether they were in or out of the water, and the shucked clothes decorated the diggings. Inland, younger women washed laundry and themselves in the trenches beside the roads. They were bare above the waist and had beautiful skin. Their breasts were heavy and well hung and their nipples were as big and individual as the ends of thumbs. I was to hear there was still a punishment for barren women. After death caterpillars fed on their breasts.

As I climbed toward Ubud, a funeral blocked my way. A priest was being cremated and the whole town had turned out. It was an elaborate and stirring ceremony. Family and friends unfurled a white cloth and held it aloft. With their arms extended, they marched under it. Their progress was awkward and the sheer cloth wavered and wobbled, like a great flag. The body came after them on a palm pallet, wrapped like a mummy, its belongings alongside.

A pyre waited at the town square for the procession. It was a series of brightly painted and papered boxes, built high and tiered from large to small like a wedding cake. The body was lifted on a crosshatch of bamboo, like a tray, and slid into a bull. Not a real bull. It had been cut and carved out of wood to hold the priest. His possessions joined him; a curtain was drawn. Barongs and drums rose in ferment. Six pots set below the bull were put to flame. The bull went up. Fire took over the sky and the smell of it consumed the air.

The priest was the last to go. Everything burned away, the wood crackling and the cloth curtain hissed and went quickly like wrapping paper, and then the mummy-like wrap until the body was left. It darkened to the color of lacquered mahogany and turned the texture of petrified wood. An arm cracked open, the skin splitting like any good hot dog, cottony and white and glistening inside. Then the white was gone and then the arm was gone and then the body was gone. All of him was gone.

When I finally got past Sayan into the central highlands I had to pull the car over and walk to Bayung Gede and the spot where Margaret Mead had settled in. It wasn't a short way, it was treacherously hot and humid, and the house was hardly a house. It sat on the side of a hill without running water or floors or glass in the windows. From the outdoor shower there was a view of the rice fields. They were tilled and cultivated like mosaics and laddered down to the Petanu River and laddered away again up the far side toward the mountains. The sun cast metallic shivers on the water in the silver and nickel and zinc shades of loose change and the tiers were a green I did not know.

It was as beautiful as any place I had seen on earth.

———

DANA HAD SPRUNG from an Irish Catholic father and an Episcopalian mother, a tricky combination. Her father manufactured plumbing fixtures and her mother was an interior decorator. She had been raised in Connecticut, attended the right schools, and looked positively all-American. She was

Mom, she was apple pie, she was the flag. She was good but she wanted to be bad—and she had been bad.

The behavior didn't show. She held it tightly reined in, kept it enjoyably under wraps beneath the manners of her up-bringing and her own cool distance and control. Her inno-cence appeared unscathed. She was like the way she often looked—as lean as a tomboy when she was dressed and ex-traordinarily voluptuous when she was naked. When she did let go she caromed and ricocheted through ravenous and risky wildness.

When we began we were swept up by the very bad notion of complete and total honesty. We started to tell each other everything, sharing (as was said then) our entire sexual histo-ries. I was older and sure I had had more experience. Very quickly that idea was disabused. After I'd met her, studying her, scoping her, I'd said confidently and foolishly, "I look at you and I know you."

"You don't know anything about me," she said.

Before she was far into enumerating her curriculum vitae I was overwhelmed and had to stop her. I said, "Just tell me how many men you've slept with."

"That's a stupid question," she said.

She was right, but I persisted and she looked at me dead on and without batting an eye said, "Well, I stopped counting at one hundred when I was seventeen."

However exaggerated, she'd made and won her point, punch-lined the conversation.

The role she played on the series fed her own growth—the two melded in a remarkable way—and led her to pull together without apology the disparate parts she had carried like a civil war inside herself. By then maybe I had seen too much and knew too much and had even become part of her old self. She was grateful for it and angry about it and ready to be rid of it like a snake needs to shed a skin.

. . .

THE TWO OF US flew first to Thailand. The United States didn't have relations with Vietnam then and we had to get our visas through Canada and pick them up in Bangkok. Only then could we fly on into Hanoi. I had read Greene and Conrad, Maugham and Kipling, and a tremendous number of books good and bad about the war.

The books kept on coming, and there was no small number of fine ones. It was a list of considerable consequence, but there was to be no *All Quiet on the Western Front*, *From Here to Eternity*, or *The Naked and the Dead*. There would be no *War and Peace*. Those big books like tent poles that staked out the territory as there had been in the literature of previous wars. Vietnam wasn't like that; it went on for too long and it was too embittered. And none of them prepared me for what I was to find.

The American conflict was but a panel in the Vietnamese triptych. Our longest war was only a small part of their struggle for independence. We were, as much as we might not like it, merely a blip in their long tale of war. For a century the French had occupied them, then if briefly the Japanese moved in, and they had been jousting with Cambodia and Laos and having at it off and on with the Chinese for even more generations. And after 1975 the Russians came.

We haven't often won honors for our historical memory. With our shortsightedness and our need for instant gratification we hadn't bothered to understand the Vietnamese or their culture. They seemed small and pliable and easily moved and not what they were and are, stubborn and durable and very used to war. They were intransigent about what was their country and we grossly underestimated them.

This wasn't new news. In the 1840s President Zachary Taylor penned a prescient letter to "His Majesty the magnificent King of Annam" which read in part:

I have only heard of lately for the first time because your country is far from mine . . . of this captain misbehaving himself four years ago by landing men from his ship in Tooroong Bay and firing on your people and killing and wounding some. I have ordered a trial of inquiry to be had upon him to be followed by every measure which justice shall require. And how could he have done so? How? When he knew that my warships and trade ships had always been received with friendship in Annam and that my own heart has always been with you and your people, brother! That captain could not have been in his senses . . .

America, my country, is very large. Very great. I have a great many war ships, fire ships and trading ships. I am now at peace with all the world, and my people are good and peaceable . . . You should forget what has passed and receive my ships and people as before to trade and you can be assured that you will never have cause to complain again.

Having unbosomed myself to you, my brother, because I am just and I am good, I hope you will listen to my words of peace and not think of revenging on the people of my nation the evil brought on by others contrary to my orders. I can now do no more. But I must let you know that if you or your officers seek to revenge yourself upon any Americans for what ought to be forgotten and forgiven after my letter has come to your hands, that then you will force me to send my warships, fire ships, and soldiers to Annam to ask you why you are so revengeful for what cannot be helped. Then upon you will devolve all the bad consequences . . .

The United States, even then, carried an imperialistic impulse, a desire to rescue tempered in righteousness. We can be a mixed blessing—the Good Samaritan who is so generous and then the part of us that yearns to be the cowboy of the world. Under the guise of defending ourselves, or saving democracy, we could put on black-and-white lenses. It wasn't the sixties that created the dichotomy, or the fifties or forties, or wherever one may reach back to try to find and fathom where the Vietnam conflict began. Way before perhaps even the nineteenth century. It's in our marrow, a cornerstone of our nature that's crossed now one more millennium.

One of our greatest fears then had been that Ho Chi Minh wasn't only a Communist, he was hooked up with the Russians and/or the Chinese, whichever tapped more into our jingoistic fears at a particular moment. The truth to fathoming Ho wasn't so easy. He made overtures in all directions, for a while as often as he changed his name. Many had been to us. He asked for our help against the Japanese and in drafting the Vietnamese Declaration of Independence; its first paragraph echoed Thomas Jefferson with remarkable fidelity. Nearly word-perfect. He wrote letters and sent emissaries repeatedly, if futilely, to Truman, Eisenhower, and Lyndon Johnson.

It was clear in country that the war was more ours than theirs, and it was falling into history, receding quickly, gaining or losing currency depending on anniversaries. But in 1991, when Dana and I went, it was still a difficult, chancy time. Our government wouldn't let us travel there, and the Vietnamese were on the lookout, cautious and repressive. They were still fumbling to find themselves. We felt watched and sometimes followed. It could be unnerving. Yet there was little anti-American sense in the people. They didn't seem to bear any grudge. Quite the contrary.

In our foreign policy America can gather up its simplistic righteousness and wield it on its sleeve, but as individuals we have a quirky ordinariness and now and again a blessed ability to laugh at ourselves and at each other. The Vietnamese knew this quality and liked it, and they found us funny. They have a sense of being the little guy who has endured by keeping on. We've become big lugs in size and as a country and we're blunderingly successful. They were built like the hare but had moved like the tortoise. We tried to move like the hare but were built like the tortoise. They recognized it and when sometimes we do, it's no small thing.

And in some way we delighted them. I think it's our towering size, openness and innocence and earnestness, and our own humor. A book was written suggesting the two countries were ultimately brothers-in-arms, but I suspect it isn't history we so much share as a quality of laughter when we allow it. They refused to take us as seriously as we sometimes took ourselves.

Something else was also happening by 1991. The liberation hadn't worked and the Vietnamese knew it and, despite themselves, were having to adjust. The process of change they called *doi moi*, or renovation (literally "the new way"), was up for grabs. The Soviet Union was imploding and the Vietnamese were glad to be rid of the Russians. They had learned to dislike, even despise, their dour heavy-handedness and lack of humor. They were cautiously ready to welcome Americans back. For good or ill, the hunger of capitalism was setting itself up to transform the backward country and bring it into the twentieth century.

EVEN BEFORE ARRIVING, I dreamt of Doug. In the dream he was the boy I had known and the young man with some acne and a steady gaze he had become. There were two of him. We were sitting in the sway of our fathers in wicker chairs on a screen porch and we only wanted to escape. Then we were on a beach, long and pale at the deepest point of dusk in the very final husk of day. The world was in gloom. Fog scumbled by, whispering and thickening. Amidst beach grass and sand dunes we caught a glimpse of his sister, Samantha. Her back was to us and she wore a tight, long, sinuous charcoal-gray dress. She looked young and fine, and next to her was another woman in a tight embroidered lace slip and thigh highs. The stockings had very wide dark tops that were held up by garters. She was wraithlike and very sexy. She turned into profile and I thought I recognized her. She didn't belong here. She had been yanked from another part of my life. This is what dreams do: dredge up disparate characters, mix and match together tantalizingly and troublingly what can't and shouldn't be. The fog grew very dense and harrowing and they turned chimera. I lost sight of them. In looking for them I lost sight of Doug. Both women and both Dougs. They all disappeared and I was left searching.

For a woman named Lay Ly Hayslip, Dana and I carried letters to a medical clinic near Da Nang. Lay Ly was helping build it. The clinic was small and plain and blindingly hot and bright with light. I knew it had to be not far from where Doug had been killed. But how near? There was no one there to ask, no one who would know. Another patrol, another day, another night, another death now decades ago. Perhaps back in the States some unknown men knew more.

I had come much because of him, but Dana and I talked little about him. His specter was only parsed out. It journeyed silently along with our troubles, and beside the sobering knowledge I had of how little I knew or remembered about his actual death this first time I went to Vietnam. (And as much as I tried to find out, I still knew little more when I went back a second time a few years later. I still wasn't ready yet.)

We delivered the letters, hoping they had a purpose and were legitimate. Second-guessing was a part of our every day. A certain amount of paranoia was legitimate then. Our travel was restricted; we were only allowed certain places. Lay Ly also had had an incredible life, surviving her childhood and escaping to settle in the United States. She was a survivor and an operator. Where she came from they went together.

We kept on driving, circling the area, and I wondered if we were getting nearer or further away. We passed what was once a cemetery for the South Vietnamese dead. After the liberation the bodies were exhumed and cremated and the site was now a rice paddy, while almost directly across from it along Highway 1 was a new cemetery for the Fallen Heroes—the VC—with a big muscular sculpture in commemoration.

For a while rice paddies were all around us. The sun laced their green into a complexity of shade. There was a chromatic wizardry to the landscape that looked fresh struck. It took me neat, as it had taken others before me.

The farmers wore the same conical hats they had for centuries. They were like shiny plates doing a slow dance; they were jiggling coins, they were wavery poker chips that turned into cymbals at a certain angle under the certain sun. The sight offered alms of beauty and metaphor. The country spun out visions in the very places that became killing fields.

Harvested rice spread along the sides of the road in wide mats. It was drying and grinding down under the tires of the traffic before being hauled away—a primitive process cheaper than milling. Unbleached, the rice hadn't a trace of white; it was the color of cornmeal flecked with burnt orange. The mud in the paddies already turned under lay like whopping drifts of cow flop. The wide sky was rife with moving clouds in shifting millishades that helped create the extraordinary hard and soft light.

Off the side of the road in an ordinary neighborhood outside of Da Nang we saw a relic. An American tank. It was partially destroyed and overgrown now and the blown-out butt end was being used as a laundry line. There was a crude, cruel beauty to it squatting amidst playing children and blowing clothes and the rampant and scrambling green growth, and a part of me, despite myself, was glad to see it. There had been a war. Kilroy was here.

While we were in Hanoi it took permission to see Ho Chi Minh. We were led to a point a block away, joined a line that wasn't allowed to stop moving, and then were escorted by a guard down the street in military fashion. The building that held him was unlike any other in Vietnam, hewn from striking black and gray granite quarried from across the country. It was engraved with a quotation, "Nothing is more precious than independence and freedom," and it had a red rug as a runner and at least one soldier at every possible place inside.

The mausoleum was cold, very cold and wet with powerful air-conditioning. Ho was under glass, or clear Lucite, lying on permanent view in a refrigerated state and blue-lit. He looked small. His arms were folded in front of him and his upper lip glistened. In the chill it gave the illusion that a fly had smuggled its way inside and settled there. More likely, it was a speck of frost caught in the polar light.

When we were through, the guard handed us back to our first guide, Giang, who walked us to another guide, Ling, for a tour of the house Ho had built beside a pond several hundred yards away. It looked like it was made of mahogany, but we were told it was ordinary wood from an ordinary Vietnamese tree. The lower floor was an open meeting area, a large table and chairs, no walls and no windows. There were books in English. Upstairs were a study, a hall, and a bedroom. All wood with some walls and shutters. It was remarkable, elegant, simplicity itself. To one side under a concrete overhang was the portico of the bunker where Ho went when the city was bombed.

At first in Hanoi we were put up in the Thong Loi Hotel, where visitors or tourists were often dumped. It was a badly conceived, instantly falling-apart bunker built by Cubans and until recently occupied by Russians. The pool was empty, nothing worked, and rats had the run of the place. Dana came down with a topsy-turvy stomach and a sudden fever, and we got out of there and found lodging in the city itself at the Hoa Binh Hotel. It was in the French colonial style then, yellow with green shutters like many of the old buildings.

The color yellow suffused Vietnam and limned its allure. It

may have come with the French but it was imbued now into the texture of the country. The Vietnamese government, especially in Hanoi, had adopted it but failed to recapture it. The new coats of paint were flat and two-dimensional, lacking ocher, while weather and age played with the old yellows, adding patina, and illustrated the way heat and rain and humidity hosted history. They had taken on many shades and wore them like emotions. Canary, citron, goldenrod, mustard, a light papaya, the mane of a lion, the look of a dulled slicker, the inside of certain plums.

I left Dana to sleep and walked downstairs in the hotel and came upon Ray. An on-the-road encounter. He was a big, gray-haired man with glasses and a book slumped in a chair completely unconscious of the noisy construction on the second floor. Not so far from dead-looking. He spied me, another American, and stopped me and started to talk. The boat he traveled on was named *The Book Ship* and while it was in dry dock for repairs he was stuck on land.

Twenty years before, he said, he had been PR director at Whittier College. He had been there when Richard Nixon was elected and that set him back because he was a Democrat (and a Lutheran) then. He was on his way to kidnap his estranged wife and ended up at Nixon's brother's restaurant and the guest speaker at this gathering didn't show and Ray ended up speaking about his own life and his wife and he broke down. The man who spoke after him asked everybody to pray for Ray and that was the first time anybody had ever done that. They gave him a little book when it was over and sometime later he was sitting in his office and he was alone and low and it was near Christmas and he didn't know what to do, which way to turn, and he reached into his pocket and found the little book and in what seemed like five minutes he had devoured it—and it was then he took Jesus into his life. The quote he remembered most, "Come with me, all ye who are heavy laden," he discovered a year later wasn't even in it. He did remember seeing it once before, he laughed, over the entrance to a nightclub in Chicago.

The King James Version of the Bible was in his hands, tremendously thumbed and annotated every which way by pen and pencil. That's what he did now, read it, talk about it, and hand it out from *The Book Ship* wherever it made landfall. He trundled to his feet and asked me to pray for him, his stomach was bad, it was bothering him, he said, but his handshake was strong. "Likewise," I said.

He may have thought my stomach hurt too, but I meant a wider prayer, for him, for Dana, for me, for all the human flotsam and souls on a wander.

The prayer must have helped, or Dana's capacity for recovery was remarkable, because when she woke she was better. By the next day she was completely well and we rode a small plane south, a rough ride. On the plane and at the airport afterwards and then in Saigon, now Ho Chi Minh City, we encountered the first trickle of returning veterans.

One, Peter Specht, had come back to spend a month on a Russian ship to analyze offshore oil possibilities. "One of those triangulation deals," he said, because no U.S. company could then be directly involved, so any arrangement had to conduit through a third country. The particulars were sketchy— he left them that way—like the old joked-up import-export job label that hung over espionage.

Peter had been a door gunner as Saigon fell, he said, and on one of the last helicopters he attached a camera to an M-60 and had this amazing footage. He was burly, with a certain wounded intensity, and a kindness that in no way made murder seem impossible. He had a mustache and a tiny ponytail and came up to Dana to ask her if she was she and to thank her. He had that shy, earnest awkwardness vets can get, maybe as close to delicate as we male oafs can be, before too many "brewskis" (as he called them later) went down the hatch. He had been a sergeant and wounded several times, bits of shrapnel here and there, once seriously, quite desperately so. He had been evac'd out to Japan and then to Travis and was in a VA hospital for four and a half months. After he got out he went back to Nam. He was in Laos and Cambodia, he said, and many of his buddies were killed. Only about four out of forty survived. He married a Laotian princess, he said, and six days later she was killed. After he came home he married a second time, he said, but moving around in the Air Force killed that. Now he had a girlfriend, five years older than he was, and she was the one who pushed him to come back. Insisted finally.

For the series *China Beach* we had conversations and interviews, by phone and in person, with Vietnam veterans that grew well up into the hundreds. One year we flew out forty, mostly women, for a weekend and videotaped them. Some came that weekend, for example, prepared to talk about their experiences for the first time; some still couldn't talk about it, their experiences still so raw that they remained undigested and undealt with. In either case what they had to say or what they tried and couldn't yet manage to say was remarkable.

The episodes of the show also loosed an outpouring of letters—from vets, and from their families, fathers, mothers, sisters, daughters, and sons. Some typed, some scrawled in pen or pencil. They came to number in the thousands and they could be equally moving or troubling or heart-wrenching, and they still come now and again without end.

Some I can't forget. Among them was a letter that arrived on fine heavy bond stationery with a famous cosmetic company letterhead from a woman named Suzanne Guglielmi. It was two pages typed and single-spaced and it flew hair-raisingly in the face of all coincidence. She enclosed a story called "Danny's Homecoming." It wasn't fiction; it was her memory of her brother coming home to Marion, Indiana, the same way and the same week that Doug had in December 1969.

"I got into the bathtub," Suzanne wrote me about the night before her brother was buried, "and the loneliness I felt as everyone else prepared for bed with someone was over-whelming. I was trying as the oldest child to be strong and all of a sudden grief overwhelmed me." Her mother, four feet eleven inches tall, discovered her twenty-eight- or twenty-nine-year-old daughter in the tub and got her out and dried her off and took a letter out of the dresser drawer and handed it to her. It was from Danny. He had written it to Suzanne in case he didn't return. Suzanne slept with the letter and in the same bed with her sister, Danny's second sister, and her husband that night and then wrote her story and put the letter and the story away for twenty years.

For other vets I met, and sometimes couldn't get away from, the war was all they talked about. Whatever had really happened became like million-dollar wounds and the Purple Hearts that went with them. They tossed their experiences around like confetti and often the truth jettisoned with so many tellings. Listening to them, it was impossible to know any longer what was true. Maybe for them as well.

These men and women who carry our gratitude were not always so with each other. Vets could turn on their own with their worst selves. The tumult over John Kerry's service was il-lustration. Three Purple Hearts, a drawer of medals called into toxic, apparently groundless issue some thirty years later. Whatever criticisms there might be of a wishy-washy or over-calculating senator, whatever his criticisms of the Vietnam War, it's not easy to understand the outburst of bile and carp-ing that arose questioning the eloquence and patriotism of the speaker of these words:

> . . . our last own determination to undertake one last mission—to search out and destroy the last vestige of this barbaric war, to pacify our own hearts, to conquer the hate and the fear that have driven this country these last

ten years and more, so when thirty years from now our brothers go down the street without a leg, without an arm, or a face, and small boys ask why, we will be able to say "Vietnam," and not mean a desert, not a filthy obscene memory, but mean instead the place where America turned and where soldiers like us helped it in the turning.

On that same plane from Hanoi there was one other veteran. His name was Dave Chevalier and we kept running into him—again in Hue and then in Vung Tau, the resort town on the South China Sea. Like Peter Specht, he had served late in the war at Camp Evans, northwest of Hue, and then back down south at Phu Lai. He flew a helicopter then and did still, in Hawaii for an outfit that he and his wife now owned. In million-dollar A Stars, they spun tourists close to the stunning waterfalls and dropped them low into the cones of the volcanoes. He was small, compact, and observant, and then he would get this light in his eye, a memory-reverie light. He would then talk about what he remembered. He didn't only talk. He was intrepid and driven and he had given himself an assignment: to find the farthest-out and hairiest firebase where he once had been. There were, of course, no choppers available to him. He rented a boat instead and took it up the Perfume River toward the mountains as far as he could. The river narrowed to a shallow thread. The boat drew too much. He had to come back. Still he wasn't ready to give up. He craved the use of the Zodiac that was being worked on at the Huoang Jiang Hotel in Hue.

Our last night in Vietnam we went to the rooftop bar at the Rex Hotel in Saigon. It was beset with a zoo of topiary in the shapes of wild animals, even an elephant. They were hulking, outrageously outsized, and made no sense, which made perfect sense. Higher still, up a winding stair a final half-story, sat a swimming pool. The bar had been a fabled gathering place during the war, tarnished and larky, and still was. The heat and the humidity remained bewilderingly oppressive. The celebrated carnival of Ho Chi Minh City was coming alive again and the squalid din rose up through the long sunset.

The letters from the vets and their experiences seemed to echo through the tumult and I wondered about the truth and fiction in Peter Specht's own war story. I wondered if Dave Chevalier had made it to that destination he so determinedly had sought. I wondered if Dana and I had helped each other and solved anything. I wondered what I had found out. And I wondered about Doug.

The color in the sky went away and the clouds built and dusk came. It was gray in all its possible permutations—pewter and mercury and smoke and the color of wet tin. There seemed hardly an end to them before dark came and shut its door.

12

THE NIGHT AFTER Doug came home Samantha awakened me. I was sleeping in Doug's room. Even squared away it was full of him, his pictures and posters, his trophies, and his clothes. The doings and makings of his young life. He was all around me and he was gone and the room, despite and because of his stuff, felt very empty.

Samantha was leaning down, whispering my name. I had had trouble sleeping and each night seemed worse than the one before. At last I was and now I heard my name. It was the sound the silence had been waiting for.

Coming up from sleep, I reached out and pulled her down to me until we lay together. She didn't fight against it. I was still waking and wanting and worried and holding back within the stealthy feel of her breath. All without moving.

She didn't pull away, very close to me, and I said her name.

"I want to see him," she said then.

"What time is it?"

"I don't know."

"Tomorrow morning."

"I want to go see him," she said.

"It's the middle of the night."

"I know. I don't care."

"It'll be okay," I said. "It can wait."

"I want to go now," she said.

We got dressed quietly and I had gone out the kitchen door before I realized she wasn't behind me anymore. I went back inside and she was going back upstairs.

"Now what is it?"

"I'm going to get my father."

"He's not going to come."

She wasn't listening and she disappeared up the stairs and I waited in the silent house not knowing what to expect. After a while she came back down the steps alone.

"You were right."

"What do you want to do?" I asked.

"I don't know." She had lost some impetus. "Where are you going?"

"You got me up. You got me going—so I'm going."

It was snowing again and quite hard. The flakes were different sizes. Large and small filled the air and fleeced the night. Fresh inches lay unblemished on the empty streets. We were the first to leave our tracks on a series of white carpets.

The parking lot of the funeral home was outsized, enormous and vacant, a cottony desert that seemed to shrink the size of the fake English Tudor building. We parked and went up to the front door and rang the bell and no one answered. We had come on a foolish quixotic mission in the middle of the night to the middle of nowhere to no avail.

But we were not done yet. We left some more tracks. We drove around to the back where there was a shipping entrance. Two hearses were there, with the snow white now, not black. The double doors were open and we went in and found ourselves where you don't normally go. The windows were painted over, as if the snow had covered them too, and the walls were nicked and blemished, an unsavory custard-colored tile. We heard the sound of toilets flushing that weren't toilets flushing. People were there working.

We didn't get far before we were intercepted.

"Doug Young," Samantha blurted.

"No," the man said. "Franklin Isley."

He was tall and skinny and had long hair pulled back into a ponytail. His skin was dark and his eyes were darker. In the hallway there was no distinction between his iris and his pupil. He wore a rubber apron and rubber gloves and low-cut L. L. Bean boots that had gum soles with a chain-link tread.

"We're here to see Doug Young," Samantha said.

"Who? Give me some help here. The night is long and I'm a little slow and behind here."

"He arrived yesterday," I said. "From Vietnam."

"Oh yes, I saw him," Franklin Isley said, and then corrected himself. "But I haven't, we haven't gotten to him yet."

He watched us falling behind him, what he meant, and with all but invisible calibrations he found a new tone: "You see, not normally, but in this case, whenever we receive someone in the military under these circumstances, they come with instructions. They've been attended to, in this case I think in Vietnam, and then the casket is sealed with instructions that say 'Viewable' or 'Non-Viewable.' But we open the casket anyway. We like to make sure. And verify regardless that the condition is satisfactory to us. We take pride in our work, and if it's going to be seen, we want to make sure that everything is all right and that the family will be all right to see . . ."

"And you haven't?" Sam asked.

"First thing in the morning."

"But which is it?" I asked.

"What do you mean?"

"Viewable or . . . non-viewable?"

"I don't know," he said. "I'm busy now." He stopped and then he said, "I'll go see."

If he looked the part he didn't play the part. He was his own kind of veteran and could've been a cliché. He must have seen a lot of death, but he was very aware this snowed-in night of all the futile urgency and crushed hope of the living we carried.

————

FOR YEARS THERE WAS a sand dune up the beach several hundred yards from ours at Fisherman's Landing. Some years it was high, some years it was wild with beach grass, and some years a winter storm had torn it so that it had a sharp edge like a miniature cliff. It could be three feet high or six—a great place to leap and die from, and maybe once a week in the summer we would journey into deep pretend and do so. Sometimes we would take our toy weapons and use them, holding off invisible hordes until at last struck down, sacrificing ourselves to whatever cause it was. I did the best falls. My bulky body was like rubber and I was daring enough or stupid enough to throw it willy-nilly into the abyss. Mason made the best screams, letting them sally forth through the air from before his leap until after his landing. Doug had an exquisite final leg spasm and death rattle.

For a while back then we had Davy Crockett coonskin caps, and then holsters with every bit of paraphernalia. I had a black-and-white gun belt with holster that I thought so cool I fitted it full of fake bullets because that was cool, and then emptied many of them (see—they've been used) because that was cool. A similar fate awaited the black-and-white gun belt and holster itself. Too showy—a cowhide one took its place. Every time I oiled my Rawlings baseball glove I oiled the holster. The neat's-foot oil deepened the shade and smoothed them both. A kid's version of hand-tooled.

Endlessly, we practiced our fast draws, wearing a gun higher or lower or wearing two (a great debate), punching an eyelet hole through the bottom end of the holster and running a rawhide strand through it to tie it down to the thigh for greater speed and efficiency. Knives were next. For a while before real ones, we carried shafts of whittled wood in thin cardboard sheaths. The cardboard was yanked from the pieces packed in with starched and folded shirts. We cut and molded and Scotch-taped them together. They looked sweet, but aged quickly and badly. The cardboard soiled and the tape turned nicotine.

About that time I heisted a paperback from my brother's room. It was falling apart, a clump of pages loose, but I can still see the cover: a man in black on horseback with a deep-cordovan-brown holster against a moody and moonless midnight-blue sky. I read it straight through in a single sitting and it pressed in deeply as a certain few books can, especially when you're young. The impact never goes away.

It was a novel, a western, short and well written, a tale told by a boy about a mysterious man. The man was dark, a knight errant who had a dangerous untold past and could not escape his quest. He had a code and with him he brought a doomed honor. He was heroic. He rode into the boy's valley in the summer of 1889, and into my consciousness, and when his work was done rode back whence he had come and he was Shane.

Those were the days our couch took a beating. The discovery it could serve as a horse led to its destruction. I leapt onto the back of it hundreds of times as if mounting my steed, playacting. The wear and tear, finally, was not small. If I was alone, a frequent thing in the winter, I played all the parts, heroes and villains. Eventually the free form of it wasn't satisfying. I decided to make up a story, write a western. I didn't know how to type so there were many starts and very few finishes. What did come into existence was chock full of action and clipped, terse, repetitive dialogue—Samuel Beckett, be proud—and without my knowing it fell very much into a script form.

The bad guys were the most fun. The more outrageous, the more so. They killed a lot and they had to be killed. There was a lot of killing. There were a lot of "Uggghhhs!" and "Aaaiiieeees!!!" pecked out a finger at a time on a portable

Underwood. A pint-sized one, less than four inches deep in its case. The enclosed part of the *e* and the *a* and the *g* filled with ribbon residue from my pounding. Repeatedly, I had to tweeze them out with the tip of a pen or the point of a letter opener or whatever tools I could heist from my brother's chemistry set.

In August of 1957 we saw *The Bridge on the River Kwai* and in a single night war replaced westerns. For a quarter (seventy-five cents, ninety, and then a dollar and a quarter as adults) we sat riveted in the balcony of the Old Colony Theatre. The movie was epic and authentic in a way we hadn't seen before. The heat felt palpable, the sweat sticky, the jungle torturous, and the characters were cut from a crustier if no less mythic cloth—a very luring combination. The next night we came back and saw it again, and then in the cold of Cape Cod Bay we forded an imagined river, ferried simulated explosives, and blew up a nonexistent bridge every day for the rest of the summer.

But most of all we hoped for a thunderstorm. They brought the sky alive and could shake the earth and gave the lightning over the water toward Provincetown a scary and electric beauty. The strokes made vivid seams, like the heavens were cracking open and what lay beyond was resplendent. We couldn't wait for one to come at night. That meant it was time for a secret mission. These were the most exciting of our sorties. Using the dark as cover we journeyed down a street that our fathers had nicknamed "Save Me Daddy Hill." Long ago one of their sisters had lost control of her horse and those were the words she had yelled out to our grandfather. It was canopied now. The maple and oak and locust trees stole the sky and the string of a road was rich with gloom. Lightning, startling and stark, laid the lines of the branches across the road like leafy X-rays. Next we found our way along an even less used road where grass still tufted in the middle. In a car the grass whisk-broomed the muffler and a rock dinged and damaged whatever it hit. All this to stalk a haunted-looking house that lay behind a decapitated stone wall and across a wild and woolly yard.

The task at hand was to take possession of the house. What we never knew was what waited for us. Was it truly abandoned and unoccupied? Were the Germans inside? Were there machine-gun nests? Were there mines in the yard and was it booby-trapped?

Even then we realized how planted our innocent misadventure was in dreamscape. We crawled across the grass like Christina in a Wyeth world toward dark and spooky windows in a Charles Burchfield house.

———

AFTER OUR VISIT AT THREE A.M., we did not make it back to the funeral home until the next afternoon. The wooden shipping box had been opened. The gaskets around the edge of the zinc Ziegler case had been released. The top overlapped the bottom and was screwed down at multiple points around the perimeter to effect a seal. They were unseated. The glass face panel had been checked for identification. The choice of a coffin had been made, though I don't know by whom or when, and Doug had been deemed Viewable. The receiving funeral director checked the arterial and cavity embalming that had been done in Da Nang and not in Germany where the government operated a larger mortuary. He had removed Doug from the Ziegler case and with some final restorative work laid him out in an open casket.

The room where he lay when we got there had double doors that slid back like those of an old parlor. It was heavily rugged and draped and the windows were smoked and tinted. There was no direct sunlight. There were chairs here and there, not in rows, set about seemingly without reason. The coffin was on a covered stand at one end.

I had been to a wake once in high school for a nine-year-old. She was the sister of a classmate and her family lived in a sprawling Tudor home that sat on a curve in the road behind a jungle of rhododendrons. The house's shabby magnificence didn't make it inside to where Lanie lay. Lanie's actual name was Alane; she had been named after her father, a doctor, whose name and credentials were set into a stone pillar at the head of the drive. Dr. Alan Wright was a wide and jovial man with a mustache, and stupendously overweight. His wife was similarly cartoon-shaped, and her hair was bleached beyond palomino, nearly white. He ran his practice from a wing of the house and his patients were mostly poor and black. Rumors drifted around that he was a bit of a quack. They had little traction until after his daughter died. They became nastier and sadder then because he had taken so long to recognize how sick Lanie was and, it was said, had misdiagnosed her.

For a while Dr. Wright was the physician for our football team. When Mason was injured we went to see him. His office had once been a sunroom; it was cold and drafty, all windows, and the floor was stone. Dr. Wright was convinced Mason's shoulder was dislocated. He hefted my brother over his own shoulder, like Falstaff hauling Hal rather than vice versa. Mason screamed in pain and passed out and his shoulder refused to reset. I had never seen my brother in such a state and it enraged me and drained me. It made me weak. My legs forgot about me and I had to sit down. For several seconds I was as useless as he was. Unfortunately for everyone, his shoulder was separated, not dislocated.

The Wrights had six children, all girls and all with male nicknames: Andy, Robbie, Ned, Chris, Stevie, and Lanie. The oldest two were cheerleaders, bright and bushily ponytailed and bleached as blond as their mother. The third daughter, my age, was heavy and sedentary. She would come into a room and find a place to sit; she'd go kerplunk. She might well have patented the expression "Can I crash?" She smoked early and ferociously; she wasn't smart or quick, but she was popular. She knew everything about everybody and was kind about what she knew and how she used it. People sought her company.

Lanie was the first dead person I had seen. She was laid out in the living room and surrounded by candles. The coffin was achingly small. Her face was misshapen; it had lost its conformation and even its features seemed to have changed. It was puffy and heavy-laden with Pan-Cake makeup and her arms were also powdered and still I could see needle jabs from IVs.

I had played with her and kidded and tickled her until she couldn't stop laughing and neither could I. I had hefted her onto my shoulders. I had carried her around upside down. She was always chock-full of questions—about her sisters and already about boys and dating and whatever it is we call love. She was tiny and funny and inquisitive and enchanting.

I have gifted her with only good qualities because she was so young and that was what I knew of her and now she was dead. Whatever else she may have been was temporarily and maybe forever forgotten. It was an easy thing to do. But who was this figure lying here?

What Alane—Lanie—died of I don't remember now. I don't know if I ever knew. I don't know what happened to her five sisters with their boy nicknames. We went on with our lives and the evening became unreal. I all but forgot kneeling beside the sweet and sad, puffy and Pan-Cakey sight of her.

But on seeing Doug—and even now, all these crowded years later—the memory of her there joined with the sight of him and returned as fresh as new weather complete with sights and smells and tastes. They arrived unabated and clustered with emotion, like the yellows in Vietnam, and accompanied by a litany of questions, so many still unanswered, set to ferment again in the blessed and cursed crannies of me.

In the funeral home the coffin beckoned us and held us away. We did not go right to Doug. Betty never went to him; both she and George kept a distance. The rest of us circled uneasily and the curious arrangement of chairs seemed now to suit our fitful paths of approach. Even after we reached him we backed away again, as if seeing him was too much in too many ways to digest. He was in uniform, Marine dress, his eyes shut, his hands folded. He rested easily yet oddly. I don't know how else to define it: it was Doug and it was not Doug. Everything about him was slightly awry. His color, his expression, the shape, or rather the shapelessness of him.

Someone may have tried to retrieve his death from what had killed him. Closed his eyes, his mouth. Washed his wounds. Sutured and stitched and pieced his blown and broken skull back together. They may have done their best work. I didn't know and I couldn't tell and it didn't matter. However hard they may have tried, they had failed. It was Doug and it was not Doug, and I could only come to one conclusion: it must not be.

I took to sitting back in one of the chairs beside a smoked window and watched him. I started to wait for him to move and became convinced he was going to. I was sure of it. If I watched closely enough, if I concentrated intensely and completely enough, he would breathe or twitch or rise up. He would do something. He would prove to be alive. He would become Doug again. The conviction was a cliché but I could not stop it.

Samantha went up to him as I sat back, watching and waiting, and stayed there. She didn't move now; she became almost as still as he was. Her back began to quiver then and I realized she must be crying. I went up and put my arm around her, and my brother approached as well. He did too. One of us on each side of her. She kept shaking until she had no tears left and then kept on shaking still. It was then that she said what I would never forget:

"That's not his ear."

IN THE SILENCE after we left the funeral home there was still disbelief. Maybe this is the way we are, the human species:

deep down into our egos we can't face that those we love are no longer, and that inevitably we won't be either. In our wrestling with denial and acceptance we try to make death palatable. We bring on makeup artists to do their best work, beseech them like Vito Corleone would to "use all their powers" to dress and doctor the corpse. Thomas Lynch, the poet and undertaker, says the dead don't care. We think they do somehow, and many funeral directors facilitate our wishes. With their blessing, we seek to make the dead look alive.

Aren't our memories the same? As Marianne Wiggins wrote, "They are all we are and all we have. Everything we've kept in life. Or everything we've lost." A person isn't dead as long as we remember him and neither are we. We save him in the billions of neural circuits in the brain we possess and thread these bundles of nerve fibers that store experience together and draw out yarn. We bind sensory images and semantic data into the sensation of a whole. There in the constellation of our memories lies the crucible where Story is born. We call them up through the fissures and faults of all that we retain. Forged from our need and in our hope, they emerge. They are a search for comfort in the deepest and not necessarily most comfortable sense and in the finding we manage to serve ourselves and by that serve others. In the best of them, however darkly charted, weaves a long-lastingness and celebration. They become history; they become prayer; they become our afterlife. We tell them so that we can live. They are what we have to refute death.

THAT WAS THE NIGHT we went out drinking and didn't drink, and for many years after I didn't drink much. A beer, a glass of wine, or nothing; it wasn't until I turned fifty that I found I was drawn back to vodka. The cold that night was still brutal; it had not let up. Darkness had come as early as it was ever going to, and it felt late even if it wasn't. The solstice and the temperature and seeing Doug did that. The snow was packed and crunchy now and seemed to emit little white dust crystals of light. It was the light of headlights in the night and the sheen of our strongest dreams. The day that had come and gone we had lost touch of and forgotten, and as we remembered it now there was no celebration in us. It was Christmas.

George and Betty stayed at the house and I don't know what they did. I'd like to think they talked or held each other or got some rest. All were unlikely true. Two friends of Samantha's joined us. They arrived separately and were a dramatic contrast.

Judy Whitcomb was a doctor's daughter, big and husky, her slenderness already fully fleshed out. She had spent a lot of time sailing and even in winter wore a tightness of skin and a smidgen of a tan. She had come from a Christmas party and was still decked out in a low-cut dress and high boots and a floor-length coat with a fur collar. The sight of her—her skin alone—set us back. We were too wrapped in crepe. The energy she brought with her we couldn't maintain and so it didn't last.

The second was Joan Holcombe. She had changed since the wedding in San Francisco. She was still a slip of a girl, flat-chested, and in her heels not five feet tall, but she was less fresh and more caustic. Some bloom was off the rose. Even in the bar she kept her gloves over her tiny hands. Her face had held on to its freckled loveliness and her lips looked even more shapely and full than before. They had nothing to do with little girls. Soft-spoken as ever, she was finger-snappingly quick and perceptive. She peeled people right open.

The drinks we ordered languished and so did our conversation. Words were very spare and we couldn't ignite high spirits. Silence felt more real and less painful. What talk there was did not wander or flower and what we said was about our hopes and our dreams; what we said were promises to keep.

Weddings are widespread with tales of how people are

caught up and couple, not just the bride and groom, coincidences and conjunctions, before it is discovered how often love can be the delivery of a promise already broken. A lot of people get laid.

The romantic notion is profoundly contagious and powerful. Around danger and grief collects the same impulse with the same force. The instinct to mate is so strong. It's like fine wine then simply to be alive and just cause for primacy.

Fiction and nonfiction are full of such stuff, and perhaps rightly so. There is such inherent drama and immediacy in these events. You could build from literature a rich syllabus of two beings coming together in unlikely circumstances. Entitle it "Survivor's Love." It is a message from the blood, how much we wish to share celebration, or how close we are and maybe in defiance of death. The act might be quick, a hurried necessity, or done in a stolen quiet like in the eye of a hurricane. It could be crude or craven, sweet and sour, for that moment or for all the moments that are left transcendent.

But not this cold night. We were hard-bitten and hard-burdened and locked inside our solitary selves. Liquor wasn't going to help, nor was literature. They couldn't help or save us. Writing wasn't yet my profession then—I was barely a wannabe—but even if it had been, we weren't ready for stories or anecdotes. Books, paintings, the best of movies have been called a force of memory we haven't fully understood or comprehended. We were a long way from there. Clocks needed to go round; seasons needed to turn. Time needed to pass. Our only refuge was each other's company. Unacknowledged and maybe even unrealized, without Doug we were in a most lonely place.

Before eleven we were in bed.

13

THE SECOND TIME I went to Vietnam it was already a different country again.

Except for the heat and the humidity nothing was the same. Capitalism had begun to run amuck and changes were already profound. Vietnam was being pulled, kicking and screaming, into at least the nineteenth century. Still the bloom was wobbling on the rose. Nothing was happening as quickly as Westerners were used to, and the Vietnamese government was struggling and arthritic, still torn itself between the old and the new.

With a few exceptions—Ho Chi Minh City, Hanoi, and Da Nang near where Doug had been killed—I had decided to go to places that I hadn't been before. I flew up to Dalat. It was a mountain resort, seventeen hundred meters above sea level, set around a lake and amidst conifers. In late October 1963, the weekend before the coup that would kill him, Ngo Dinh Diem had come to Dalat with the American ambassador to dedicate a nuclear research center. It was his last major public act. The American ambassador by his side, Henry Cabot Lodge, once a Kennedy foe, had turned very tough. He knew well a clock was ticking and a conspiracy was underway and that America supported it, and that without us it wouldn't have happened. At least not then, not the way it would pathetically and unfortunately unfold.

By the late nineties Dalat was growing fast. Its population had spurted suddenly to 150,000 from fewer than 100,000 twenty years before. It was aclatter with expansion and the outlines of new rooflines skewered the sky. Its French heritage was fading; the hunting was largely over, the wild animals extinct. During the sixties there had been a zoo, and suddenly there was a drive to bring it back and a new one was being planned. Domestic tourism was now the leading industry, many from the north; it had become a favorite honeymoon spot.

Clouds were plentiful and there was a pleasantness to the air that was bewitching. The shiftings of the sky were leisurely and lambent. The pines whispered and offered their scent. Who could have imagined pleasant could be such a pleasant thing? I went to see Vien Thuc, a monk who was an artist and wore a woolen cap in the shape of the old leather aviator ones. He had these lit-up eyes and a smile that made age impossible to guess and thousands of paintings stacked and hung about his windy Japanese-like garden and his studio, a series of low rooms with a tin roof and leaky skylights. I had heard about him and I wasn't alone. He had been at Lam Ty Ni, a pagoda, since 1961 and had made a tourist book or two.

The last emperor of Vietnam (such as he was), Bao Dai, had hunted lions and elephants and summered in Dalat. After his exile Bao Dai had outmarried and outlived scores of his successors, whatever their title, and was still alive in 1991 and living in France. His summer palace had been started in 1933 and "accomplished" in 1937. It looked rinky-dink from the outside, hardly a palace. It was a forty-eight-crayon box full of eroded yellows and had circles within its structure, in the shapes of its rooms, its windows, and even its furniture. The truth was its round shapes were art deco. Transplanted and refurbished, it could have sat in small splendor in Miami Beach.

Underneath its run-down patina and the meddling museum fixings and abysmal care it was quite beautiful.

I returned to Hue and settled into another circular room on Le Loi Boulevard that had been an embassy house at some point and now was claiming to be a hotel. Some splendor gone to squalor. At five the city began to wake. The sounds of car horns and backfires crackled from all sides like fireworks and the smell of exhaust joined the wet and fermenting aroma of the Perfume River. Hue was the way I remembered, tumid and torporous. I went to the site of the Ancient Capital and walked where, during the Tet Offensive, the Americans and the Vietnamese had fought for one of the few times in the war hand to hand and yard by yard.

In the morning I crossed over to Dong Ha and found Highway 9 and the road to Khe Sanh. Here and there, erratically, the road was under construction. Red earth and mud splayed out like a messy wake. A boy stood alongside the road atop one mound. He placed his carved wooden sword into a pretend scabbard at his waist and stood guard as I drove by. Fifteen kilometers in from the coast the construction stopped and the road leveled and then started to climb. Past a working quarry; past geese on the road; past motor scooters ridden by boys actually wearing helmets and glass masks, a very unusual sight; past the Rockpile; past what looked like an army base flying a host of Vietnamese flags, the yellow star in the field of red; past women carrying long logs, beams perhaps, in baskets on their backs; past a man on a bicycle; past a water buffalo, and a young man with a wooden crutch and one leg and one stump, but riding the buffalo uphill, the crutch really a wooden stick, and he held it out in his left arm, as if probing with it for balance. Now the road started to wind as well as to climb as it ran alongside the Da Krong River. The windshield wettened and the cloud cover was darker and lower, closing in, and I passed the Ho Chi Minh Trail. The growth around the road was thick and dense now, a jungle that in places looked impossible to penetrate. I stopped to ensure I was on the right track and in broken language pointed and pronouncing it "Ch-shong" a man said Khe Sanh was still ten kilometers ahead. Soon there were no people left on the road. There was only the potholed and pitted, worsening, narrow, twisty, and climbing way. The wind came and the clouds were so low and close they might as well have been fog. The jungle pulled back and faded away. Bamboo thinned out and disappeared and there were young fir trees and the earth warmed in hue and became red. Not a simple red; it was practically roan and like laterite. The ascent grew in pitch. The road turned to dirt and rock, the rocks small and packed close together, and made for rugged going.

Without the boy hawking souvenirs beside the road I wouldn't have known I was there. Nothing else was in sight. I left and locked the car and made my way along an irregular path. The ground was damp but hard and the shade of fresh rust. It had a grainy, mottled surface like a beach after a hard rain. Until recently the notorious landing strip lingered, and sometimes in the early mornings or late in the steamy afternoons the phosphorus still smoked from what was left of it, as if it were a volcanic site. In 1992 strawberries had been planted around the perimeter, and then in 1994 and 1995 coffee arrived back, the same crop the hated French had once harvested within a click or two. The embattled runway, the killing ground, was transforming into a coffee plantation. Inland, away from the city and the hot spots, the tourist destinations, Vietnam was returning to and remaining itself. In many ways what it had been it was again. Or it always had been. It refuted our quick and needy sense of progress. The beans on the bushes were green and occasionally in scarlet clusters. The scarlet, like Chinese red, was so fiery and lurid it seemed fake.

I looked out across the plain. Not far away, on the other side of the road, a community had begun to spring up. Not this way. There were no traces left—only the shapes of the land and the fog gathering in its clefts and groins like a sea of white water surging into its inlets.

I remembered the news reports and the Robert Ellison photographs from the siege in 1968. They had gained the cover of *Newsweek* and spread across eight pages inside. I went back not long ago and looked at them. The issue had faded and chipped and the khaki and burnt sienna colors of the pictures had lost their luster, but not their poignancy or power.

Here was the sky full of parachutes blooming like poppies as they dropped in supplies. Here were the sandbags and the raw earth and the concertina. Here was the endless sea of expended and shucked 105-mm shell casings, here was the smoldering husk of a crashed chopper, here was the blistering fireball of an ammunition dump exploding, and here were the men, the clusters of stranded men, the men huddled and the men dug in. A line of them pressed to the ground in a bunker, holding their helmets on tight, cigarette packs crumpled and tucked in, the coppery granules of earth the men clung to razor sharp in focus in one picture, the dirt-crammed stubs of a soldier's fingers in another.

And here were the shots of the men's young faces. Some had fresh stubble and some didn't and couldn't; they had no need to shave yet. The eyes of the men were young and tough and weary and numb and staring.

They were eviscerating photographs and had a rough grueling beauty as such images can. Wars make for stunning pictures. They vivify, agitate, rend. But these photos weren't of the wounded or the dead. They apprehended a different drama—what it was to be pinned down and have to wait, not knowing what was to come, survival or death; what in the eyes became known as the thousand-yard stare. That same week the photographs had been published Ellison and forty-seven others had lost their lives in the crash of a C-123. He was twenty-three years old.

What else was left of the base where the infamous siege

from the American war had taken place? A few rotted scraps of camo sandbags and tarpaulins, a worn-away combat boot and a shoe or two, some shells, by this time probably strategically dropped so something at all was there. And a couple more kids hawking dog tags, Marine insignias, bullets, and a quarter. The quarter was dated 1984.

This was Vietnam, and even Khe Sanh's mud slopped with controversy. Why had we picked it? Why did we hold it? Why did we abandon it? What was the objective? Was it necessary? What was it about? Winning and losing were still in contention, impossible to sort out.

The next day I hired a driver. The skinny roads were worn and wearing and crammed. This first driver, named Hai, drove slowly and badly and returning after dark drove fast and badly. He knocked off two chickens on the way back. In driving in Vietnam, it was said, there were three goods: good horn, good brakes, and good luck.

Later, reaching from Hanoi further north, the driver I drew was an artist and a maniac. He provided me with a hair-raising three hours. Horns beeping, tooting, sounding, calling, warning, having at it a thousand times as we tore down a one-lane road full of buses, bikes, motor scooters, people on foot, animals, and often oncoming trucks. His name was Nguyen, the equivalent of Smith if Smith were a given name, and he never changed expressions. No panic, inches from disaster, the whole road like the ultimate video game.

Every day on the roads it felt like a two-way evacuation was underway, but it was just business as usual.

In these journeys I went along the back road to Dong Ha and then up to the Ben Hai River which cut along the seventeenth parallel and the center of what had been the DMZ and forked at the Hien Luong Bridge. Here again were the rice paddies with their greens and yellows so vibrant and packing such a poetic punch. Late afternoon played on the webs of water and tessellated the light. Distant rains began to build.

They brooded over the land and then began to broom it. Spectacularly they came and swept over us.

The Hien Luong Bridge used to be one-half red and one-half yellow as a symbol of the separation of the country and the land was stripped around it until the bridge was destroyed in 1967. The bridge that replaced it was now being replaced. The building of a new one was under way and the rice paddies had come back to surround it. There was a memorial on the North side, with Ho Chi Minh's head of course, the remnants of a bunker, some sampans, and the bright shades of laundry hanging not far away. We stopped once along the way. I had a cup of coffee brewed on a small aluminum plate in a small aluminum cup and then dropped into a jelly glass. Colorful polka dots were on the glass and the coffee was very black and very strong and very good. I was glad to be out of the car for a while.

The handicapped worked at a shop next door. I could see them and hear them through an open doorway. There was one with no legs, and one with a clubfoot, and a hunchback. All were whacking away at hunks of stone. They were making paperweights and mobiles and sculptures to sell. The gewgaws hung from the ceiling and filled the sills and doorway and littered the yard. They were cheap and ordinary and yet the odd good one among them was simple and moving and took you by surprise.

Across the cranny of a street an old man sat in a window. His skin was a dusky shade, like a milky shadow. A boy was getting a haircut, his head leaned all the way forward and a razor going up the back of his neck, shaving it clean. A girl in an *ao dai* and long gloves that stretched nearly to her elbows mounted a motor scooter. Her complexion was pale and luminous like fine linen and her hair was long and black and looked still damp. It hung straight and true and she adjusted the back panel of her dress under her, folding it quickly onto the seat so it wouldn't blow or get caught. The motion was practiced, casual, done, and she set off down the puddly road and disappeared from sight.

My destination was the tunnels at Vinh Moc where a whole town had once lived. They were in Quang Tri Province near Vinh Linh and, unlike the famous tunnels at Cu Chi, they had been occupied by civilians and had been restored at their original location. At Cu Chi the tunnels you could get into as a tourist weren't the real ones and not even in the same place. These at Vinh Moc, created after the town was bombed and completely wiped out, were on three levels and at three different depths. They were roomier and airier and seemed friendlier and less claustrophobic, less brutal. Perhaps it was the red earth and the nearness of the ocean. One of the tunnels opened out onto the beach.

There was no such relief at Cu Chi. The tunnels there, whether real or rebuilt, were dark and wet and sweat-popping. They were very tight fitting; there was no way or place to stand up. The dirt stained whatever it touched like smears from a wet crayon. In seconds I was full of fear and wanted out. In minutes I was soaked, my neck was sore, my back cramped, and I wanted *out*. I knew quickly and thoroughly and harrowingly just how big and cumbrous, if not fat, a two-hundred-pound American can be.

At Vinh Moc the whole village settled in. Seventeen babies were reputedly born in the tunnels. Families had niches the size of car trunks to live in. Children played near the mouths of the tunnels in the seepage of daylight. They had a hospital space, a conference hall that could squeeze in fifty. There were four ventilation shafts, two watch posts, three wells, and thirteen entrances, seven toward the sea and six up the bluff. The deepest of the three stages ran twenty-three meters down into the earth and the main backbone of the tunnels stretched for 768 meters, nearly half a mile.

On the way there, close by, an aging man stepped out into the road suddenly and stopped us and made us pay a toll. He loomed up in our path like a nightmarish visage from the war, military in bearing and all business, even dangerous-looking except for his black-rimmed glasses, which hung awkward and askew. He had not a note of humor or additional conversation. Pay up. No questions, no hesitations. He set off the worst and most atavistic alarms in me. The young guide and driver were also shaken. He was a sobering guy.

Way north, the other side of the hair-raising car ride, lay Halong Bay. Offshore, great oblong limestone hunks rose out of the sea. Their vertical assault was dramatic and they hid caves and tunnels, nesting birds and even animals. Stalactites like fossilized tears hung from some. The craggy monoliths were stunning and streaked and stained with iron oxide, rust that had found a rough-hewn beauty.

General Vo Nguyen Giap, who had once commanded the North Vietnamese troops, had a small place overlooking the bay. He was a tiny, crinkly, courtly man, old now; a doctor and an attendant always close by. Before he was a general he'd been a professor of history and after Le Duan, the leader after the liberation, bumped him from the politburo in 1982 he had retained his military rank and for a number of years served as Vice Premier of Science and Technology. He didn't wear a uniform this particular day or much any longer, just a pressed shortsleeve shirt. His skin was as gray as sleet and so was his hair. He didn't want to talk about the war. He had had his say in any number of interviews in recent years with American reporters or returning factotums. The war was behind him now, he had said his piece, and he was more interested in his war with his tiny, scraggly garden, admiring the view, and wondering what made his tea so dark. He peered into it as he stirred it. He didn't use a spoon; he had a root for a swizzle stick.

He did mention Allison Kent Thomas, an American who had parachuted into the northern highland jungle of Vietnam in 1945 and landed in a sacred tree. Thomas had been with the OSS, the leader of the "Deer Team" that had dropped in to help the Vietnamese after another group had attempted to walk in and failed. Plucked out of the tree, Thomas had been cordially welcomed and served a cow (slaughtered in his honor) and given a case of Hanoi beer (recently captured), and he had met one "Mr. Van" and discovered a very skinny and ill man called "Mr. C. M. Hoo."

Mr. Hoo was a mysterious fellow, who spoke English and liked to glom American cigarettes and to ask questions. He was very inquisitive. "The best teachers are the best listeners," Allison Thomas told me in one of the phone conversations we had had in the 1980s. Mr. Hoo claimed to have once been to Boston and New York and worked in the kitchens of restaurants. The remainder of Thomas's team—there were seven men in all—flew the same route from Poseh, China, on a DC-3 and parachuted in about ten days later. The Americans, including a medic, Paul Hoagland, who later joined the CIA and died in 1970, helped nurse Mr. Hoo back to health in the mountain caves near Kimlung. While there the Americans had trained the Vietnamese, both men and women, in the use of rifles and grenades. With Mr. Van, then, the Americans had begun to march to Hanoi. At Thai Nguyen they encountered the Japanese. The battle, a running skirmish really, lasted several days and helped bond Thomas and Mr. Van. After that, the Americans followed both Vietnamese men into Hanoi, arriving in the wake of Mr. Hoo's declaring his country's independence. They had a celebratory dinner then, the Americans still in uniform but Mr. Van in a suit and a well-worn and well-loved fedora hat.

Mr. Van, of course, really wasn't Mr. Van. He was Vo Nguyen Giap, and as we sat his memory reached back across those more than fifty years and warmed. The time together in the "forest" had linked Giap and Allison Thomas, forged a kinship, and only a few years before, when Thomas had come back to Vietnam, the two aging men had had a reunion. After the war, Thomas, a major, had returned to East Lansing,

Michigan, and the law. In the photographs taken back then, he had looked young and rakish, sporting a mustache as he sat with Mr. Hoo and Mr. Van. Almost all the Americans had grown mustaches, well nurtured and some with wild and beautiful handlebars; a few of the men had even sprouted beards. The facial hair wasn't about rebellion. It was about style and protection. They'd try anything to combat mosquitoes. Forty years later, when I talked to him and in the letters we exchanged, Allison Thomas sounded very solid and thoughtful, the best of conservative Middle America.

From that same time there were other survivors, and in the eighties I sought out several of them: Henry Prunier, a bricklayer and mason in Massachusetts, also on the Deer Team, who had spoken French and some Vietnamese and had had a spectacular mustache and lost forty pounds in the jungle; a very tiny, vital, funny Chinese-American man named Frankie Tan, who had cut Allison Thomas down from the tree, and who brewed for the mysterious Mr. Hoo a concoction called LoFuGo, which was concentrated extract of tiger bone marinated with alcohol; and in a cellar in Orlando, Florida, I spent time with an outlandish character with an outlandish name, Archimedes L. A. Patti. He had a huge head and the skin of a cadaver and he parked himself at a desk that wrapped 360 degrees around him. The desk was massively clotted. He was a very serious, cautious, courtly man, a little arrogant, a little obsessed and a little alone, ringed in by piles of books and papers and clippings, and now deeply entrenched and trying to complete a biography of Ho Chi Minh. It was overdue and he still had a long way to go and he was worried and a bit haunted that Random House (the umbrella company of the publisher) was impatient or, worse yet, losing interest. He would never finish the book. Patti had been in Hanoi ahead of the others, the one American to witness the delivery of the Vietnamese Declaration of Independence on September 1, 1945, that so closely followed in its opening words our own.

Allison Thomas sent me remarkable photographs, a copy of his diary, notes in French he had received from Giap after the war, and the final report he'd filed when the Deer Team's mission was complete. He had distilled his diary into the final report and it concluded:

> Our friend of the forest, Mr. C. M. Hoo, now Mr. Ho Chi Minh, was made President of the Provisional Government and Minister of Foreign Affairs. Another friend of the forest, Mr. Van, now Vo Nguyen Giap, became Minister of Interior. The new government appears to be enthusiastically supported by the majority of the population in every province of Indo-China . . .
>
> The people know the French intend to come back but they keep saying if they come back with arms they will fight to the death.
>
> The story of our experiences in Indo-China is melodramatic in the following sense. On 16 July we were living in the forests of Indo-China with the Chief of the VIETMINH party. Less than two months later, this same chief had become President of the new Provisional Government and was installed in the former home of the French "Resident Superior" in Hanoi.

These men, and the others who'd been there then, saw Ho Chi Minh in a different light than he was cast in thereafter. They had seen the determination and they had seen the human being. He hadn't denied he was a Communist, but his interests weren't Russian or Chinese. They were Vietnamese. He was uppermost a Nationalist. Freedom for his country drove him and he pursued whatever course would get it done. He admired the Americans and wanted our help. His goal wasn't our presence. His interest was in our ideas and our support. We gave it to him and then took it back. We also began to lie. We supported the French out of fear and for economic reasons, and used the Cold War and the Iron Curtain and the domino theory as cover. When the French lost at Dien Bien Phu, we participated in the Geneva accord that installed an American-educated Vietnamese Catholic, Ngo Dinh Diem, as president of South Vietnam and guaranteed elections within eighteen months. We helped cancel the elections, violating the agreement, lying some more, and then helped rig the elections when they were finally held. Whatever the legitimacy of our enemies—and maybe there was plenty—we saw them as all of one accord and joined in conspiracy. We traded our black-and-white lenses then for Red-colored ones. We ignored contrary evidence and attacked anyone who presented it. We shot a lot of messengers. We burrowed deeper into the depths of our own deception.

I remembered an interview with Aaron Bank, an Army colonel who lived past one hundred, and the man hailed and subsequently honored as the father of the Green Berets. He had been with the OSS on crazy, daring missions in Germany and Italy, and then he too had come to Southeast Asia near the end of the war in 1945. His reputation was simple. He made no bones, took no prisoners, one tough right-wing soldier. "Ho was a commie and we knew it," he said, "but supporting him were not just commies. He was very friendly to the Americans he ran across and he could have been right in our lap. Let's face it. We cut our throat; we backed the wrong side."

THE GUIDES AND THE DRIVERS I had after Khe Sanh knew some English but little about the American war and nothing about 1945. Both were long ago, far away, and irrelevant. They were history. They belonged to their parents' and their grandparents' generations.

I had a second driver named Hai, and his wife's uncle had been a pilot in the Army of the Republic of South Vietnam.

When the war was over he had been placed in a re-education camp for thirteen years and now lived outside Boston. But Hai didn't know him. He was proud and careful of his English and as I left he asked for confirmation in pronouncing his next client's remarkable name: C. Pudge. Another, Toan, had lost her father. He had been an Army journalist and while he was driving near Hue an explosion had ripped apart his car and killed him. Neither carried the incidents as grief or deep history. They were shared as if they were filling out forms. Both were living very much now, professionals eager to get ahead and make a living.

Saigon was rip-roaring with young foreigners the same vintage as Hai and Toan, living on such dreams and cell phones, and who thought like the companies that employed them they were only a breath away from making a killing. But the going had gotten tougher. There was a truth that was a truth: Vietnam had more miles of untapped and untouched beach than anywhere else in the world. And there was a joke that wasn't such a joke: Michael Eisner, the head of Walt Disney, was going to buy the country lock, stock, and barrel and make of it the biggest Disneyland yet. The fly in the ointment was Vietnam itself. There was an irreducible and thorny lesson to learn even as the Middle East turned sour and treacherous and Vietnam once again seemed enticingly attractive. Whatever was done to it, whoever did it, didn't matter; the country had its own fitful pace of progress.

By 1997 Americans weren't just revisiting. A number had settled in Vietnam. In Dalat by chance—and then by design in Hanoi—I met Chuck Searcy. He had served in 1968, largely in Saigon, gone home, married and divorced, and started from scratch a small weekly newspaper in Athens, Georgia. For twelve years before he sold it the paper consumed him. In 1992 he came back to Vietnam with an Army buddy. He didn't have the classic symptoms of post-traumatic stress. He didn't think he was trying to work through any heavy issue.

He didn't think he was trying to solve or resolve anything. But he was struck through by a tremendous sadness. It overwhelmed him. For the first time he put behind him the frozen images that he had carried since 1968 and he found himself coming back again. Several times. In January 1995, in conjunction with the Vietnam Veterans of America Foundation, he opened a one-man office to help provide Vietnamese with artificial limbs and wheelchairs. The need was tremendous. The office expanded. By 1997 there were seven employees— two Vietnamese, four doctors, and Sarah Pfeiffer, the daughter of a vet. Now they were outreaching across the country North and South.

One of Chuck Searcy's friends was Bobby Mueller. Small, electric-quick, a galvanizing speaker, Bobby had been the first head of the Vietnam Veterans of America. In that post he had taken it upon himself to visit high schools and talk to the students about the war. For a while he did it incessantly and for a reason. Bobby was a paraplegic, wounded on a hill with no name in I Corps, shot through the lungs and spinal cord and paralyzed, but the wheelchair wasn't enough: the kids still didn't get it. When I met him he told me how he had to take them back into the time and into the jungle, into the rice paddies and into the foxholes and into the mud, into the fear into the lostness into the death. He had to make them see it and taste it and feel it. Only then was there recognition of what it had been and what it meant.

Bobby's wife had had a very rugged bout with cancer. It was a difficult, dismal time for him before and after she died and it devastated him. Of all things then he discovered scuba diving. He was crazy about it. It helped bring him back to life and to Vietnam. The two men, Chuck and Bobby, had worked out a deal with a well-sized, sturdily handsome boat down at Nha Trang to take the disabled, both American and Vietnamese, on dives.

It was a sight to contemplate, these men and women, im-

mersed in water, in the engulfing silence of scuba diving, doing an underwater dance as they explored the beauty that often lies there—the coral and the slow shimmying weeds and
the bright flashes of fish and the slow streaming dazzle of the
sun that plays down into the depths. Clean and pure and shivering and very white and churchlike.

———

IT WAS IN THAT KIND of celestial light that we set out at last
to lay Doug into the ground. The late-December day was
white. The Fairview Cemetery was white. The sky and
ground were white. The sun was brilliant and its light on the
frozen snow that capped the frozen earth was white. The
branches of the trees were white, encrusted in ice and snow,
and the tips hung heavy like icicled fingers. The gloves on the
Marines were white. The reflections off the rifles seemed
white. The whiteness was lime and beyond lime; it was one of
hallucination and headaches. It was searing and blinding, gor-
geous and ghastly, and squinted eyes right down to slits. Only
the glare was its own color, a white out of Melville, a white
beyond white.

> . . . In many natural objects, whiteness refiningly en-
> hances beauty, as if imparting some special virtue of its
> own . . . yet for all these accumulated associations, with
> whatever is sweet, and honorable, and sublime, there yet
> lurks an elusive something in the innermost idea of this
> hue which strikes more of panic to the soul than that
> redness which affrights in blood . . .
>
> Is it that by its indefiniteness it shadows for the
> heartless voids and immensities of the universe, and thus
> stabs us from behind with the thought of annihila-
> tion . . .
>
> Or is it, that as in essence whiteness is not so much a
> color as the visible absence of color, and at the same

time the concrete of all colors; is it for these reasons that there is such a dumb blankness, full of meaning, in a wide landscape of Snows . . . ?

The coffin waited on a dropcloth that looked like a fake plastic putting green and the ceremony was short. A hymn, a prayer, rifle fire, taps. The salutes were tight. The volleys of shots ripped at the frigidity like ice cracking underfoot. The American flag as it was lifted from the coffin snapped first in the air and then in the hands of the Marines. It was tightly folded and three-cornered and presented to Betty. The sharp crisp wind ran across and through us and it was over. The body would be lowered after we left and it all felt too little, too short, too austere, and out of time and out of place, but at least and at what seemed at long last it would be done.

Mason and I changed and quickly packed. We were eager to get home, close the door on these slow free-falling few days that had seemed to last forever and to leave them behind. We needed to knit ourselves back into our lives. We were set to go when the phone rang. Doug still wasn't at rest. The ground still couldn't be dug. Excavation remained impossible.

For the first time George and Betty learned there had been no hole under the fake putting green. No one had told them. Nor that the day before the backhoe's engine had stalled in the cold and refused to start again. And now the blade it dug with, like the one Mason had tried to use in the side yard nights before, had snapped. The ground, packed solid, had sheared it off. The frozen earth had rejected it.

"Where is he?" Betty demanded.

"I don't know," George said.

"Call them back. I want to know where he is."

Before he could get an answer she took the folded flag upstairs and came back down with a blanket. She put on her coat and took the phone from George's hands and hung it up.

"Drive me," she said. "Wherever he is, I won't have my boy being cold."

So Doug had to wait a while longer, and it was while he was waiting that it was decided to take him on one more journey and lay him in the family plot in Massachusetts.

Three

14

VERY EARLY THAT NEXT MORNING on the Big Island in Hawaii after I received the news about George, before getting on the telephone, I drove up toward Waimea and then out the Hawi road. A low-grazing stratus settled across the tricky highway like the image of smoke over a battlefield. The sun was already up; it rises very early in Hawaii. When it could it filtered through and coated the arms of the prickly pear cactus along the road with a freshly minted platinum. Then it was gone as I turned downhill and into deeper clouds again.

I passed Upolu Point and the single-lane airstrip set next to the sea where small planes had come and gone in flurries during World War II, and found myself on a narrow, rutted dirt road that led toward King Kamehameha's birthplace. There was one other struggling vehicle in sight. It gave up and fell away and I was alone. Soon the road required four-wheel drive. I had to walk and the red earth clotted on my shoes. There was a tossing wind. The ocean roared just out of sight.

The *mo'okini heiau* appeared like a cairn. It was nearly thirty feet high, flat-topped, a place of prayer and sacrifice now nearly two thousand years old. Legend said it had been built in a single night by a chain of fifteen thousand men carrying the salt-beaten lava stones the fourteen miles from Pololu Valley.

The battered rocks had been stacked and layered and had the spidery-faced surface of enormous cantaloupes.

At some time the *heiau* had been restored, but it was again falling down. It was a powerful place, dark and wounded and abandoned. It felt holy and bereft. I knew I had come like those before me to seek a sign and reach after hope. Rain blew across my path, one of the quick showers that come especially in the afternoons. It left in its wake the rising sun and a rainbow, stark and perfectly struck, its jagged end landing in a neighboring field of wild grass and scattered sugar cane. The pot of gold was only a hundred yards away.

I walked after it and it kept walking away from me. The faster I went the faster it did. I couldn't catch it and turned back to the *heiau*. The weather wouldn't hold; it refused to clear. Sun and rain took turns coming and going, battling with one another. After a while there was no rainbow left and the sun had hiked up the sky.

I started back and when I reached Wailea Bay I picked up the phone and made the phone calls I didn't want to make, first to my mother and then to Betty, only to discover George had died just before one a.m. eastern time. It was the same hour that the grandfather clock he wound every week stopped and the same hour I was swimming at dusk in Hawaii.

Next I got Jenny on the phone: "You know?"

"I know," she said.

"I'm leaving here, but it's going to take me nearly twenty-four hours to get to West Hartford."

"Why are you bothering? You didn't fly back when he was sick."

"I knew he was sick, not *that* sick."

"It wasn't too hard to figure out."

"I'm sorry I called."

"Isn't that nice to say."

So many of these conversations degenerated badly. I wanted to say her name again. Call her and us back from sniping, and our own frozen tundra. I had plenty of remorse, so much so it was cotton in my mouth. But she knew; she always knew.

"I suppose you want me to come."

"You don't have to do that."

"You don't want me to?"

"I didn't say that."

"Wouldn't it be great if you once actually said something. Actually asked, and felt good about asking. How different things might be."

"I'll call you when I get to L.A."

"You don't have to bother."

"I'll call you anyway."

"What does *that* mean?"

"I'll call you."

"Maybe I'll be here," she said.

———

IN THAT SAME YEAR we videotaped Percy reminiscing by the bluff, a few of us thought it would be a great idea to also film all the members of his generation who had gathered that summer. Our parents and the rest of the surviving brothers and sisters. They didn't agree; they insisted they had nothing to say. They refused. It took me a while to understand what they didn't say: it would link them to Percy. They weren't going to die; and even more, they weren't going to think about it. Their refusal was about denial and their blockage manifested itself as certainty: a tried-and-true New England trait that ran as deep and as long as the winters.

We chose to ignore them and set the cameras going after the ice was literally and figuratively broken at one more cocktail party. They were gathered in a semicircle in the living room where I had tried that one morning to talk to my father about his drinking. Its mud-shade walls were unchanged except for a new set or two of moisture stains, but it was afternoon and there was light. In the west-falling sun the brown bloomed briefly. I sat on the floor and asked them to introduce themselves. Right away they started in.

Next to Percy, the oldest of my father's ten siblings was Dorothy, and she announced that she'd been conceived right here in this very house where we were and born on September 15, 1908, though she spent the first years of her life in Forest Hills, a section of Newark, while my grandfather worked in New Jersey. That was as far as she got before George interrupted her:

"You were born on September fifteenth, right?"

"Yes," Dorothy said. "That's right."

"Right. So going back in time and geography, right—"

"Sounds like Christmas," I said.

"Conceived in December," said George.

"Oh, I think you're getting very technical," my mother said, sensing trouble, and deeply liking to smooth things over. It was to no avail.

"I was born in September," Dorothy reiterated stubbornly.

"Right," George said. "But nine months before, it wasn't here because it was winter and we weren't here in the winters then, and nine months before, it wasn't here in this house because it wasn't here. It wasn't built yet."

"That's what I've always been told."

"Who was doing the telling?" I asked.

"Could be difficult to prove," George said, sipping his drink, over the lip of his glass, and my question went unanswered.

"George is a mathematical man," his wife cracked. "A genius, after all. You gotta look out."

"You don't have to be a mathematical genius," said George, "to figure that one out."

His taking his sister's story apart was a talent, maybe even a gift; it was also a cutting tool. He knew it, sipping his drink, his face trying to stay deadpan and not show self-satisfaction.

In the eight or nine years since Dorothy's cockamamie

mathematics the casualty list among those in the room had been extreme. More than half had gone, and for Dorothy, who recently died, it may have been an early warning of what was to happen to her, a heart that wouldn't stop but a mind that lost itself. She lingered for several years unable to talk or recognize anyone. Without our knowing it, we were witnesses at a last gathering.

When I looked at the video later I discovered that one of the cameras caught George in profile. A close-up. An old man, a vital man, with smooth skin, some tan, and no hair on his head. A few wrinkles knit about his eyes and across his forehead and a nest of veins wormed near his temple. A delicate divot of growth sprouted from his ear. His clothes were summer ones, well worn and familiar. Nothing was new; nothing had been for years. His pants were checked, and because he was so tall and his legs were so long there were a lot of checks. Until you saw his smile, it was his nose that was most arresting. It was a beak, a proboscis, a prow. This half-Roman, half-hooked hunk set like Gibraltar in the midst of his face.

The next winter at Percy's funeral his skin lost any color, drained to fish-belly white, and he keeled over. It was a shocking sight, a whole lot of height toppling. For a while, what seemed an unbelievably long while, the service continued. Everyone let him be. It got to be too much for me. I was close by, so I climbed over a pew and loosened his tie and checked his mouth to make sure he hadn't swallowed his tongue. Now everyone pitched in. The paramedics were called. We considered mouth-to-mouth, but there was a wispy breathing. Within minutes he was on his way to the hospital.

The diagnosis was dehydration. They plugged in an IV and for a couple of hours he was beyond kidding. He looked old and tired and a little bewildered. The better he got then, the more embarrassed he was by the incident and the more he wanted it over and forgotten. The jokes came then. They didn't last either. The next day George and Betty left early and he was well on his way to eradicating the experience. It had never happened.

But I had the memory of holding his head in my hands, feeling the shape of his skull. The way the bones set under the skin. The way it was wet at first and a disturbing color and heavy. That was it most of all, that heaviness. So heavy and unresponsive, as if it were only an object. A way-outsized cue ball, a leaden coconut, a rock the size of an enormous melon.

———

THE PLANE FROM KONA was delayed and I had to run from one terminal to another, then the long way down to the gate to catch the flight to Boston. I was still in shorts and soaked with sweat and I realized I hadn't had a chance to call Jenny. I tried from the plane and got a machine. I didn't leave a message and then spent another ten dollars to say I was sorry.

After landing in Boston I tried again. She picked up in the middle of my talking to her machine:

"How are you?"

"A little rattled."

I had expected the worst, but whenever I thought we were in a rhythm—bad or good—she would fool me. She had a corner on defying expectation.

"I'm not surprised," she said.

"I'm sorry again. I had to run—"

"I know how important he was to you."

Completely to my surprise I started to cry. More chokes really; my throat was making noises without my consent. I lost the power of speech.

"Say hello to your mother for me."

"I will."

"Send her my love."

"I will."

"Even Betty."

"I will," I said. "Can you come?"

"I don't know, John. We'll see."

FOR SEVERAL DAYS after the operation, if slowly, George had gotten better. The doctors were cautious but said in doctor-speak all the right things and optimism reigned. Everyone got busy forgetting the rule that surgery is an invasion, especially when you're older. An American artillery officer in Vietnam coined what became an infamous line about a place called Ben Tre. "We had to burn the ville to save it," he said. Surgery can share the same dark comic horror.

George was stuck with tubes—in his stomach, in his anus, up his nose, and down his throat. IVs, catheters, drains, oxygen. The tumor had been larger than suspected and it had taken a lot of cutting-away. His abdomen had been opened sternum to hip, and there trouble began. The stitches refused to heal. They wouldn't take and the acids started to leak through and poison his body. It was blamed on his age, not on any lack of surgeon's skill. It hadn't been mentioned before but now it was presented as unsurprising. It meant infection was all but certain and slowly it became clear the incision would possibly never close. They would have to keep George alive in a sterile environment and bypass his stomach and feed him intravenously.

This whole time George was conscious. So tubed up, he was not comfortable or happy and with a regulator jammed down his throat he couldn't talk, but he was awake and aware. From his bed he watched the activity around him. Nobody addressed him much directly and when they did they tended to shout. They thought somehow that if he couldn't speak he couldn't hear.

He was surrounded by a wishful chorus, saying to each other and to him he was getting better. For the first while it seemed he was, but even when it was clear he wasn't they were still saying it, wanting to believe it themselves. Betty wasn't tracking well. Not so surprising. Denial was in her bones, her very genes, and the doctors were sending a mixed message. The surgery that had been declared a success now was revealed to have been much more extensive than they had foreseen. Samantha, just arriving from California, didn't know what to do. For years she had struggled against her father and then, growing older, growing more conservative, growing more like her mother, she had acceded. Again he became the giant in her life, as he had been in her childhood.

The depleted and deflated sight of him now wouldn't compute. She didn't know how to handle it. What worked, her solution, was to refuse the truth of his condition. However dire he looked, it was temporary, an illusion. He was Big George and indestructible. The strength of her vision of him beat back the truth. She rejected reality. He was going to get better; he was not going to die. The blockage was exhausting. At the end of each day she went back to the house she had grown up in and where her parents still lived, and fell asleep like a stone. Only in the middle of the night, waking, was she suddenly rife with doubts. Alone in the dark she would break down. In the daylight again she refound her ability to just say no.

In the midst of this Mason and Beth drove over to see George. Now under a full oxygen mask George recognized them. He knew who they were, but they were shocked and alarmed. No one had prepared them for the condition he was in because those so close—Betty and Samantha—weren't accepting it.

After he was moved from ICU to semi-ICU there was a way to communicate with George. The hospital had a book-size tablet like a small blackboard. The alphabet, letter by letter, was printed around it and you could scribble words or phrases on it. While everyone was still full of encouragement, while the regulator still rendered him speechless, George took to pointing at the alphabet. One of the nurses, Trisha, no bigger than a gnat but with energy and attitude to burn, was amused that he always seemed to point to the same letters. Two of them, B and S. She didn't know why but he certainly was stubborn about it. Over and over. His long fingers would crook at them and, as he wasn't understood, they began to stab. S and B and B and S.

I don't know who caught on first—the answer was obvious, of course—but maybe that was because here was one more thing no one wanted to get. For three days this went on, the pointing and the growing deliberate lack of comprehension. Each day George was worse and each day the need to make a choice about his survival became more crucial.

While Beth was at the hospital visiting again, George grew animated. He was alert, his eyes were very alive, and he kept gesturing with his hand. Beth retrieved the blackboard but he didn't point. He waved off the blackboard. Instead, he made a new gesture: he drew his finger across his throat. Beth thought he must be thirsty. She offered him water, but wasn't sure how best to give it to him. The oxygen mask and the regulator were in the way. She peeled back a corner of the mask and with a moist cloth wiped the corners of his mouth and what she could of the rest of his face and his pale bald head. The skin was gelid and loose across his skull. He shook his head as she did and drew his finger across his throat once more. Beth stopped what she was doing, confused. A second thought occurred to her. There was talking around her—that certain chat we all fall into with patients in hospitals. He must be tired of it. Some quiet, please. She shushed everyone, but even before she could turn back George drew his finger across his throat a third time. Fearing what he meant now, wanting to be sure, Beth called Trisha over to the bed. With the two of them beside him George did it again. Very simply and very clearly. The two women looked at each other and knew.

Within hours the ventilator was pulled and he was taken off life support and within hours more, that same night, that same time as the grandfather clock stopped, that same time as I was swimming, he was gone.

———

IN THAT GREATEST GENERATION George came from everyone seemed to smoke. Both my parents, most every aunt and uncle, so many of their close friends. It was a drinking time and a smoking time. Ashtrays were as plentiful as place settings of china. People collected them and every flat surface wore one, purchased or piked or amassed from gifts. Every morning after they were heaped with butts. The smell of them fouled the air. It permeated everything, clothes, slipcovers, rugs, even the wallpaper.

It was Camels and Chesterfields and Lucky Strikes, regular and then king-size, and then there was a switch, the women first, to filters: L&Ms, Winstons, Marlboros, and then eventually the ones that claimed lower tar and nicotine, Kents and Salems. These were also the years of ripe-colored lipsticks. The stubs in the ashtrays, wherever they finally landed, were ringed in remnants of reds, ruby and garnet and crimson, and even shades as dark as blood.

My father prided himself on not getting sick, not admitting it anyway. Whatever his condition—whether a cold, a fever, or the aftereffects of his drinking—he never missed a day of work. Pleurisy changed that. It knocked him out, put him on his back in bed for two weeks. The first time I had ever seen him like that. The last thing he hungered for then was a cigarette. His Chesterfields lay on the table by the bed untouched. He was not interested in smoking, couldn't; he was too sick. Recovering at last, he found even then the thought of them was repellent. He said to himself and to us later, that was that. When he was well he would stop forever, and he did.

That was how my dad was with his word. If he gave it he kept it, but on his own terms and in his own time. For years he was a man, whether he admitted it or not, who had to know he was an alcoholic. Nothing stopped his drinking; it ran on, worsening, and out of control. It was only his stroke that changed that. In the illness, like before, he found the way to stop. After he was better—as better as he would get—he didn't talk about it. He never said a word, but he didn't drink again.

Once I asked George when and why he had quit smoking. For years, he said, people had ragged on him about its nasty effects and consequences. They didn't bother or defray him. He ignored them. This was long before the connection to cancer had been clinched. What stopped him was so typical and true of him.

On the golf course one day, getting out his driver, setting himself, George put his lit cigarette down in the grass. He happened to have a cold and a nagging cough. It was affecting his concentration and his play. It was hurting his game. He didn't like that. The man George was with had already quit smoking and was playing well. He didn't like that. George ripped into the ball, it made that sweet *swock* and sailed out well past two hundred and fifty yards, and he forgot the cigarette. He left it behind. He walked up the fairway feeling better, feeling good. His cough diminished, his play improved. So busy competing, he didn't make the connection at first. When he did, still playing, on the back nine now, winning now, he decided right then to stop, and he never smoked again.

I think back to George in his last years sitting on the stool he had set out beside his garden and his having trouble on the steps the summer my father died and only a winter before he did. His competitive fires never flagged. How could he not have wanted to outlive his brother, gain one last victory? And he had. If he wanted to live to the millennium, that was one thing he didn't achieve, but perhaps that wasn't a driving force. His survival was about his control and pride in himself, his own personal and private sense of space and grace, and when that was done—gone, taken from him—he made his decision the way he saw fit and the same way he had with cigarettes. Cut his losses, and when it came time, that included himself.

As with my father, I can wonder what George thought as he lay in the hospital those last days unable to talk but still clear in his mind. I have no idea except this was an immensely practical man, even more than an egotistical one. He was an actuary—he knew the odds—and I think he knew chillingly the actuality.

It is the nature of man to believe—at least in the fresh, sweet early years—that we are in charge of life's journey, that the course we plot, the wind we follow, what we say and what we do, is in control and ruled by the odds and will bring success and some safe harbor. Especially talented men, and certainly this one.

That was one of the things that had thrown George about Doug. His son's character and his son's destiny didn't fit the tables he knew so well and had lived by. Sometimes even created. Forget for a minute love, or the entrenched, unresolved battles that divided them and that were never repaired in time, so not ever. Stuck without reparations. You don't long outlive your own son. Doug shouldn't have died. It didn't make sense then and never would.

———

THE MEMORIAL SERVICE at the First Church of Christ wasn't well attended. It was only now that I realized suddenly how depleted our family had become. The remainder gathered in the front few pews. The rows behind us were empty, and then a few others scattered about the back of the church. George's peers were largely gone; he had outlived them, too.

The minister had a beard and was softly formed and softly mannered. No eulogy was planned and he confessed he was new to the parish and hadn't known George. "But in what I've heard in the last few days," he said, "I gather he was a man who was successful in business and he loved his family and his golf. I know you're all thinking of him. And that's what we're here for—to remember him. So now if anyone would like to share, memories or feelings or whatever, they're most welcome." He waited, and when no one spoke or rose he proceeded with the service.

Very quickly, it was all but complete. Again then the minister turned to us and inquired a last time if anyone wished to speak. I looked around, waiting—at his wife, his living son, his daughter, their spouses, his children's children. But silence answered him. No one moved. There were twenty-two of us first cousins on this side of the family. Close to a dozen of us were here, but we were frozen in what John Cheever called "the deep cartilage of our decorum." No one moved.

When we were children we sang a song in church:

> *I sing a song of the saints of God,*
> *patient and brave and true,*
> *who toiled and fought and lived and died*
> *for the Lord they loved and knew.*
> *And one was a doctor, . . .*
> *And one was a soldier and one was a priest,*
> *and one was slain by a fierce wild beast . . .*

Drop the saints and lose the fierce wild beast and our family fulfilled its verses. What had started as a Pilgrim woman mating with an English immigrant had spawned children and grandchildren that had spread across the country and splattered into surprising lifestyles, professions, and religions. Among us was practically one of everything, including a cousin who'd become a Quaker.

During her wedding ceremony, as in their meetings, there was a period of silence. It was long enough to make me, young then, uncomfortable. The quiet of the meeting room stretched until it changed. It became meditation. The room filled with breathing and the silence grew audible. Within it—

as hokey as it may sound—bred a bonding, a togetherness. And then people began to talk, a soft-spoken chorus wishing bride and groom well.

This silence brought that one to mind, but it felt different, hamstrung and haunted. It flew in the face of who George was: so long hale and hearty, so towering not only at the net but also in our lives.

A lesson to be had: be happy outlasting everyone who has anything to say about you, or die a lot earlier.

The minister said, "In that case let us conclude our remembrance of George Woolridge Young with the saying of the Lord's Prayer . . ."

I found myself standing then and walking forward and turning. The church looked very empty and I stood there. I realized I was angry, I was furious. How could this man go unspoken about? It was an insult, a travesty. I was still angry with him and I knew how important he was and I felt it now and I realized I had no choice. I had to say something, and it was about my dad and my uncle, and it was about the Spider and how large he was in several meanings of the word. How we loved and looked to him and fought against him and at times hated him and how big he had been for all of us. From these two men, and especially him, we had taken ferocious and coded, begotten and misbegotten lessons about what it was to be a man. Once again, I don't remember the exact words I said. I don't remember at all. I know what it would be in a script: the character would have trouble getting started, would gain purchase and, rising to the occasion, would cinch together his speech into eloquence and simple, moving human shape.

The others in the film would be there and they would be stirred and hopefully the audience—whether on television or in the theater—would be also and the music would rise and it would be another moment, one that would offer insight, release, tears, and culmination. Maybe even epiphany. I had seen the scene, I had written the scene myself, and I would see the scene again and many more times. This is how it concludes—with such a speech—and I had heard often as I watched such a scene the rustlings, those sounds in a crowd that seem like restlessness until you know them and know they're the cloaked sounds of weeping, even when I feel and I know it isn't done very well. It's expected, it finishes the sentence, it concludes the movie; it fills out the periodic table.

So why don't I remember and why does it matter? It doesn't, and maybe that's the point. I don't know whether I wrote and performed the scene well because I didn't have the distance. I don't remember because I was there, only there, too close and laid open and only there.

JENNY AND I WALKED from the church together and, make no mistake, I was glad she was there. I was still wrought up.

"I was afraid no one was going to speak."

"Do you want a compliment?"

"For doing so. Yes."

"You got a compliment."

"But why? He was so . . ." I fished for it again, what he was, and couldn't catch it.

"You did good."

"No, that's not what I mean."

"Others did speak after you did. Maybe because of you."

"No, it's not that either."

"I know," she said. "It is the end of something. First your dad. Now George. A one-two punch."

Back at the house after the service, the surfeit of food was as overwhelming as when Doug had come home. (Can't it be proved that casseroles came into existence simply to obliterate those who have survived?) It was summer, not winter, and the maples swung shadows across the screen porch and the house inside was sticky and wilting. The day was bright and my memories of 1969—other than the frozen day we had first tried to put Doug in the ground—all felt dark and of the night. Many of us who had been here then were here now. We were much older now—more than half of many of our lives had taken place since then—and looking around my mother felt it necessary to point out that all the males of my generation now had "potbellies." Some of us still looked good, worked out, but it was true. Skinniness was gone. There was this collection of stomachs on display. Including mine.

For a second time that night I found myself sleeping in Doug's room. It had long since become a sewing room and a storage space. His bed and almost all his things were gone. Only one shelf still memorialized him. His high-school diploma remained there along with three photographs. The copper-headed boy on the beach making a face into the camera and squinting into the sun. The Marine private standing with his mother the day he graduated from Camp LaJeune. The third picture, though, wasn't of Doug. He wasn't in it; his father was. In crisp black-and-white Lieutenant Colonel George W. Young being awarded the Legion of Merit by General Hoyt Vandenburg in September 1945.

There was yet one more thing on the shelf—Doug's Purple Heart for the wound "resulting in his death."

I looked at the row of them as I went to sleep and I couldn't help seeing them in the ghostly light when I woke in the night and in the first glary reflections of daylight when I woke again in the morning.

THE NEXT DAY, back in Massachusetts and before we left again for California, I went with Jenny to see where Doug lay and where George soon would. My father was just down the hill.

I asked, "What will happen to us?"

"Isn't that up to you?"

"Is it?"

I remembered one of the first times I had led her to cry she had put her head under my arm and toward my back so I couldn't see her face.

"Are you crying?" I had asked.

"No."

"What's that noise?"

"That's misting," she had said.

"What's the difference?"

"Misting is singular. When there is only one tear."

"That's cute."

"It's nothing."

"I hate it when you cry."

"You like it when I cry."

"That's bullshit."

"Is it?"

Her head and face reappeared. The tears—because that's what they were—brought rose and ginger up from the bottom of her complexion. She looked young, wounded, and quite beautiful, and I wanted to lick the wet from her face and suck the sorrow out of her eyes.

"Yes," I had answered to the same question, but I wondered now and wasn't so sure.

These many years later in the cemetery Jen considered a moment and then she said, "I don't know why I loved you in the first place and I don't know how I loved you for so long. Just when you were being awful you'd do something, sometimes *ridiculously* small, and redeem yourself." She looked at me, maybe to protect herself, somewhere between laughter and disdain. "Now you want another compliment, don't you? An example. Okay. It could be so small. A look. You'd notice something I had done or cared about when I was sure you hadn't or wouldn't. You're a very good noticer. It could be with the kids and you'd be being so obnoxious and they'd want to go somewhere and you just wanted to watch television and you'd ignore them until I'd want to scream or was screaming and you'd roll your eyes and call them over. You'd make them sit on you, all of them, all on you and you'd hold them and start talking to them and not let them go, and they'd be laughing and bearable and happy again. Of course, you'd still be watching the television the whole time."

We had a heavy-laden history, inextricable yet beyond quietus.

"What should we do?" I said again, plaintively.

"You have a vote in this, you know."

I turned her around dramatically and looked at her fine and weathered face and said for the first time: "I fucked up, you know that. And that's not it. I lost myself along the way as much as I tried to hold on. You know I held on to you and blamed you, and couldn't see you at last for you. I know now I love you and I always will, more than I ever knew and ever showed, but I need to find out now how to go on and not carry with me all that my family—not you but George and Bill and Doug and my mother and all the others—has set ticking inside me."

15

THE THURSDAY AFTER my father died Betty got a letter in the mail. It wasn't the first such communication she and George had received. Sometime before, a phone call from a man looking for the parents of Douglas W. Young. The man claimed to have served with him and said he would like to come and talk to them. Why? What did he want? It was Betty's nature to be wary and suspicious. Thirty years and now he calls. She wasn't buying it. She called the local Marine office and they bore out her caution. In the wind like a virus was an outbreak of fleecing attempts against aging parents of men who had served in Nam: I was with your son, he was great, can you make a contribution to dot-dot-dot? Here, give me your credit-card number. And the expiration date? But the man had never called back. Now this letter.

Betty read it and didn't show it to George. She threw the letter away, done with it. It sat in the trash but she kept checking to see if it was still there. For three days the wastebasket altered her normal path around the house and then, largely disgusted at herself, she took the letter back out of the trash and read it a second time.

A man named Rae Sincennes had written it and he lived on the Gulf Coast near Houston, Texas. He had looked up the ledger of the Vietnam War Memorial on the Internet and found Doug's information and was asking permission to come up from Texas to see them. It would be at their convenience. He wouldn't take up much of their time. It was something he needed to do, he said. Here is my phone number. Please call me.

Betty wasn't easy pickings. She was hardy New England stock; her genes intimated she could live to be a hundred. Her handsome face was scribbled with a thicket of tight-knit lines, very fine ones like a spider's web, and her mouth had started to fold in on itself. She could be warm and winning, surprisingly tender, or she could be scathing. Her moods were impossible to predict. She'd blurt out whatever she thought without censorship or apology, and without realizing it. A quick sample of the menu: at one gathering Betty called out from across the room plenty loud enough for all to hear, "What's the matter, John, aren't you going to kiss me? It's okay. I won't bite." So I went to her and she puckered up. "See, I've had my shots," she said. At another, thinking she must be tired, I let my hand fall to her shoulder consolingly and she spun away. "What's the matter with you?" she hissed, teeth bared. "Don't touch me."

Repression wound her up tight. She was parsimonious and at times unwrapped. A year after Doug died I received a letter on his stationery. I'm looking at the name and return address of a dead man. It was unsettling and it was crazy; it gave me the heebie-jeebies. It was from Betty and I wasn't alone. So it wouldn't go to waste, she used his stationery, crossing out his name at the top of each page, until it was all gone.

Her son's death was something she didn't talk about. In her mind she had successfully dealt with it. She willed it away; she shut down thinking about it until she no longer did, until on as many conscious and unconscious levels as she could muster and wring into control it didn't exist. The letter was a can opener. The words and even the writing of this boy—well, no longer a boy—from Texas. The letter found its way into her pocket. She shoved it there and carried it around, moving it out of dirty clothes and into clean clothes when she changed. She still didn't tell George. On a rainy day, after marketing, she discovered the letter had gotten wet. The ink had smeared and the phone number was no longer clear. She started to cry. She didn't know it was happening until a drop further dampened the page. She went to the phone and on the fourth guess at what the number was she found herself talking to Rae Sincennes. He was on a Delta flight the next morning.

It was only then that she approached her husband in the garden.

"The rabbits aren't getting in this year," he said as she approached.

"It looks like a prison."

He had rigged a fence around the rectangular area and a second one around the lettuce. The fencing wasn't high, but the crosshatch of the wire was close-knit.

"They're pretty enterprising. They may look cute—"

"I never said that."

"They're a damn nuisance."

"Surprised you don't have—what's that wire called?"

"What wire?"

"They use it in prisons and it comes in coils." She was taking her time getting to it.

"Concertina."

"That's it."

"If it'll work I'll use it."

He had been weeding with a rig he had tinkered together, clippers set with a spring and clamped to a forty-two-inch-long handle. It looked a little like a dinky posthole digger. With it he could pluck, cut, or chop the weeds while still standing up. The days of full-on bending were over. Now he was checking the netting over the blueberries that kept the birds at bay and getting the hose ready to water.

"There's some man coming by this afternoon."

"Oh. Where's the water pressure?"

"The hose is scrunched."

"Give it a kick, will you. What do you think about more beefsteaks next year?"

"He says he knew Doug."

"Give it another kick." It began to register. "What?"

"That's what he says."

"I've got to go to Agway." The name then of the garden supply store.

"That's what he says."

"Who's going to drive me?" He had given up driving a year before.

"I'm going to see him."

"I'll guess I'll have to drive myself."

"I'm not going to let you drive."

"Doug."

"That's what he says."

"Elizabeth, you can include me out."

"What do you think—he'll take advantage of me?" She said it gaily, as if she were talking about sex, not duplicity.

He realized what few others would have: she was dressed up. It wasn't fancy; she was just cleanly and carefully dressed. Clearly, the fat was in the fire. "I don't like this."

"George, you're staying right here. You're not going to run out on me."

"I don't want to stir things up."

"Hah!"

"I don't want to fight."

"Fighting? Who's fighting? You want to see fighting?"

"I'm going to turn the hose off and put it away and put the tools away and clean up. Maybe I'll go over and see how Mason's garden is doing."

"It's too late."

A car had pulled up and a man was getting out. He wore a sports jacket that was wrinkled from flying and driving and an open-collared shirt. His head was shaved smooth and his skin was malt shade. Deep dusty-gray circles under his eyes were beginning to crepe and he had a dark splotch of a birthmark like a splattered tear below his left eye. He was African-American.

"Mr. and Mrs. Young," he said. "I'm Rae Sincennes."

It was George who stepped forward and spoke first and shook his hand: "George Young, and this is my wife. What can we offer you to drink? I was about to have a cocktail myself."

BY HAPPENSTANCE, knowing nothing, I arrived as Rae Sincennes left and couldn't stop myself from asking: "Who was that?"

"That was something," said Betty. I could see how undone she was. She'd been crying and she was laughing now. Her perennial shifts were even more sudden and electric than normal. "Who knew?"

"Knew what?"

"That was Rae Sincennes."

"Who?"

"He's from Texas."

"Who?" I might as well have been an owl. "What was he doing here?"

"He's going back now. He couldn't stay. He said he was his angel."

I dropped in some more futile whos and whats.

"I guess that takes care of that."

"I don't understand, Betty."

"All the way from Texas to say for twenty-nine years he's been waiting to tell. He was so new—he had some word for it . . ."

"FNG?"

"Is that a word?"

"An acronym."

"For what?"

"For a New Guy." I omitted a word; I didn't say Fucking New Guy.

"He was so new, so new, and he begged off. Doug went in his place. Doug volunteered. He walked on point, that's what he called it. For twenty-nine years, he says, Doug's been his guardian angel. Can you imagine that?"

I realized George was curiously absent. The meeter and greeter with his perfected ebullience always on display. "Is George here?" I asked.

"Oh, he's inside somewhere."

"Did he hear too?"

"He wouldn't go back to work. That George. George after it happened, after our Dougy was killed. To have all those people try and say something to you and have to answer *something*. He couldn't stand it. He kept putting it off." The can was way open now. "His friends, his secretary, he didn't want to see them. And everybody knew. Even those from other companies. He was a big guy and they all wanted him to know how they felt. How sorry they were. Even the golf club wasn't safe. He felt too naked. He wouldn't leave the house. I had to kick him out finally and then I was alone. I'm always alone but then I was, I really was, and I had nothing to do and I cried and cried and cried. And then—that was that."

George came outside now from inside the house. I wondered for a moment if he had needed time to re-collect himself and fit the parts that had been so long compounded into smiling denial back into the shape he was so used to. He didn't notice me.

"Well, Elizabeth," he said, "let's get going. I need that fertilizer, the Agway closes at five."

"I'm not going to get fertilizer this afternoon."

"I can't let this whole afternoon go by like this and get nothing done."

"Nothing done." She wasn't really asking a question. She was disagreeing.

"You know what I mean."

"I have no idea what you mean. I've never had any idea."

"Let's not go down that road."

"I'll go down any road I want."

They were snapping at each other, getting their rhythm and habit going, but it felt phoned-in and benign, and George didn't respond to her. He set the piece of paper he had been holding down on a table on the screen porch and walked out into the yard. He reached the edge of the bluff and stopped and stood facing away from us. I found myself looking at the paper on the table. It was a Xerox of an old mimeograph, the sort that once would have been purple and when it was freshly printed had a sweet mixed-up scent of perfume and glue. It was a copy of the memorial service the men of the third platoon, C Company, First Marines, had held for Doug in the province of Quang Nam in the vicinity of Da Nang after he died and that Rae Sincennes had saved ever since. Twenty-nine years later it finally reached the parents of the boy-man it honored.

After a while I put the paper down again. George was still at the edge of the bluff and I joined him there. For the first time he became aware of me.

"John, hey, hi. I didn't know you were here. Did you just get back?"

"I flew back yesterday." I had returned briefly to Los Angeles following my father's funeral.

He wasn't really listening to me. He could have been listening to the light surf and for the faint wind, but he wasn't.

After Doug had gone to Vietnam, he wrote his parents a number of letters I've never seen, and they may well be long gone. Apparently at first they were long, descriptive and sardonic, and then they grew shorter and shorter. The last few were only a paragraph or two and the last it was said held only one sentence and four words. "I'm okay. Love, Doug."

George kept putting off writing back to him. He meant to, he had every intention to, but he didn't know what to say. George didn't understand Vietnam and he didn't understand his son and he didn't understand how his son had ended up there. For years they had had trouble and it had gotten worse. When Doug lost interest in college and flunked out, mostly intentionally, George was vituperative. They had a horrendous shouting match and then they both withdrew and George wouldn't speak to his son. Once Doug was drafted the rupture calmed down; it was no longer explosive, but it wasn't any better and in some ways worse. They couldn't find a way to say anything to each other. The parting when Doug went into the Marines was all but silent and once sent to California Doug never made it back home before he shipped out. I ended up being the last one to see him alive.

Finally, George sat down and wrote a letter. He put on his business hat to do it, dictated it to his secretary, and then delayed mailing it. Even to him it felt stiff. He tried again, writing it himself in longhand, but the letter was still on his desk when Doug was killed. He wasn't alone. I hadn't written him either.

In a sense Rae Sincennes had brought three decades later a letter back from Doug. George had covered his grief. The well of it had been set underground, long planted, he thought, and now it was open again and despite all his disciplined acumen at distancing it felt deeper than ever.

I said, "I came by to hit some golf balls."

"Now that's a good idea," he said.

So once again we drove some. There was no black night this time. This was the middle of the day and George was much older. His hips didn't work well. The plastic replacement parts didn't like to rotate or swivel. Arthritis bound the loose elasticity of his swing. But there was still the loose wiggle-waggle and his pleasure at any well-hit one and amused tolerance or laughter at my enduring ineptitude. We hit a number and before we were done were joined by the next generation, Jake and his cousin Bill and some of his friends. We dotted the beach and the shallows of the Atlantic with old balls.

The street was hot as Jake and I walked home. It had been repaved since Doug and I had walked it, daring each other barefoot along its baking blacktop. The childhood scent of tar felt like it was still in my nostrils—I could exactly recollect it—but it wasn't so hot and I wasn't barefoot anymore. We had left the house my grandfather had built and my aunt and uncle now owned and we passed the house Mason had bought on the way to our own, and I thought again of Doug as I often did and always would on this street.

On this day when Rae Sincennes had come you'd think such a thought would have to be deep or meaningful or revelatory, but it wasn't. Before we were teenagers we had taken the ferry over from Woods Hole to Nantucket to stay with Betty's mother, Doug's grandmother, for a few days. The island had no movie theatre then. An old meeting hall, a swatch of wooden floor with a stage at one end, served the purpose: on weekends a place to show films. The movies could be old or new, the seats were folding wooden chairs, and the screen was high up and the space was always jammed.

The night we went only the front row was left. We sat wedged against our neighbors and each other with our necks craned back, gazing heavenwards. I'm trying to remember why we even went and can't. The movie that was showing was ancient; it was silent, in black-and-white, and we'd never heard of it. We were uncomfortable, sure we would be bored, and we almost left. We kept hesitating, debating, and I don't know why we didn't.

In the movie Charlie Chaplin carved up an old shoe that sat on a plate. He was going to eat it. The shoe didn't want to be cut or stay on the plate. He was desperately hungry and the leather was complete gristle. Chaplin hacked at it, sawed it, pounded it, and chewed it with increasing frenzy and futility. Doug started to laugh, both of us did, everyone did. His crackling laugh was like his father's in this way: it was wonderfully contagious, and we laughed and could not stop. We laughed until our sides ached and our tears ran, and we could not stop.

16

IN AUGUST 1969, even before I moved to California, Doug wrote me from Monterey where he was waiting to be shipped out, getting a crash course in the Vietnamese language. He liked California, he said, it was "definitely decent" and suggested we get together if I came west.

His letter was full of tales about the craziness of the military. It was funny to him how upside down and petty the Marines were. At boot camp every minute had been taken up. There was no escape and no free time and no "slack." He had then made his way through infantry training, staging (which was supposed to be final preparation for Vietnam), and now this detour to language school. Each step and each place proved to be less regimented, more chaotic and rife with waste. Slack (a word he liked) and more slack. One thing to be learned at all costs seemed to be how to "skate," slide out of work. "Drinking beer and shooting shit for a lifetime? WOW. I just don't need it," he wrote.

It was insane to him, and dangerous. Was Vietnam going to be like that? Still he was undaunted. He wanted to see the world and what a war was. He had never seen death. Destruction, he wrote, fascinated him as much as creation.

His letter was handwritten, several pages long, and young—

as we both were—and he ended it with "beating the draft is worth just about anything. Chao ong. Doug."

IN LATE OCTOBER, the last weekend before he shipped out, Doug did come to visit me. I had been in Los Angeles for maybe a month by then and he came down by plane from the Monterey Peninsula. He didn't bring his uniform and he only wanted to do the simplest of things: go to the beach, see the movie *Easy Rider,* drive a car the length of Sunset Boulevard to the Pacific Coast Highway.

That Friday night was his twenty-first birthday. The proper thing was to fete him, but I hadn't much to offer him in the way of celebration. So recently arrived, I knew hardly anyone yet. For me, and many, Los Angeles proved a difficult place to make friends and find a community. That would take years, and even then, at least in my case, it seemed circumscribed around work. Doug didn't think the date or what it popularly meant was such a large deal (his phrase). No matter, we foraged to a bar for his first legal drink and to a strip show at a joint ridden with tourists—not so much from across the country as from West Covina and Torrance and El Segundo—called the Body Shop that I think is still there.

Before long we abandoned it and drove along the crowded length of Hollywood Boulevard and the Sunset Strip. It was 1969 and drifting about the famous sidewalks with the stars set into them were motorcycle kings; cases of red, lost, dope-soaked eyes; the young and the married stepping out for the evening; Salvation Army singers; and beggars with beards, musicians with beards, hipsters with beards, beards with beards.

At one point we stopped for gas and attempted to find a bathroom. The gas station, we discovered, shut and locked theirs at dusk. Friday-night jams of people on the Strip and no cans. And why did it seem unsurprising that in attempting to restart the car we found the battery had died? While an attendant was working with jumper cables I made another futile search down the block. When I returned, hip-hopping, Doug was sitting in the front seat laughing. At first I thought it was at me (though certainly it was at the failure on my face and in my body language), but really it was at the predicament. A laughter without rancor and one I couldn't help joining.

Saturday we went up into the Hollywood Hills to help in the making of a student movie. It was a dry and crystal-clear day, clean and unusual, especially then, for L.A. Most of making a movie, even a student film, is about waiting, and we waited and ate and occasionally got our faces photographed in the background of a party scene. The film was about the masks we wear and hide behind in our everyday lives. It was full of masks, literal and figurative, and was heavy with symbols and metaphors and supposed meaning. This was a world I was just becoming part of, but much of the point was beyond me and I'm sure beyond Doug. The whole enterprise must have left him askance. Coming from where he was, going where he was going, it had to seem silly. That night we went and saw westerns at a retrospective and all around was talk of movies.

When we came back to the empty apartment it was late. We sat in the small, bare living room. There were two director's chairs, a desk, a lamp, and some big throw pillows on the floor. We sat in the chairs and put our feet up on opposite sides of the desk. Doug seemed very removed and distant.

"Any earthshaking thoughts?" I asked.

He smiled what seemed self-sufficiently. "Not yet."

We were silent for a while, as we had been many times before, in the Sailfish, in the garage or attic of our grandmother's house, on the balcony in San Francisco before jumping into the pool that one time we had been in California together before, and that was an inherited and inevitable part of ourselves. We leaned back in the chairs, balancing on the back legs, our feet extending toward each other across the desk.

"I was throwing away junk before all this," he said then,

"and I came across a list we made which you sent me years ago but years after we made it in the Big House. What were the two letters?"

He looked at me as if I would remember (which I did) and he wouldn't, but it was he who answered his own question. "C.S.," he said.

We started then calling off the adjectives we had tagged onto these opening letters what even then seemed long ago—"Cork Screw," "Certified Snob," "Crusted Scab," "Complete Shit"— and we began to laugh once again. This was a different laughter than earlier, less loud and less funny, a bit struggled, but a conscious hitching together by Doug of our memories together.

We didn't talk about girls. We seldom had. So much time together before they mattered but not much time afterward. Separate schools and different summer jobs had kept us increasingly apart. We fell back again on the subjects that had once hinged us and been enough. I think it was something else too: a mutual naïveté and inexperience. We were both alone and didn't know enough and weren't secure enough to even brag.

Sunday we saw the movie he wanted to see, *Easy Rider*. I never saw it again and had long since dismissed it—a movie of then, about then and only then—until recently I happened onto it in deep cable. It was true; it looked amateurish and antique. What I had forgotten, though, was its immediacy. The parts that were funny, freshly funny, then were still funny now, and its visceral impact was surprisingly intact, if in a different way. Time had altered its reason to be shocking. The ending, manipulative and melodramatic, had meant to be a statement then about the reactionary forces loose in the country. How dangerous they were, how they couldn't stand nonconformity. How they didn't understand freedom. A little gratuitous, even darkly wishful, a rebel's romantic statement. But today you just don't end movies that way anymore. It would be a far braver act or a far stupider one. The call for a happy or victorious ending is sweeping and mandatory, lashed to the unforgiving currency of the bottom line.

After the movie Doug and I borrowed an acquaintance's Peugeot station wagon and drove the rest of the length of Sunset Boulevard to the sea and north on the Pacific Coast Highway. We stopped out beyond Malibu where the wildness was still then. Parked above the ocean, we watched the sun fall in a canyon that was desperately waiting for rain. The air seemed dusty with dry earth and late light and smelled like sheepskin with a twist of menthol from eucalyptus. We talked about our parents and our families and the rest of our lives. As close as we had been those two days, that weekend showed us we weren't so much any longer. Our link of nostalgia and disillusionment wasn't sufficient. He was on the change, not the same as he had been in San Francisco. The highjinks were gone from him. His experience and the possible foolishness of what I was up to, writing and writing for movies, had begun to separate us.

This was his last weekend before Vietnam and I realized I hadn't gotten him a date, helped him get laid, or have, if not a remarkable time, maybe just a good one.

"I guess this film stuff is pretty silly," I said limply.

"I guess it is. A lot of games." He smiled his protected smile that seemed to hold back a final bit of information. Then he made an open palm gesture with his hands as if accepting the various kinds of human foolishness. "But what isn't?"

"Maybe what you're up to."

"I wouldn't go that far."

After another while I asked, "Any ideas on what you're going to do eventually?"

"Maybe I should take up golf."

"That'll never happen."

"You're right," he said. "Maybe try college again."

"Maybe you shouldn't go."

"To Vietnam? It's a little late for that."

"Don't go."

"You're serious."

"I don't know. The war sucks and it's not even a war really. Undeclared."

"What, are you picketing and occupying buildings?"

"Not enough, maybe."

"What do you really think?"

"I think I don't know and it sucks."

"I think I don't know, but I've got nothing here and I want to go. There are things to see and I want to see them."

I started to argue with him, not about anything foretold, not about wanting to see things, but the how and the where, the choices we had made. But what was mine so far after all? Doug seemed to know my mind and the answer anyway:

"You know, I'm not like you," he said. "I think you know who you are, or at least what you want to do, and I can mock it, but I also envy it. I don't. And I'm not really a part of the family. I don't know what I am. I hate my father. I hate my mother. And of course I love them."

"Jesus," I said.

"I know," he said. "I just want to go, get on with it and find out."

"Find out what?" I asked.

"I don't know." He laughed before growing serious again. "Something. Something other than all the shit of our growing up."

"This may sound stupid," I said, "but if you find out anything you didn't know, let me know."

He felt through the words for their meaning and then gave a short laugh. "Okay. If I find out anything I didn't know."

When we got to the airport we shook hands—we didn't hug—and Doug without any more words walked through the gate toward the future, decent (as he would say) and curious, with an equanimity that under far easier circumstances I could not muster.

Beyond any politics, the truth was I didn't know who I was

yet, and the not knowing and the love and not knowing even how to say that silenced me. But he was at this moment— however subjugated in a crushing bureaucracy, the U.S. military, specifically the Marines—contemplating a true radicalism. His own kind of revolutionary. He was, within the limits of his not inconsiderable abilities and his upbringing, ready to chuck it all for he knew not yet what. He looked conservative; his hair was crew-cut while I was letting mine grow to the shoulders, in lockstep with the rebellion of the time. A rebellion that threatened to change everything but that in fact changed little, including me. My luck and gift was to have a chance to write about it, sometimes sending it up, sometimes trying to make meaning of the country that had formed us both. Yet I can only wonder now where his uninterrupted journey might have taken him.

I never heard from him again except for a single postcard with a picture of a water buffalo on it and this on the flip side:

There's this Colonel who has sod flown in and some grunt to cut it and take care of it so he can drive golf balls or putt or some such bullshit.

There's no escape.

———

I THINK OF THE TRICKS memory plays on us and the tricks we play on it.

When I was in college I was very taken by Lillian Hellman's life as portrayed in her memoirs. Her tough relish for truth, her romance with Hammett, even photographs of her. Her plays I knew little about. She had a great jaw, an ugly beauty of a face beset with creases and whorls that seemed well earned, and when I saw her interviewed once on television there was this deep, guttural, rip-roaring, head-thrown-back howl. She was famous for not naming names, for not cutting her conscience to this year's fashion. She carried honesty and integrity with what seemed great, fought-for, almost primitive pride. She looked rough-hewn and her prose had a struggled yet chiseled plainness. There was clearly art in it but no fuss, no fanciness. She cornered anti-bullshit.

And then the stories began to come. The words she had so notably spoken she hadn't really, not exactly. The ones best known and most quoted were written, or at least polished, after the fact. The slow leakage of fabrication picked up speed, turned from a trickle into a torrent. Some, maybe much, even all, of what she had written was called into question. So famous for truth, in John Gregory Dunne's words, she became infamous for fiddling with it. For lying. It seemed in no small way she had made herself and her life up. She had cut the cloth of it to suit her own fashion. She had made a whole new coat. Hellman, rather desperately by the end, airbrushed her spoor. She used forgetting as well as remembering. She not only covered her tracks, she created new ones. Fiction offered, honored, and sold as truth, as nonfiction, as autobiography. Still, even reading *Pentimento* now knowing that, it remains powerful, alluring, and seductive. What did that finally mean?

One thing I came to know: she wasn't alone. The literary and not only literary giants of my youth, the icons, made themselves up and over, and the more mythic, the more successfully so. Their lives were their stories and they were the storytellers. Hellman, Hemingway, Karen Blixen, Muhammad Ali, John Ford, Sam Peckinpah, to name a few (not to mention Lincoln, Kennedy, Billy Tipton, Howard Cosell, and probably John Dillinger). I had lived in a place—Hollywood—that coveted and practically prided itself on such successful makeovers to escape their original selves and in their prodigal pursuit of the Big Recognition. And who is to say that it hasn't always been and won't always be true?

Was it the same in a sense with Doug and myself? Is this a memoir or in some sense an anti-memoir? Or even, as one friend insisted, a *man-war*. More than that, as Dunne had gone on to say, isn't that what we all do—"invoke the possibilities of nuances beyond the facts"? I had known the kid, the boy, and the adolescent. I never knew the man. There was not yet a man to know. I didn't know his last years, the end of school and the day-to-day in the Marines. I did not know what he had seen and thought and wondered and discovered in Vietnam. I did not know exactly how he had died nor what "friendly fire" finally meant except it was deadly and he wasn't alone in it. The estimates of those it consumed were disputed and disturbingly high.

When we are young we think it will last forever and when we look back it seems like it lasted only a minute and a half. For Doug it did last forever. And it is easy when someone young dies, especially one we love, to ennoble him. The images we have freeze and engrave in our minds and we invest them. They are at once left in time and yanked out of time. The promise becomes our vision and becomes a defining moment touched with illusion not unlike the captivating allure of Katharine Ross's initial screen appearance in *The Graduate*.

Would Doug be bald and bellied and living in Connecticut now with 2.5 children and voting Republican? Would he be telling war stories? Would he be the one reading the "fractured French" coasters? Would he have seen too much and, as in my father's tale of risk, have turned away? Would he be on an island, living out where life had taken him, marriages come and gone, tinkering on I know not what, and not caring about what still holds me and so many of us, the roots of ourselves? And where would that twin be, the one we all carry with us, that quality of fear that controls us or goads us and that at our choice grants us light or steals it?

There was no way to know, and my lack of knowledge is manifest. I don't even have the tarot cards. Yet I hold on to and ruminate and write about the crumbs of him that are left in the shiftings of my memory, to save them from perishing and to piece them together impossibly into a whole, and I cannot stop.

———

IN NOVEMBER 1982 I went to the dedication of the Vietnam Memorial in Washington. I didn't know what to expect. Its design had engendered a firestorm; it had been scathingly christened "the Black Gash" by some, an intended insult that soon would melt away.

It was a lazy modern V cut into the earth like a great Braque bird, its black marble slabs, its two wings, together nearly two football fields long. The walkways and curbing were dark gray granite and the grass was already trampled, made mud by feet and rain even before the official ceremony and by the time I descended into it.

And that's what you did. Descend.

The truth and power of it was that it took you underground. It buried you along with those who had died. It was a wall, a foxhole, dark and dour and dank, and it was a sculpture—which was undeniable as you stood next to its magnitude and its simplicity—and a work of art. It was nearly ten and a half feet high at its vertex and yet the trees beyond and above it were at play, that day the leaves alive with wind and the last of autumn, and above them there was a rush of light and the gift of the sky.

But first and finally there were the names. Each man and woman who had died was etched on the Wall. Here the dead were not forgotten and here I was not alone. Many stood beside me that first time, and many were beside me when I came later in the day and then in the night and then in the years to come. In sunlight or in snow, whatever the weather, I was never alone and we would look at the names. We would silently read them in the reflective apparition of our own faces. Wasps and Italians and Armenians and Jews and Blacks and Chicanos and Indians and officers and grunts. All these Americans. In their absence and presence we felt the loss of them and the recognition of them at once. We were part with the names—along with the Wall that carried them and called them out, along with the carved-out earth within which we stood—of what is ours, what is us, good and bad, there and here, Vietnam and D.C., American.

The Wall offered them up—these marble names in an American church, 57,939 then, 58,238 now, and more to come still—to those who came in sorrow and rage and need and grief and in search of solace, and they wept and they spat and they laughed and in reunion and release they relived the best and the worst of what they and we had, and they kept on coming and haven't stopped yet. "Remember . . . remember . . . remember . . ." one man in battered camo fatigues kept saying that day, and couldn't stop saying it. What was said there often became refrains, cantos of sorrow and release.

The faces of these men and women who had come to the Wall to find a name made their own etchings. I had seen again the photographs of the faces of the men at Khe Sanh, and I couldn't help seeing those who were here now. They were the families of the names and they were those who had served with the names and some were old and some had grown old and some were still young, and they reached out, reached their hands out, reached out with large or small, smooth or gnarled or knuckly fingers to the names on the Wall. One man traced the nook and cranny of each bevel of each letter of a name. Another had to climb a ladder to reach a name. Another got down on his knees as if in prayer to get close to a name. One took his fatigue sleeve and rubbed a name, small concentrated concentric circles, as if to rub the name not only clean but out.

All manner of feeling was here—as there would be each time I came—and it roiled me up inside, brought it all back, the horror and the anger and the uncertainty, the terrible sadness, the waste, and I found Doug's name. I touched it and traced it too and remembered him and mourned him, and not immediately or instantly, I'm not even sure exactly when, there was and would be a piece of healing and a particle of letting go.

———

IT WASN'T SURPRISING, I guess, that I dreamt of Doug again not long after that. There was a gathering, a memorial to mark his death ten or fifteen years after it had happened, which meant in that time in the early eighties. The shock was that Doug was there. I was holding him around the neck in what seemed a playful, affectionate sort of full nelson. There was an edge to it. It could have been a stranglehold; and in a dream, certainly this dream, there was an awareness of the cutthroat potential even in the affection. George Jr. said some words, a speech, something I couldn't imagine in life, and his father did something that by morning I couldn't remember and could only wonder why not. The wind gusted Sam's skirt to her and she lowered it and began to dance. Her pantyhose were translucent and she wore no underwear and the shapes of her were clearly visible and the sheen of the nylon was phosphorescent. She did not stop. In her movements she seemed to gather heat and light and collect around her those indecipherable touchstones of desire. She danced in troubling radiance, awash in light that didn't seem seamy or beneath board. It bathed her, played through her, and seemed to issue from her divined with both beauty and terror.

And Doug? Was it Doug? I was never quite sure it was Doug. Or whether it was a body I was holding up, or even a tall skinny dummy. In the dream I never saw him face-front. I only got to see the back of his head, his reddish hair, some pale skin, and an ear, the ear that Sam had looked at and commented on when he was in his coffin.

The dream felt true and far too enigmatic. Its allure outstripped its meaning, and left me without answers of any kind.

ACROSS THE YEARS I had tried somewhat haphazardly to find out about the day Doug died and what had happened.

The truth is I hadn't tried hard—and at some level that wasn't the source or object of my interest. The particulars of his death were not my exact obsession, not then. I don't know when or how we first found out that Doug was listed as killed by "friendly fire," and on one website as "murdered by accident." It opened the possibility of mystery, but it also made his death sadder and more useless. It blew the head off of the tragedy of it and made it pathetic. It was no wonder my aunt and uncle, and maybe all of us, wanted it to go away.

That second time I was in Vietnam I thought at least I could find where Doug had died. It was a misguided hope. I had by now found out what information the Marines had to offer. It was in a kind of shorthand: mysterious to the layman and not much less so when it was explicated. The data they offered didn't add up to much. It had Doug classified as a language specialist in one place and a file clerk in another. It had his place of death as Quang Nam Province, which included Da Nang, but was no more specific. Searching further, as far as you could easily go, it had his death categorized as "by other than enemy fire."

Not even then, only later, only now as I was writing did I bear down to investigate. Official records exhausted, I came to question my aunt Betty about what she remembered. I hoped to see again the copy of the memorial service that I had glimpsed on the table on the screen porch and get Rae Sincennes's phone number and call him. It didn't take Betty long to respond. Her answer was unequivocal, she said no. She wouldn't show me or help me. It was done. She didn't want to dredge up the past anymore. It was done. It did no good. It was done. Done. Remains Non-Viewable.

No.

I asked Samantha to intervene. She said she would approach her mother and ask her again. She never called back, and finally I called her again, only to learn her mother had said the same thing to her.

No.

"But I think I have a copy of the service," Samantha said as we talked.

"Could you make me one?" I asked.

"I know it's around here somewhere."

"You could just send it to me."

"No, that's all right." She was on a cordless phone and walking. "I can find it."

"I don't want to put you out." Which was very true but not the whole truth.

"Here it is."

"Great. Fax it if you want."

"It's not very clear. I don't know if it will copy or fax very well."

"Well," I said, "read it to me then."

"How do I describe it?"

"What size is it? What does it look like?"

"I guess it's eight-and-a-half by eleven and typewritten— you know, like those old mimeograph machines."

"The ones that were purple and smelled at first. Smelled good at first."

"Like that, and folded. On the outside, I guess like a cover, is some sort of picture or drawing. Whatever it is it's very black and it photocopied very poorly. My mother thought it was soldiers, a line of them in the grass. Anyway, it's not very clear. Grass, blue sky, a lot of foreground, and these shapes."

"What does it say?"

"'In Memoriam. Douglas Young.' And the dates, a summary of his career, awards, survived by . . .'" She came to a stop.

"Where was it held?"

"Logistic Command Da Nang. 26 December 1969. And then there's a prayer."

"What prayer?" I felt, as I had sometimes before, like the question man, but I wanted to know as much as I could.

"'I will fear no evil for thou art with me.' Psalm 23:4, and then there's an opening sentence and an invocation . . .'"

There was a pause, a silence, and even through the cordless phone, a less-than-superior piece of merchandise now some staticky distance from its cradle, I could hear her take a breath.

"I changed my mind," she said then. "I can't do it."

I said nothing, I'm sure wondering how we had suddenly gotten to here and how I could change her mind, but had no chance to before she said, "Why are you doing this?"

I said, "I'm not trying to do anything. I started writing, not only about Doug, and I suddenly realized how little I knew and in some cases remembered."

"But what do you want to know, and why, and what does it matter now and what good does it do now?"

"I'm not trying to dig up ghosts. I just want to know what happened. 'Friendly fire' sticks in my craw—did somebody fuck up, who was it, how come we didn't ask, and how come they didn't have to pay, *and we know nothing.* The records don't make sense." I stopped and amended myself. "Yes, I want to know that, all that, and I'm angry and angry that I didn't ask sooner and I feel stupid, stupid not to have done so. But it's not only that. I want to know, Was it quick? Was he in pain? Could he talk? What did he say? Was anyone there with him? Did he hurt? Was he alone?" I stopped again and amended myself again. "But that's not exactly it either. Even if nothing can be done, even if it's too late, even if there are no answers, I want to know how he was, what he was thinking, reading, talking about those last days, what music he was listening to. Was he okay? And if I never have asked or said it, I don't think a month or a week or maybe even a day goes by when I don't think of him and wonder."

I could hear the catchings of Samantha's breaths and was having trouble with my own. She recovered first. "I know there are different ways of dealing with it, trying to make it better." She tried to laugh, not very well. It sounded like something brittle and delicate breaking inside her. "But—and the strange thing is, I agree with my mother—it doesn't change the past, the fact that it happened. It's done. I'm not going to do this."

AFTER OUR HOUSE IN Massachusetts burned in the late 1980s, and before we rebuilt it, I found some scribbled notes that had survived the fire. The house had been a one-story cottage before we added in stages a screen porch and a second floor. It was in the summer after the work was done and before the house burned that Samantha and I had sat down to talk, among other things about Doug, and got sidetracked into tennis. From where we sat in two freshly reupholstered chairs on the new second floor we could see the breadth of the Cape's curl. The spires of Provincetown—a church, a lighthouse, and a monument—stuck up like a miniature picket fence. The water was restive and lay on the green side of teal. The sun in striking it scattered diamonds across the bay. We were alone, one on one, one of the few times since Alabama we had been so, and we have never been again since.

The jottings on the paper I had scavenged were smudged. The ink must have gotten wet from the fire hoses and the paper had browned and curled from the heat and from the smoke. The edges were tobacco and umber and the smidgens that were darker still, truly black, crumbled into my hand into ash. The words were impossible to read any longer. It was frustrating and ironic and somehow appropriate.

The two of us had such a history. On and off, it traced all the way back to birth. We had been close, innocently and not quite so innocently, and at times we had not seen each other for years. What I had written that day I couldn't make out or decipher, but I remembered she hadn't been comfortable. I had tried to kid it away, to reach back to when we were young and easy. But maybe we never were.

After she left she had telephoned and said, "I want to apologize. Maybe I can do it better this way. On the phone. You know you've always intimidated me. I don't know what it is. Maybe it's the way you look at me, and I of course don't, can't, look at anybody."

She was trying to joke, and she laughed a little, but it wasn't quite right. It didn't come off. She had said to me, and would again, how lucky her life had been, and then recanted, doubled back, because of Doug, but in so many other ways she said it had been. Her marriage, her children, her job, her garden, her home. Yet even if her life was "happy" I sensed that day before the fire, and sometimes since, that in some undefined way she felt as if she had missed something, some recognition she could well have had, a splash in a bigger pond, a larger and greater spotlight. And that, like our fathers, with our competitive natures, and in the way I looked at her, touched disappointment and the diminution of her dreams.

I had called Samantha for another reason as well. I had located the videotapes that we had made that one summer, the one of Percy and the one that included so much of her father, and wondered whether she wanted a copy. She did. I made one and sent it to her and a month later she sent me a graceful letter rich and concise with feeling and gratitude for the gift of it, not the gift from me, but the gift of visiting with these fundamental and irascible people in our lives, so many gone now, especially her dad. I wanted to quote from it and she agreed and then a second time and then sadly withdrew permission.

BUT HER LETTER set me deeply wondering. What were the differences between my sending the video and Betty and Samantha refusing to send the memorial service? What was my wanting to know? Was I invading their privacy? Or Doug's? Was it untoward? Out of line? Was I trying in some way to trump their sorrow with my own? Were we in turn dwelling, denying, or dealing?

What was certain to me was they didn't even want to go to the asking of the questions that drove and haunted me, not to mention the answering of them. This is where I had come from—a world where there was a clamping down on information and emotion, where I couldn't now or maybe ever have approval to write or offer what was true. To tell the truth I'd have to create fiction that captured truth. Or omit it.

What I knew was I had no idea how exactly this boy, this man, I had loved had died. What I knew was I had no idea how many people his life had touched. What I knew was I would never have all the pieces of the puzzle now. I would never be satisfied with that.

I asked my daughter Jacy, savvy and now in her twenties, what she thought. She said it was clear. My questions—my need to know—were about death. The video wasn't about watching the dead—that startling casualty list that it now illustrated—but about seeing the people alive.

She was right, and yet after all my wondering and asking who can finally measure the truffle cake we carry with all its layers and secret nooks and crannies of our grief and our guilt?

17

I'M NOT EXACTLY SURE when I knew I had to find Rae Sincennes on my own. The need didn't dawn; it just became an actuality.

I thought it wouldn't be hard to locate him, a snap really, but the search proved far more difficult than I imagined. The Marines were unhelpful, and I couldn't determine whether it was conscious obstruction or bureaucratic malaise. In the world of military records there are a huge number of variables, I learned from a *Boston Globe* reporter. It often takes, he said, many weeks or months of visits to various archives. I filed a Freedom of Information Act request, even though I wasn't literally the next of kin. The time it took was daunting; I'm still waiting for a response.

And the truth was, I had forgotten his name and my aunt Betty had misidentified the town he had come from. It wasn't Houston—it was Galveston, Texas. A lot, increasingly, slips through mental cracks. Call it research, call it skip tracing, call it a kind of hunting, there are those who are good at such things. Finding even one of them wasn't so easy, but when I did they found the man who had come to call on my aunt and uncle.

They didn't like to talk about their methods—how they did

it—and the writer in me was intrigued. All they would admit was that between licenses, tax bills, credit cards, computerized records, surfing the Internet, and maybe some hacking, it's hard not to leave astonishingly accessible tracks. Within the Marines too is an unofficial network that's as effective (and as protective) a gatherer of information as the CIA.

They found a wrong man before they found a right one, a platoon sergeant, Duke Rushing, who claimed to know everyone who was killed the same day as Doug and who was now married to a woman who had been engaged to one of those who had been. I had an e-mail address and the town he lived in. Still it took a while to unearth him and I tried several phone numbers futilely. I got no answer and no machine at one and got an upset, confused, and perhaps drunken woman at another who shouted she'd never heard of Duke Rushing. With the next and what was the last possible listed number I got another woman:

"May I please speak with Duke Rushing?"

"My husband has hearing problems, so I take messages for him."

"But you can take messages for Duke Rushing?"

"My husband is Dock Rushing, honey."

"Was your husband in the Vietnam War?"

"Are you kidding? My husband's far too old to have been in that. He was in World War II."

"Your husband's not named Duke Rushing?"

"Dock, honey. We used to get calls for Duke Rushing here, but it's been a while. A long while."

I tried an e-mail address and my messages were never opened, until I found an Army captain to triangulate them through. But when I did finally make contact, Duke Rushing didn't know Doug.

And then came Rae Sincennes.

. . .

RAE SINCENNES HAD FLOWN up and now I flew down. Houston sat in a smear of smog and even Galveston, an hour south, lacked much of a sky. Like Miami Beach, Galveston sat across a causeway, a similarly long thin strand of sand that was still waiting rediscovery. Fought over during the Civil War, it had become a leading port and the terminal point for two railroads. It had even prospered during the Depression and Prohibition, rife with rum runners and bootleggers. Galveston had once been a booming, bawdy place.

In 1929 a University of Texas graduate student, Granville Price, did some remarkable math for his thesis. He counted the houses of prostitution in Galveston and uncovered fifty-five. Next he averaged the number of women per establishment, added in the independent operators in nightclubs down the island and spread along the beach, and toted them up. London had a ratio of hooker per citizen of 1:960, Berlin 1:580, Paris 1:481, Chicago 1:430, Tokyo 1:250, and Shanghai 1:130. But this island, a ribbon of sediment as flat as a penny, put them to shame. Galveston's ratio was 1:55.

That time had long since passed by. There was no such thing as fifty-five now. The trains were gone, and the opera at the opera house, and much of the gambling. A railroad museum was left and a block or two of the great sprawling stone and wood Victorian homes. A few were tourist attractions and the rest were gone or were worn dinosaurs waiting for rehabilitation or extinction.

Toward the Strand and the seawall there was a funky section and a beachy section bunched with motels and maybe twenty blocks of clapboard bungalows. Long after the mansions, the first of these bungalows had shot up in the boom of World War II and the rest filled in quietly during the Eisenhower years. In one of these, one that was a cream and a faded sea green, one that had well-worn, slatted, wooden storm shutters that like isinglass could come right down, lived Rae Sincennes.

Once he must have been a short, slight, small man, but the years had packed on weight. He was round now. The shaving of his head only made him more so. His kids were grown and gone. They had cleared out, and now it was his stuff that filled the rooms. The clutter was immense. He had LPs—Junior Walker, Bobby Moore, Sam and Dave, a scattergun shot of Motown—a collection of *National Geographics*, myriad encyclopedias, and in binders every issue of *Ebony* and *Playboy* ever published. His wife was also gone. He was alone now with his gathering of things, and his books and magazines and possessions had become his family. He had had many jobs and he now had one more, on the water, and after leaving the boat and after drinking, but not too much, he came home and they were close by and it was within them that he lived.

I rang the bell and Rae Sincennes let me into his house. Uncomfortable then, he sat us outside on two beach chairs on the front porch. They were aluminum, weathered and salt-stained, and with a weave of grisly green and yellow plastic strips. We didn't last long there either. Soon enough in his restlessness he moved us on to the Elbow Room, a comfy wreck of a place that poked out over the Gulf of Mexico.

"Thank you for seeing me," I said.

"I wasn't sure at first," Rae Sincennes said. "I don't like talking about Vietnam. For years I never talked about it. I don't know why I couldn't. It was in there, locked up in there, driving me crazy, fucking me up. I tried drinking. I tried drugs. I tried women. I was a lousy husband, a lousy father, and lousy at work. It's gotten easier now. I've gotten better. At least in some ways. And then when you said who you were . . ."

He didn't mean only my relationship to Doug. He knew of my work, the television series, and even if it was gone there was still some wattage lingering in its wake.

"You were there?" he asked.

"Vietnam?"

"Yeah."

"Twice."

"You did two tours?" His gaze hardened and homed in and he answered in correction before I could: "You weren't there. You weren't in country. Not then. Not during the war."

"No, only since then."

"I knew it," he said. "You were there, but you weren't really there. There was no way. I can tell. I know that deal. People come at me all the time, asking and telling, and they don't know anything. They'll never know. I met a guy the other day and we had served in the same war, in the same fucking war. He would understand, wouldn't he? No. We had nothing in common. We weren't there at the same time or the same place. It wasn't even the same war. You know what he did? Laid sod. He laid sod at some practice tee at some fucking officer's driving range."

I said, "I went in '91 and '97."

"I saw your show. Your show was good." He basked for a moment in the touch of it, even if it was a rather dwindling glimmer of fame, and yet he was leery of it. "But that's what it was. A television show."

"We knew that," I said.

"It wasn't real," he said. "It wasn't there."

"We just tried to tell some stories," I said. "There were a lot to tell. A lot that deserved to be told. Still are."

"Stories?"

"We were grateful at least we got to tell a few."

"You want *stories*? I've got *stories*. I could tell you *stories*."

"Maybe that's why I'm here," I said, but I felt as if we had veered a wrong way unaccountably and I didn't know why. I hadn't seen it coming, either his deference or his dangerousness. These loose shards of his pathology.

"What was she like?"

"Who?"

"That pretty nurse. She was something. I'd like to crawl up her carpet and do some munching."

"I'm sure," I said, very carefully, "but I'll tell you what: let's start again." And I tried to: "I want to thank you for calling and seeing my aunt and uncle when you did. It meant a great deal, and I'd also like to hear what happened. Whatever you know or remember."

He took his time, quieting down. He had a beer and a chaser and he tasted both of them and withdrew back into himself, defusing, and didn't hurry back. "Is it luck?" he asked finally. "Or is it a curse?"

"What?"

"I wish I knew," he said. "To carry around the fact that I shouldn't be alive. Except for your cousin. I should be dead. Except for him. He was my Guardian Angel and I was such a Fucking New Guy. I was lucky, so lucky. I thank God every day. And, guess what, here I am alone, all alone. I didn't tell your family that. They didn't need to know that. All alone. Except for Nick the bartender, and you of course. Some luck." His mood swings were quicksilver and unpredictable. His easygoing roundness was shallow cover, only skin deep. "And I don't know why he volunteered. He was what, a shipping clerk?"

"I thought Doug was a language specialist. He went to language school in Monterey."

"That's the Nam."

"What do you mean?"

"Train for one thing, end up doing another. Didn't make sense. Not a lot made sense." He corrected himself, again growing dark. The birthmark that splotched along the side of his dusky face seemed to pulse. Even after decades he was packed tight with baffled feelings and they led him into troubled places. "Nothing made sense."

"How well did you know Doug?"

"I didn't know him. Not really. I didn't know anybody. I was so wet. I was still falling off the fucking turnip-fucking truck."

"Then how did it happen?"

"Good luck with that question," he said. "I know you're going to think I'm crazy, but I ask myself that and I don't quite know. Sometimes I think my mind, this fucked-up head, I think it's going. I'm losing it, my memory for sure." He laughed ruefully. "Sometimes I think it's all I got left."

"Tell me about that day."

"'What kind of day was it? A day like all days, filled with those events—'" he said, and stopped short, leaving the quote hanging behind. A chunk of his cover fell away. "It was wet, it had been raining, and there was mud everywhere. I'd never seen anything like it. Where we were that's all there was. Take a step and you stuck in it. Pulling your boot out made these wet smacks, like farting noises. One kid had a piece of aluminum, like a saucer, like you use on snow, and he was sliding around on it. It was crazy. And yet the sun was out, it had come out, it had finally come out. Everybody started kidding me right away. They said I'd brought the sun. So they dubbed me Rain Man. Makes sense, doesn't it. I told you. I make no bones about it. I was scared and shitting everywhere. I was one hundred and thirty-seven pounds of flying feces. Before I even had a bunk I was living in the latrine. That's where I met Doug. He thought it was pretty humorous. It wasn't fucking humorous to me! Wading through shit that looked exactly like the shit that wouldn't stop coming out of me. He just offered to go. I don't know why. I don't know. I don't. He was completely laid-back and he said what the hell. I want to see. I didn't believe him. I wasn't buying it. Then there he was, locked and loaded, ready to go. This guy who struck me as shy and yet knowing, do you know what I mean?"

"I think so."

"He was funny."

"Funny?"

"Not funny exactly. I can't define it. He shone."

It wasn't a word I would have used or applied, but it ran through me and rang quietly through the Elbow Room with an echo that carried across more than thirty years. "Not only doesn't it make sense," Rae Sincennes said then. "But there is no justice. That's what got me for years, worked on me, came down and downright chewed and ground down upon me, fucked with me, until I realized of course justice isn't real. It's an idea."

"What is real?"

"A dumb question and the only fucking question. My kids are real, my friend. My family. I know because I lost mine. I lost them and can't get them back, and I have to live with that even as your cousin is my Guardian Angel."

"But maybe what's real *is* Doug or you, or me, if it happened to happen, getting shot at. Even killed. Because if justice, if ideas, don't mean anything, why should he have been killed, or why should you have been shot at?"

"I think about a lot. I think about too much. Believe me I do. But I don't think about that. I don't think about things like that. I don't think. I try not to think. I fail, but I try not to think."

"Maybe," I said then, "I should just drop it. I shouldn't ask any more questions. I should just drop the whole thing."

"Now there's an idea. And you think you can? You think *I* can? You think I haven't tried? That God knows I haven't tried? It can be a costly business, curiosity. Wanting to know. I learned that the very hard way."

He was so different than I had imagined, and so different than he must have been with George and Betty. That had been an act of consummate grace. He had given them a great gift and the cost of the trip must have been substantial as well as the benefits. That important to him. He had held himself in, hidden from them what was still seething inside, what he didn't or couldn't hide from me.

Even in his drinking and his denial he saw right into me. The heavy, hardscrabble tread of exhaustion lay like scar tissue under his eyes, but his vision was unimpaired.

"I had to go up there. I had to go up and tell them. It did me some good. It may even have kept me alive just one more time." He tried on another laugh. "But it didn't change the entire fucking world."

"Someone once said to me, 'Few things matter and fewer still matter very much.' This is one."

"Someone once said to me, 'Maybe he's the guy on the other end of the saw.'"

"I don't understand," I said. "What did he mean?"

"Your cousin," he said.

"That you were opposites?"

"Not me, not just me," he said. "You. You and Douglas W. Young are connected and so am I and so I guess we are connected to each other. Fucks with your head, I told you."

"Tell me about that day," I said again.

"I saw them go out, but I didn't see them come back," he said, and ordered another drink, another scotch. "It was night by then and I didn't think about it—that he was out there and I wasn't. I was still scared for me because when he came back safely soon enough I was going to have to go out. Some private couldn't do it for me forever."

"Corporal."

"Only after. That's what you get when you die. Promoted."

"How did you find out? Who told you?"

"No one. That's the thing. No one did. No one wanted to talk about it. No one ever did. Ever. It was just in the air and I fucking knew."

"But—"

"When somebody got greased we didn't talk. Listen, if somebody talked about the New York Yankees on a day, if somebody talked about pears, the fucking pears we had in C-rats on a day, if somebody talked about Christmas on a day, that was it. They were gone. Never mentioned again. Never fucking again. I wanted to know what happened and I didn't want to know. So many years now and it's no different. He was wasted, *wasted*, shot in the head, and you know how, not exactly, we'll never know exactly, how or who fucked up. Shot in the head by one of us, down and dead, dead bang." He looked back to his drink and this time he finished it. "And then I heard, months later I heard, he was alive, and someone talked to him on the way back. In the medevac chopper. And he died there."

It was like an earthquake. All my conceptions, every one I'd ever had, tilted. "What?!"

"I don't know," he said.

"Which was it?"

"I don't know," he said.

"I want to know."

I was ready to leap down his throat, my own loose shards, and he ignored me and turned to the bartender. "One last one, Nick." The bartender poured another shot and Rae Sincennes drained it. Only then did he turn to my gyrating impatience and me.

"When I was short, waiting to come back to the world, waiting for a chopper to get me out of the boonies and back to Da Nang where I was going to be one motherfucking happy pig in rear-echelon-motherfucking-shit, and there was this little Portable Rican turd waiting too. He'd lost—"

"What does this have to do with—"

"Nothing. Everything. You want to know what I know?"

"Yes."

I was pissed off and he saw it and he came right back at it.

"Then listen and listen fucking tight cause this is what I know," he said. "He'd lost both legs. He'd lost his right arm. He'd lost an eye. He had a frag in his skull. A kidney was gone, his spleen. His balls. He was a collection of tubes pasted back together and being shipped off to Tokyo on his way home. I tried to ignore him, but he looks up from his gurney and starts talking to me. You know what he said? The little turd looked at me and he said, 'You know it could be worse. I'm lucky.'

Could be worse. Lucky?! *He was lucky!* I've carried that and I've carried your cousin, however he died, and I know, every fucking day I know, I know he lost his life and I got mine. The world lost him just to get a little more of me. It was a bad trade. Life should've been easy but it wasn't. That was my destiny. I felt guilty, and I ate all the guilt and all the shitty self-pity I could suck down, and it's taken me all this goddamn time, all these years, to feel worth it and be glad to be alive."

He had struggled all these years with why some die and some don't and what that meant, and to find what was genuine—maybe so had I—and it had distilled at last to livable essence. Only peace was not yet and maybe never would be.

18

MY LIFE HAD TAKEN ME to California, where Doug and I had seen each other that last time. I had stayed and written novels and then had fallen sideways into movies and television. Times had changed. The dream of being a novelist, a large goal earlier in the twentieth century, wasn't so much. In some sense movies had replaced it.

When I first had some success I soon discovered I was a target. Everybody was writing a screenplay. The bartender, the car salesman, the reporter, the overweight psychic, the neighbor down the street, the plumber who called the Hollywood Hills the Swish Alps, the so many drunks at so many parties all buttonholed me wanting to tell their story. They were writing it or wanted me to write it. Instantly, I became their audience and possible ghostwriter, and beyond their conviction I came to realize how often they were close to plea.

The screenplay—that was where to make your mark in this day and age, tell your story, and find your pot of gold, and the illusion in the dream wasn't apprehended. The big screen. The stars. The chair with your name on it. Hobnobbing, rubbing elbows with the famous. The splendid lives. The filthy lucre. The supposed filthy lucre. It dovetailed neatly into the sweepstakes instinct in all of us, the possibility of the long shot coming home, the rainbow and the pot of gold.

One tracked down my mother even before she had a chance to read an article about her son in the Boston newspaper. His name was Bill Kearney and in one of his subsequent letters to me he wrote:

> I know your [sic] busy and I don't want to be a bother to you, but I'm a very unhappy man and I *pray* [underlined twice] every day that I succeed in my efforts as a writer.

> P.S. I just finished my first book, I think it's very good. I'm sending a copy to Mormon [sic] Mailer because he has read some of my other material and has given me some fabulous comments.

The first script Bill Kearney sent me, *The Flying Car*, was a comedy-fantasy and I didn't feel qualified to critique it. When I wrote him so, he immediately fired a letter back:

> I don't want to take advantage of your kindness but I wrote a Walter Matthau type comedy that my toughest critics love. Could I send you this one last script?

Except it wasn't the last. There was another after it, and likely there could have been more.

Once upon a time the novel had had such a place. No longer. The news is long since out now that books don't spawn giants much anymore and by and large don't sell and aren't read and seldom define a time or cut along any leading edge. They've lost their crucial place in telling stories in our culture and abandoned their central seat in our imaginations. No single or landmark work bestrides a time. They've lost the magic. The world has fractured and fractionalized and so has art.

Even screenplays right now pale before the blasting melodrama of reality. It has come to dwarf the deeper excitement and possible propinquity of fiction and drama, a place sacramental with emotions and truths we didn't know we carried and hadn't yet known about the exquisite sadness of being human and alive. These are the stakes and they are still with us. This yen to discover and share, to tell and to be heard crouches within, waiting to beckon. The need remains, wed to our shaky faith in our uniqueness, and won't go away. We worry at the marrow of what we can't let go of. Our stories hackle at us. We scratch at them, whatever they are, adapting and altering, polishing and planishing, seeking their palliative promise, and I was no different.

Doug's death altered the course of my journey. It struck me and forged me, like my father's risky swim, and the tales of George and Bill and Bill and George. The sum I will never exactly know, like the exact place and circumstances of his death. It's inestimable, who he was and how he died a gnawing cipher that refused closure, and aren't those the things that define us? And as we search for their meaning, literally or symbolically, we often attempt to create that closure over and over in our lives, whether through sex or art or violence or service or psychological paralysis, or the quest his death set me on that was finally as much about me as it was about him.

"In even the best of caskets, it never all fits," Thomas Lynch also wrote. "All that we'd like to bury in them: the hurt and forgiveness, the anger and pain, the praise and thanksgiving, the emptiness and exaltations, the untidy feelings when someone dies." This is what we had felt that December day looking at him. This is what had silenced us that Christmas night when we didn't drink. We couldn't sort it out, any more than I can catch all of Doug or my dad or George in a book. But Doug's fate became a part of my biography and painted my work.

Why did he die and why didn't we? Why didn't *I*? The edge of that dime was preciously thin and unanswerable. It's part of loss and a reason loss is such a wily and unruly thing. It plays on our luck, our own survival, as it wounds us, and it can't be measured and we can't control the rabbit punch of when it will come, but come it will. It wrenched at us then and wrenched at Rae Sincennes still, and it goaded me to attempt what I hadn't and needed to do: find a fit into Doug's boots. And not only Doug's. The reach beyond "me" into the lives of others gave up a great, blessed, humbling and emancipating gift.

It took me a long time, many years, before I realized this and to discover that there was a map in what I had been up to. The twenties, the Depression, and World War II had molded my parents, and those events rubbed through what I knew, the second half of the twentieth century. Even in television and movies, an industry of escape, I had kept turning back to these years and places that had formed me and the times within which I had lived. They were my territory. My search and wrestling wasn't finally as much about who I was as about what was the common experience I was part of—this time when there was no renaissance or obvious revolution, no good or great or out-and-out war. Nothing so simple or clear-cut.

Success didn't by any means lie here; it was booby-trapped by truths we often didn't want to hear. But for me there was no choice. With the tools that I had, these small black marks, these awkward, imperfect, infuriating, beautiful things called words, I needed to chip away to the best of my ability at the calculus of memory and love.

IN ITS CURIOUS and chastened path it had led me to Hawaii and to start to write as best I could this story of a father and a son, two cousins and two brothers, and to track down at last one of the Marines who had known Doug, Rae Sincennes in Galveston, Texas, who should have gone that December day in 1969 and didn't. I had sought to find out what I didn't know and discovered what I would never know about Doug's death. What I learned and what I felt had set itself down fast and slow and then stopped when I met my son, Jake, in Sun Valley, Idaho. A senior in college now, he was driving his car, a 1998 Trans Am, to Princeton and we began to drive together.

Jake had switched majors and was suddenly devouring literature. He had gone into college premed. One night when he was a senior in high school, he had spent a night in an ER with a doctor who was also a technical adviser on a television show. The prospect of the night sounded exciting to me, though emergency rooms, like war, usually provide fathoms more boredom than carnage. He never talked much about it afterward and I don't know if that's where his interest began to flag. In college for the first time in his life he had a difficult semester. He had trouble with molecular biology, broke up with his girlfriend, and tried drinking too much. A bad grade, a broken heart, and a wake-up in the infirmary. Suddenly, he turned to reading. He announced that he was thinking of becoming a writer.

When I told him what I had been writing he nodded and said nothing awhile, a while in this case not seconds or minutes but days, and then he said, "Dad, how come you always write about Vietnam?"

The question had a kick to it as Jacy, my elder daughter, had once asked me, "How come you always write about death?" Even my younger one had gotten into the act in her own way by inquiring, "How come you never write anything about kids, Dad?"

They were also asking implicitly, and other times explicitly, about who I was and why inevitably and by my choices I had missed no small chunks of their lives, the day-to-day, the ordinary, the invaluable shit and string beans.

I said to Jake, "I don't know. I guess it's what I know."

He was silent again awhile, a shorter while, before he said, "You know we have nothing like it."

"Like what?"

"Nothing has happened like Vietnam or the sixties or anything to my generation."

"Maybe that's not all bad."

"But will we have anything to write about?"

"That's true," I said. "That could be a problem. Or that could be your subject. Or—something will happen." I was being more glib than prescient, though world events would change that soon enough.

In Ketchum we took sight of Hemingway's grave. He lay beneath two pines and under a broad, flat, smooth, life-size chunk of granite. A pitch of pennies scattered across it. At the beginning and end of *For Whom the Bell Tolls,* Robert Jordan lay flat on the pine-needled floor of a forest, but there was no forest here. The two firs were ragtag and not sizable or grand. Since Hemingway's death the highway had expanded and drawn near and his fourth wife and great-niece had come to set hard by.

It was only a month or so later that Gregory Hemingway, once a doctor, died in a Key Biscayne, Florida, jail of a heart attack. He had been arrested wandering the streets naked way after midnight, a black velvet dress and shredded panty hose over one arm and high-heeled shoes in his other hand. His nails were painted a plum color. Looking drunk, looking happily demented. At first, to the arresting officer, Nelia Real, he said his name was Gloria. He died without making bail and while waiting for a pretrial hearing. During his life, it turned out, he had suffered from manic depression and had shock treatments. He had written a highly praised book. At age eleven he had been the Cuban pigeon-shooting champion and later a professional game hunter in Africa. He had had a sex-change operation and cross-dressed. He had been married

five times, and still lived with his last wife in a Coconut Grove
cottage. One of his daughters said, "He was not a sideshow
oddity; he was a man with problems. He was a good human
being." It's not so easy being the son to a famous father; not
always easy to be a son, period.

As the shadows grew long and dark, Jake and I reached the
Craters of the Moon National Monument. I had never been
there or heard of it. The shapes of lava were crude and sinuous and the wind picked up and zithered across them. They
seemed to draw the end of the day into themselves and send
an insolent chill through the barrenness. We saw the sun die in
a blaze near Arco, Idaho, and the moon, a day from full, poke
its ruddy and pitted countenance above the horizon. It was
enormous, larger than the sun. It shrank and whitened until it
was luminous alabaster and a rich, round, normal size. We
were in country now where the weather and the rituals of
every day still ruled. We reached Idaho Falls, with its long and
low waterfall stretching hundreds of yards through the center
of town, and stopped for the night.

The next morning we followed the Snake River and then
survived the tourist-choked Jackson, Wyoming. It was
mobbed and very discovered. We tried lunch at the Silver
Dollar Bar in the Wort Hotel. They claimed there were two
thousand three hundred and two silver dollars laid into the
clear surface of the bar. It didn't take us long in these states to
discover there were a lot of silver dollars in a lot of bars.

We passed into the Tetons. This was the country where
George Stevens, the director, had shot the movie version of
Shane fifty years ago. The film achieved considerable stature.
The lesions and nobility of the landscape were well caught,
but the cast of the movie paled before what had in reading
dug so crucially into my imagination. By chance we realized
we were on course to pass close by a dude ranch, the Triangle
X, tucked up and back from the highway, overseeing the strik-

ing shale-and-slate-shade range. It was the same ranch where we had gone and stayed for a week when Jake was only six.

I took a photograph there and then that has always stayed close at hand. It's been on my desk, on a nearby bookcase, in my bathroom. In it Jake's sitting on a slat of the corral right before rain. The storm clouds are practically charcoal and look like fists, yet he's still lit by the sun. He's aglow. His hair's bleached blond. He looks like nothing so much as the boy played by Brandon de Wilde in *Shane*.

We sidetracked now to the ranch, a return that felt like synchronicity, bought a disposable camera, and I took photographs again, trying to replicate the originals. This day was its own, though. The sun was glaring, there was no circus of clouds, and the light was flat. Afterwards, I popped the camera into the glove compartment, where it was promptly forgotten and eventually disappeared, and I never saw the pictures.

While we were there then, when Jake was six, he hiked and square-danced and rode down the Snake before dawn and saw a moose. He wore a colorful bandanna that was too big for him and a buffalo-plaid fake-down vest that was too big for him and rode a horse that was too big for him. His hair was much darker now and he was tall, tight, and lean. The profound changes hardly existed and didn't matter to my subjective eye. The two were so connected. Both were my son.

Yellowstone was slow going and singed from the fires of 1988. The evidence was still very strong. Whole landscapes of trees were bare stalks. The sun, lowering again, ricocheted through them, as if they were still burning. There had been more fires in the summer of 2000, brutal and huge, that swept away thousands more acres. The drought continued. New ones were burning in Glacier National Park to the north. Smaller ones, closer and under control now, flavored a slice of the sky with a bright dry haze, a brown smear, as if we had never escaped the San Fernando Valley. Sunset did away with it. The light became richer and declension returned and it became beautiful again.

We rung low on gas as night fell and, miscalculating the miles from Cooke City to Red Lodge, began climbing the Beartooth Highway. A misleading sign didn't help. Cooke City was like that. Almost nobody lived there, yet it was gripped with a funky pride and an ornery nature. It lay four miles outside of Yellowstone, in a deep cleft of the Absaroka Range with a single four-block-long main street. A couple of motels and rental cabins—the Soda Butte Lodge, the eight-unit Elk Horn Lodge, and of course the Grizzly Pad—a café and bar or two and a single Exxon station. In what there was of summer, Cooke City was wall-to-wall with trailers and mobile homes, but it was in the winters where it was carving a legend out for itself. They were unending and snow-driven, lasting seven months and longer, and the snow fell in the hundreds of inches. After the fires, the bull market for snow, dry as dust, turned the scored mountainsides into a hot spot for a new sport called high-marking, a brain-and-gravity-defying plunging about on the latest and most loaded snowmobiles.

Leaving Cooke City, Jake and I kept working our way through a series of switchbacks, turning and reversing and having to turn again. The route was scenic, famously so, but we couldn't tell. The subtle subtractions of light stole the spectacular surroundings. We could no longer see it. In the gloaming heaven and earth turned inchoate. The ascent assaulted miles per gallon. The gauge kept dropping and the dark enveloped us. We made light of it. This was adventure, guys together, and it was good to be daring, take a risk. We had to be near the summit.

But we weren't.

We always had to switch back once more. I began to worry and tried not to show it. But I could feel that sweat, the crawling flop sweat that comes with worry, and Jake knew it. He was such an exceptional portal for my emotions. There wasn't

much traffic but we let even trucks pass us. The needle wobbled into the red. We kept the RPMs as low as we could. We
worried now we would run out. We worried about the embarrassment if we did. We worried more that there would be
no other cars left at all to help us. Outside, the wind was thin
and there had to be scatters of snow. Patches lingered all summer along the plateaus. It was up here in his life or in his fiction that Hemingway had buried the gun his father had killed
himself with. He had climbed a rock overlooking a lake, holding the pistol, seen his own face in the still water, and dropped
the gun and watched it fall and fall away. It was up here he had
placed some of his early stories, the ones where he found for
a while what the best of writers and moviemakers seek, what
Stephen Spender called "the unceasing inter-relationship of
the page (or the screen) with the life within and beyond
them—the battle, the landscape, or the love affair."

We rose above ten thousand feet, grinding toward eleven,
and we seemed for a moment to recapture the day. So high, its
very end still buttered the clouds and warmed the western
edge of the sky. The gauge pointed at E. Then below E.

The crest of Beartooth Pass came at last and we could think
of only one thing to do. We shoved the gearshift into neutral
and began the long, very long and very winding, way back
down. Running on fumes, we coasted down the mountain. It
wasn't easy going either. The road still followed the convulsive
contours of the land. There were just as many hairpin turns as
before and the last miles were black. Dense pines and the deep
blue night enveloped us now. There was no escaping it and it
seemed without end. We were going to be stranded. At last
then the road began to straighten and level and we knew we
were going to make it. We found ourselves laughing, ecstatic,
in relief.

At the end of our coast, far below Granite Peak now, we
rolled into Red Lodge, Montana. At the first gas station we
stopped and filled the car's tank. We were tired now and felt

good and we found a restaurant about to close. They had had a hectic night but it was quieting now. Everyone was tired and ready to get home, yet they were gracious. We felt the same way. They served us well and the meal turned out to be a surprising and relaxing pleasure. I collared the last eight-ounce filet of salmon and Jake had a cut of trout. Both were superb.

By now it was late, after ten on a Labor Day weekend. All the motels in and around Red Lodge were sold out. There was one No Vacancy sign after another. Only a refurbished hotel, the Pollard, had a room. It looked well done, even overdone, and expensive. We debated whether to stay. I had driven up and down the Beartooth Pass and then had a wonderful piece of salmon and a martini. I was ready to stop; I had had enough excitement for one day. Jake was reinvigorated and keen to keep going. He wanted to forge ahead for a couple of hours. I could sleep. I relented. He began to drive and I kept an eye out through some construction along Route 212. It was a two-lane road in the middle of resurfacing. After that I let my seat back and lay back and closed my eyes.

I came up too sharply out of too short a sleep to the sight of a large mule deer through the windshield. Jake was yelling and the car was swerving. His reactions were extremely fast. He twisted to the right, accelerating, and we shot past the deer. We missed it and, as if it had been a mirage, never saw it again. We were suddenly on the gravel shoulder of the road. Now Jake braked hard—he stomped it—and we started to slide. The rear of the car swung. Jake turned the wheel left, and turned it too hard. He didn't let off the brakes. They seized and the skid took us over. In its sway, rubber screeching, we shot back across the highway.

"I can't control it!" he shouted.

On this opposite side there was a gully and we went down into it. Rocks ripped open the bottom of the car and ruptured the radiator and, still sliding and fishtailing, we took out a barbed-wire fence. Two fence posts were severed and vanished. We mowed them down. They were churned and chewed up under us, spinning the already spinning car, and the wire reamed my side of the car and sheared the two right side tires from what was left of the wheels and hung us up a foot from a vast antlerlike sculpture of dead branches and a chilling, life-ending trunk of a tree a foot further on still.

It all came in slow and fast motion, and I knew finally there was nothing I could do about it. The brake on or off was irrelevant now. Wherever we were going we would go. We were in free fall and fate had us in its sharp panic, its deep fear, and its bizarre exhilaration. I didn't have time for dread. I did all I could do and what I most wanted to do. In that eternity in a microsecond, I reached out to my son's shoulder and touched him in an attempt to say, I'm with you, I love you, it's not your fault, it may well be your grace, and what will be will be. I let go of all else.

It was an upside-down gift graven into my imagination and my memory, this moment with him, this what could have been a fatal experience that I had never had even safe and right side up with my own father.

None of which Jake remembered.

BUT I REALIZE NOW, and I may have realized in that field in Montana, even way back then on the Big Island's beach, that this is a New England story, and that I am part of it and it is part of me, and so is Jake. Death, even natural death, may be the order of things, what is inevitable, but it is violent and has violence in it. It can lead to an acting out, or acting in, and to grief. I have written here about my family and silence and I know now that in it has always been grief as well as reticence and tradition. Grief has such strength and it never heals. Its surface closes in imperfect scars. It scores our lives. It is a whisper in the world and a clamor within, someone wrote. More than sex, more than faith, even more than its usher death, grief is unspoken. And as we live on we come to know a less sharp but larger and more enduring thing called loss that shapes and marks our lives like God has marked the landscape of the earth and it has no end.

And so I must go back from time to time to see those living and those dead who have helped form me and from whom there is no more escape now even after they are gone than there was when they were alive. The echo they make— the memory of them—so stirs with my own and only increases as I draw closer to the place where they have come to and where we all go. These are the things we carry and bequeath, good and bad, heroic and fallen, noble and otherwise, to those who come after us, even as they need to let go and leave us for their own journey into the times in which they will live.

So it is now that I am driving through and around the Big Dig, the endless construction that is intended someday to reshape Boston, and head down I-93 in one more rental car to Route 3 to Route 3A, and reach now as the oak leaves turn russet and cinnamon and brown and fall and close upon themselves on the ground the cemetery that has plots remaining and waiting, including one for me, and one for Jake and all of my children, on the side of a sort of hill beside my father, and where not so far away at last the two of them, George and Doug, lay again side by side.

Acknowledgments

The journey of this book would've been incomplete without the thoughts and insight of Thomas Lynch, Jonathan Galassi, John Glusman, Henry Reath, Brian Dennehy, Deborah Aal, George Diskant, Brandon Stoddard, Mary Anne Dolan, Michelle Stoneburn, Sam Alura, Lynette Danylchuk, Karen Fried, my brother Mason, and Michael Connelly, who offered up as well a title.

It also couldn't exist without the forbearance of my family—including my sister Margy, my brother Peter, and especially my mother.

Certain names and places have been changed in instances when I couldn't locate the person, or at an individual's request.